RESEARCH IN SOCIOLOGY OF EDUCATION AND SOCIALIZATION

A Research Annual

SELECTED METHODOLOGICAL ISSUES

Editors: **KRISHNAN NAMBOODIRI**
RONALD G. CORWIN
Department of Sociology
The Ohio State University

VOLUME 8 • 1989

  JAI PRESS INC.

Greenwich, Connecticut   *London, England*

CONTENTS

LIST OF CONTRIBUTORS

Alan C. Acock

Center for Life Cycle and Population
Studies
Department of Sociology
Louisiana State University
Baton Rouge, Louisiana

Karl L. Alexander

Department of Sociology
The Johns Hopkins University
Baltimore, Maryland

Charles E. Bidwell

Department of Sociology
University of Chicago
Chicago, Illinois

Hubert M. Blalock, Jr.

Department of Sociology
University of Washington
Seattle, Washington

Ronald G. Corwin

Department of Sociology
The Ohio State University
Columbus, Ohio

Doris R. Entwisle

Department of Sociology
The Johns Hopkins University
Baltimore, Maryland

Krishnan Namboodiri

Department of Sociology
The Ohio State University
Columbus, Ohio

Aaron M. Pallas

Department of Sociology and Education
Teachers College
Columbia University

vii

Robert W. Pearson   Social Science Research Council
                                    New York, New York

Aage B. Sørensen   Department of Sociology
                                    Harvard University
                                    Cambridge, Massachusetts

PREFACE

Many of the questions raised in the literature on education are linked to the effectiveness of the school and the educational system. A basic criticism has been, for example, that the schools are not doing what they are supposed to do. If everyone is agreed as to what the school and the educational system are supposed to do, it becomes primarily a technical question as to how the effectiveness in question is to be assessed. But unfortunately there is no such agreement. To some, education is something that a person has once he or she has received a certificate, a diploma, or a degree. To some others, the important thing is what the courses and curricula completed make one capable of doing. Those of this latter camp are worried, for example, that every year American high schools graduate large numbers of students who are functionally illiterate. To some, educational quality is linked to international competition. This was a critical issue in the 1950s in the United States when the

Soviet Union launched the first space rocket. It has regained centrality again recently, with the realization that the preeminence of the United States in science and technology has weakened. The April 1983 report of the National Commission on Excellence in Education (''A Nation at Risk: The Imperative of Educational Reform'') contains international comparisons of student achievement completed in the 1970s, which reveal that on nineteen academic tests American students were never first or second, and, in comparison with other industrialized nations, were last seven times.

To many, the present educational model is predicated on the assumption that formal educational institutions are supposed to focus on intellectual and skill development, while the rest of the socialization and training is left to parents, communities, churches, and the like. Others believe, on the other hand, that school curriculum has a formal part concerned with the contents of the various subjects such as history, biology, and mathematics, and an informal part concerned with values, norms, life styles, and social relationships. Other issues that have received attention include the following: Should schools train students to fit into the existing social structure or help them develop the capacity to evaluate it and develop alternatives to the status quo? Should schools treat each student identically or provide different learning opportunities for students of different backgrounds so as to compensate for the handicaps created by the background? Should schools be concerned with producing well rounded, critically thinking, intelligent citizens or inculcating students with the skills needed to become an engineer, a physician, or a certified public accountant?

Different chapters in this volume address one aspect or another of the school effect question. Sørensen analyzes the concept of educational opportunity. His basic thesis is that schooling involves a complex interaction among the abilities and efforts on the part of students, the exposure they receive in the school to curricular materials, and the outputs in terms of educational credentials. The curricular materials determine the ''opportunities for learning,'' and the credentials inform employers, parents, and others what the holders thereof are supposed to have learned. Through devices such as ability grouping a positive association between opportunities for learning and ability is fostered. Schools can thus affect the distribution of learning outcomes directly by allocating opportunities for learning differentially among students and indirectly by affecting the distribution of abilities or aptitudes. Schools generally choose an output distribution of credentials (e.g., 40 percent prepared for college, 30 percent for specific vocations, and the remaining for life in general), and personnel recruitment and facility creations are accordingly structured. Once this choice is made, there is a tendency to keep it from changing no matter what the student body composition is. Public and private schools, for example, may differ in the distribution of credentials, even when the ability distributions do not differ, thereby providing different opportunities for credentials for students of the same ability composition. A student's access to opportunities for learning will depend on which other students he or she is competing with for this access. The stronger this association, the greater the inequalities in opportunities created by differences in student body composition. The inequalities of opportunity within and among schools demand close scrutiny in any study of school effects.

Entwisle and Alexander suggest that schools do affect children differentially, but this happens particularly in the early part of the school career, when children are learning basic skills and their academic self-images are first taking shape. In making the transition from home to full-time schooling, children develop different patterns of learning and different patterns of reliance on significant others to support learning. Children thus enter achievement trajectories early in their school career, and these place boundaries on their attainment later on. Furthermore, the patterns of learning and the social relations established early in the school career persist. Entwisle and Alexander call this the critical period notion, and demonstrate that this notion helps to bring some order to the extant literature.

Blalock poses the following problem: Granted that school effect is to be assessed in terms of student outcome variables, how should one proceed to develop appropriate models and estimate them? There is general agreement that student outcomes are basically micro-level phenomena, affected by, among others, individual-level factors operating within and outside the school context. Given that the phenomena studied operate at the micro-level, it is only logical that analysts think in terms of micro-level frameworks. If one's model is formulated at the micro-level, the proper unit of analysis should be at that level. But many of the variables that are manipulable operate at the macro-level. The question thus arises whether models can be developed at the macro-level with some assurance that changes in the macro-level variables will actually produce desired changes in the micro-level student outcomes.

There is a vast literature bearing on this problem. Blalock distills the message of that literature in terms of a few guidelines. But he makes an important suggestion that a framework involving an interdependent set of equations be adopted, different equations pertaining to different actors (students, teachers, parents, peers, etc.). Why the emphasis on interdependence? Because a student as a test taker may be influenced by his or her teacher, parent, and peers; but he or she in turn may influence each of the other actors involved (teacher, parent, peers). Models that take the individual student's behaviors as strictly dependent, and the characteristics of parents, peers, etc., as strictly independent are based on the faulty assumption that parents are uninfluenced by their own children, peers are not influencing each other, and so on. The interdependent system of equations, on the other hand, allows the two-way influences involved. But what about macro-level analyses of schools, school districts, or systems? Blalock's recommendation is that the first priority should be to develop micro-level models. Then work upwards to increasingly macro levels. The more we are sure of the micro-level processes, the more justified we can be in making the simplifying assumptions necessary to make defensible inferences from macro-level models.

The phenomenon of school dropout enters the discussion of school effect for several reasons. First the exit pattern from school by duration of enrollment reflects school effectiveness. Thus one might hold that if the school is successful in keeping pupils well motivated, very few of them would exit before completing a cycle (e.g., senior high). Second, dropout is similar to transition to disability in physical and mental well-being, and hence it enters the calculation of school life expectancy (a measure parallel to active life expectancy) reflecting school effectiveness. For reasons such as these high dropout rates are sometimes in some places a political embarrassment. Educational statisticians use the term "wastage" or "inefficiency" when they refer to levels of grade repetition and dropout. It is questionable whether these terms in their usual meaning apply to grade repetition or dropout. For a pupil may, by repeating a grade, be able to perform much better later on in the educational system and in adult life. Furthermore, if all pupils are not capable of successfully completing a cycle, which is very likely to be true, it might be argued that the efficiency of the system is in fact increased by some pupils leaving the system early.

Be that as it may, the dropout pattern and grade repetitions if present are characteristic features of the educational system. How to record these features and how to analyze their covariates are therefore of interest. Pallas addresses some of the conceptual and measurement issues involved, discusses the production of dropout statistics, and reviews the literature on school dropouts. He points out among other things that in the United States, some school systems provide alternative ways to get a high school diploma or equivalents. (Does the existence of these alternatives promote dropping out?) Usually those who follow an alternative route to high school diploma or equivalent attain their goal at an older age compared to their counterparts who stay in school and obtain the diploma in the more usual way. Does this delay in obtaining the diploma or its equivalent make a significant difference in the life chances of the recipients? An appropriate methodology for addressing such questions is the multistate life table technique. Pallas forecasts frequent use in the future of this methodology in the analysis of school enrollment patterns and their covariates.

In his chapter, Charles Bidwell tackles a thorny question. What is it about educational attainment that affects status attainment? He observes that there is little about the experience in school (as measured) that can be specified unequivocally as the factor responsible for status attainment. While socialization effects cannot be ruled out, we must look more deeply into the process involved for the answers. The measure of educational attainment typically is simply the number of years of schooling that someone has completed. But what happens during those years that gives people with more formal education an edge in the labor market? It is by no means clear what else is being measured beyond the sheer amount of education. Is it, for example, a proxy for other attributes, such as motivation to work, useful work habits, or knowledge about available jobs?

Bidwell approaches this issue from several directions, taking his readers on an illuminating tour through theories of Weber and Sorokin, an analysis of patterns of allocation thresholds that structure the education system, a review of the symbolic and substantive meanings of educational attainment, and ending with a discussion of the formation of human capacity. At various points in the discussion variables are mentioned that deserve more attention in the research models. They include: change of values and other moral commitments, gains in ratiocinative powers, motivation to work, work habits, knowledge about jobs and how to find and keep them, participation in socially strategic social networks, capacity for competition and group loyalty, styles of dress and manners, and command of a class or occupational argot. He concludes that education affects mobility in two primary ways—through thresholds in the educational system at which individuals are evaluated and screened for the market place, and the socialization and credentialing effects on the person.

We are reminded that the education-occupation connection takes place within vocationally specialized, bureaucratized societies where education has become less an emblem of elite social status than an instrument preparing people for technically specialized occupations. It has, to a great extent, replaced ascription and particularism as a selection mechanism. However, Bidwell observes that our measure, number of years of education completed, does not accurately reflect the educational structure that has evolved. On the occupational side, educationally advanced occupations generally are also the more technically specialized. On the educational side of this equation are courses of study of varying length. It is the completion of these programs that is important, not just years in school. The hierarchical nature of this threshold attainment structure is associated with other attributes, such as how tightly the strata are coupled and the selection criteria used, which in turn affects the flow of people from one curricular stage to the next. Curricular differentiation takes on a life of its own, at each transition point channeling graduates into still other stages of the process. There are several implications, but the one that seems most fundamental is that the variable, years of education completed, is insensitive to the discontinuous nature of educational transitions and cannot reveal much about the mechanisms that block entry into various sectors of the labor market. Numerous studies have used number of years of schooling completed. But, as Bidwell stresses, this measure produces measurement error and invalid inferences because it treats each year as being of equal value when in fact schooling is completed in blocks of years and courses. The effects of education are most powerful at the transition points. For example, an employer probably will be more likely to define a person with one year of high school as having no high school than as having completed one third of high school.

Bidwell then turns to the alternative meanings attributed to educational attainment by human capital theorists, signalling theorists, and cultural capital theorists. He suggests that the cultural capital argument encompasses the other two. Certificates signal that desirable habits and life styles have been acquired (whether through socialization or screening), and at the same time the cultural traits acquired (e.g., language fluency) may prove to be useful in doing the work. Correspondingly, selective criteria include these cultural traits. The debate between theorists of the human capital and signalling persuasions will be difficult to resolve without better measures, and in particular it would be important to see how what is learned in school—whether general attributes or specific skills—is actually mobilized in work settings. Finally he calls for more work on: the mechanisms regulating threshold structures, how education affects human capacity, and the relationship between the substance of capacity and the way it symbolized.

Some of the issues raised in the preceding discussion are pursued by the present writers in the chapter that follows Bidwell's. We review a variety of ways in which the education-occupation connection has been explained. Most of the attention has been devoted to individual level explanations, such as ability, acquisition of social and cultural capital, and interpersonal skills and values. Also, some attention has been given to institutional explanations which focus on the agencies responsible for assigning individuals to social positions and the existing structural constraints. In addition, we suggest that it would be instructive to give more attention to macro-level structural approaches that seek the causes of mobility in labor market structures, legal constraints, and demographic conditions. In particular, we advocate using cohort analysis techniques to examine relationships between aggregate levels of education and occupational status.

But the link between education and occupation can be explained differently depending upon the outcome measured. We maintain that social scientists have placed too much reliance on test scores as the primary dependent variable. Just as Bidwell raises questions about the meaning of years of education completed, so we question the meaning of test scores. Perhaps because social scientists favor explanations that emphasize the individual's ability and perhaps because of availability, test scores have been indiscriminately used, notwithstanding their numerous shortcomings reviewed in the chapter. We believe that failure to recognize this measure is not sensitive to the full range of school effects and may have deflected attention from other fundamental issues that deserve to be addressed.

Our criticism of test scores naturally leads us to ask, what outcomes should be measured? In addition to their intellectual mission, educational organizations have always been expected to affect character by providing moral, normative, and political forms of socialization. A taxonomy is provided which summarizes the sweep of outcomes that one can attribute to the education system. Doubtful that the essence of the educational process can be captured with existing measures, we propose some measures that are needed. Another taxonomy is included which summarizes critical dimensions of the schooling process. More and better measures are needed which tap non-cognitive outcomes and which are more representative of crucial intervening variables such as school structures and processes. It will be impossible to determine the full impact of school effects unless such variables are included in the models. By contrast, it is noted, the existing data bases are inadequate for several reasons, including shortages of measures of the type we propose. It is concluded that whereas most studies examine one dependent variable at a time, in reality outcomes form complex, highly interdependent patterns. And, in addition, even though it is generally recognized that educational systems consist of hierarchical layers of classrooms, school, and the like nested in one another, formal models reflecting this structure seldom have been employed. A multi-layer model is described.

Given that learning is a time consuming process, and that a large part of it takes place in the school, it follows that one aspect of the study of school effects concerns the impact of the school on the time pattern of learning. Longitudinal surveys, which collect data on the same persons or other units over successive points in time, are aimed at providing the needed measurement of time pattern of change and development. Pearson discusses the advantages and disadvantages of longitudinal surveys. He points out among other things that longitudinal surveys do not, contrary to the popular belief, permit unequivocal inference about causation. The main problem is that although longitudinal studies permit the analyst to trace the duration of individual conditions and to order them in a sequence that suggests causation, causal inference in such instances nonetheless cannot be made without making certain untestable assumptions. There are scholars who seriously question the wisdom of uncritically viewing longitudinal data as a panacea. Pearson points out that in recent years with increasing frequency attention has been given to coupling longitudinal designs with experimental designs so as to permit the follow-up of cohorts of subjects randomly assigned to treatments or interventions. This technology, however, has not gone far beyond the initial stage at which its strengths and weaknesses are being discussed.

Acock's essay on measurement error in secondary data analysis does not deal directly with school effect. But the general problem he addresses is highly pertinent for studies of school effects based on the usual type of data. Acock mentions a number of common sources of measurement error in survey data. Asking inappropriate interview questions may yield skewed response distributions when in reality the corresponding distribution is not skewed. Asking very few questions about a topic results in the domain of a complex concept being inadequately tapped. In interview surveys coverage errors occur when those who are supposed to be interviewed are not interviewed. Thus males and members of certain race or ethnic groups may be more difficult to be located than others. Information obtained through one person (e.g., a child) about another (e.g., a parent) may differ from that obtained directly from the latter. Of course there is no guarantee that the information about a person obtained from himself or herself will be accurate. Thus misstatement of one's age is a common error in survey data. In interview surveys the sequence of questions asked often influences the responses obtained. Treating an interval scale as ordinal and collapsing categories of a categorical variable are other possible sources of measurement error. Acock discusses these and a number of other sources of measurement error and addresses their implications for statistical inference. He points out that procedures such as analysis of covariance structure allow analysts to incorporate measurement-error models into data analysis. He advocates the use of a multi-level conceptualization of measurement to bridge the gap between empirical research and theory construction. This involves, for example, assuming that a theoretical variable of interest is causally linked to a latent variable, which, in turn, is causally linked to indicators that are imperfectly measured.

In chapter 10, outputs of the education system are examined using the perspectives of three types of input-output approaches. One approach focuses on individual pupils, classrooms, schools, etc. It is common to focus on test scores (reflecting various skills, attitudes, etc.) when thinking of individual pupils as the units of analysis. A vector of scores is attached to each individual pupil. Each individual is thought of as producing the vector of scores using as inputs his (her) ability, time investment, and goods and services received. At the classroom level, the corresponding output becomes a vector of distributions, representing, for example, scores received by the pupils in various tests. At the school level, there are as many vectors of distributions as there are classrooms. And so on. One form of input-output analysis of educational outcomes treats as *explanandum* any such output complex. The explanatory variables chosen usually are interpreted as inputs. Many of the studies that focus on school effect can be thought of within this framework.

Another type of input-output analysis focuses on the flow of pupils through different levels (grades) of the school system. This approach permits linking different processes (birth, education, and entrance to the labor force) with each other. It permits also an examination of school effects insofar as the flow pattern differs between schools or over time within a school. Study of wastage is an example. Differences in socioeconomic background, readiness, family environment, and the like are known to account for intra- and inter-cohort variations in the flow pattern.

Yet another type of input-output analysis is concerned with sectorial interdependence in society. Households, classrooms, schools, etc. can be treated as sectors analogous to industrial sectors for this purpose. Also, instead of treating households as a single sector, it makes sense to stratify them on the basis of socio-economic status or similar criteria and treat each stratum as a sector in its own right. The same applies to classrooms, tracks, and schools etc. This approach permits linking the output of the education system with the flow of various goods and services in society. In this way the education system is viewed as part of a broader social system. The parameters of the education system that receive particular attention in this approach include teacher-pupil ratio, the number of leavers from the education system at different levels (e.g., high school graduates), and level-specific duration coefficients (the average number of school years of life at each level per leaver at the end of the cycle involved). By considering different regions and different sectors of the education system within each region, this type of input-output analysis can be used to examine variation of parameters of the education system between regions and between sectors (e.g., public and private) within regions.

Krishnan Namboodiri
Ronald G. Corwin
Editors

PART I

CONCEPTUAL ISSUES

SCHOOLS AND THE DISTRIBUTION OF EDUCATIONAL OPPORTUNITIES

Aage B. Sørensen

INTRODUCTION

Most sociological research on educational processes in some manner focuses on the provision of educational opportunities by schools to students from different backgrounds. The present chapter follows this tradition of research. However, it departs from the tradition by focussing explicitly on the concept of educational opportunity, a concept that despite its frequent use has not been much discussed in sociological research.

The conceptual analysis to be evaluated raises the question of what deter-

Research in the Sociology of Education and Socialization,
Volume 8, pages 3–26.
Copyright © 1989 by JAI Press Inc.
All rights of reproduction in any form reserved.
ISBN: 0-89232-929-7

mines the distribution of opportunities. In this chapter the distribution among and within schools shall be emphasized, rather than the distribution among social classes which has occupied so much attention in past research. This is not to deny the importance of studying the allocation of educational opportunities to children with different social origins. But the exclusive attention on the social origin issue has led research to ignore other and important sources of inequality of opportunity, especially those inequalities produced by unequal access for similar students to learning opportunities and educational credentials within a single school and among different schools—these inequalities that can be called inequality of opportunity by locale.

Variation in educational opportunities among schools should cause variation among schools in educational outcomes. Thus identical students obtain different outcomes in different schools—such variation in the outcome among schools is referred to by sociological literature as school effects. This is a topic that has received nearly as much attention as the analysis of relation between social origins and educational opportunities and outcomes. Originating in a concern for how expenditures on schools affect educational outcomes (Coleman et al. 1966), sociological research has tended to conclude that most variation in educational outcomes is within schools, that it is related to family background variables, and that the variation in outcomes among students is difficult to affect by school policies. The controversies about this have once again reemerged, because of the research associated with Coleman (Coleman, Kilgore and Hoffer 1982), now about the different educational outcomes produced by public and by private schools.

The main activity of research on school effects has been documenting the presence and absence of the variations between schools in learning outcomes, rather than explaining the variation or the absence of the variation. The recent research comparing public and private schools is perhaps an exception. Coleman and his associates suggest several mechanisms explaining why private schools may be superior to public schools. But the theory suggested by Coleman and associates (see also Coleman and Hoffer 1986) is very much tied to the public versus private school comparison. And, again the controversy has been mainly about methodological issues such as the degree to which adequate controls for selectivity have been employed (see for example Goldberger and Cain 1982).

In general, there are very few systematic sociological theories that focus on explaining quantitatively measured school differences in educational outcomes (for a recent exception, see Bidwell and Friedkin (1987)). Such a theory should be much concerned with educational opportunities and their distribution. It is the objective of this chapter to contribute to the formulation of such a theory.

In summary, the argument is this. Children enter schools with backgrounds that will be relevant for what happens to them in school. Once in the schools, they are taught a variety of subjects and the amount they learn from this teaching depends on how able they are and how hard they try. The quantity of material they are taught determines their opportunities for learning. Both the opportunities and the subjects students are taught are in some manner related to what schools desire to produce in terms of educational credentials. The credentials are meant to provide information to employers, parents, and the wider society about what students should have learned and what they know. Schooling then is a complex interaction between the abilities and efforts of students, the organization of the teaching materials in the curricula which determine the opportunities for learning, and the organization of the curricula in the educational credentials that provide the opportunities for leaving school with certain assumed qualifications.

The process of schooling is a long one for most, and students change over this period. An ideal school effects study would first compare the inputs students bring to schools with the outputs in terms of credentials and knowledge produced by those schools for the same children. The ideal study would show how the relation between these distributions varied across schools. This has never been attempted and evidently would be very difficult to do. At best, short snapshots of the schooling process are feasible. To provide useful information, such studies have to rely on an adequate conceptualization on the interaction between educational opportunities and individual characteristics that constitute the schooling process. It is this interaction that is of interest here.

THE CONCEPT OF EDUCATIONAL OPPORTUNITY

The dictionary defines opportunity as a favorable combination of circumstances. In other words, the chance to obtain something desired. In the context of education, opportunity is the chance to realize a certain educational outcome. Two types of outcomes are relevant. One is a certain credential, such as a degree. The other is mastery of some material, which is usually measured with an achievement test. Evidently there are other educational outcomes of importance such as personality development and the acquisition of certain social skills. I shall concentrate here on the outcomes that most directly reflect what schools explicitly are organized around—these are the learning outcomes and the provision of credentials.

It is important to understand that an opportunity is the chance to realize a desired outcome, not the outcome in itself. Opportunities are characteristics of a system. If it is claimed that person A had better opportunities than person B, this is meant to say something about the systems A and B are part of. If A realizes a different outcome than B, say a higher score on an achievement test, then the cause is unequal opportunities when A was in the system with better or more opportunities, not when B was less able or showed less effort.

Systems differ in the number of opportunities they provide, individuals differ in their ability to take advantage of these opportunities. The measurement of opportunities is often confounded with the measurement of outcomes because it is easier to measure outcomes than it is to measure the opportunities that interact with the ability and efforts of individuals producing these outcomes. Thus, information about learning outcomes in the form of achievement tests are usually more available than the measurement of the opportunities for learning that made these outcomes possible. Indeed past research, as noted, often states that it addresses issues of educational opportunities. However, this research usually measures and analyzes only actual observed educational outcomes in the form of achievement tests or educational credentials.

There are two strategies for focussing on opportunities more directly. One is to measure those opportunities directly, the other is to mathematically specify the interaction between individual characteristics and system or structural opportunities that produce the observed outcomes. Assuming the validity of this specification, inferences about the number of opportunities are possible. Both strategies, of course, assume a reasonably precise concept of what is meant by an educational opportunity. I will now consider this concept more closely for the two types of educational opportunities of interest: opportunities for learning relevant to measured academic achievement and opportunities for credentials.

Opportunities for Learning

There are elaborate theories of learning, emphasizing cognitive structures, memory processes, and motivational states. There is also an elementary fact about learning: one cannot learn what one has not had an opportunity to learn. An opportunity for learning is the presentation of a certain amount of instructional material. There is learning that involves invention and re-invention of knowledge and techniques not directly presented, but to learn this way assumes the presentation of problems and situations that facilitates the learning of new materials. Schools present most of the opportunities for learning through teaching. The quantity of the opportunities for learning available in a given instructional setting is determined by what students could have learned in this instructional setting in a given period of time. Students are exposed to opportunities from learning outside the instructional settings of schools. They may be taught by parents, experiences and experimentation, and by each other. All these sources of opportunities for learning are relevant, but for the learning outcomes most relevant for educational attainment, schools have quite an extensive monopoly. Most opportunities for learning relevant to the results obtained on the conventional achievement tests are determined by the amount and the content of what teachers teach in classrooms and other instructional settings. This in turn is a function of the amount of time devoted to a given topic, the pacing of instruction, the curriculum that decides the subject matter, and the amount of instructional material devoted to that topic. Some of these quantities are determined by teacher ability and effort, others like the curriculum are usually decided by the schools and the local governments that regulate what schools should do and which credentials schooling should result in.

It is in principle possible to obtain measures of how many opportunities for learning have been presented to a given group of students in a period of time, say a school year. But it is difficult to obtain such measures and it is rarely done, the main exception being short term educational studies of pacing and other attributes of instructional efforts (for sociological examples see Barr and Dreben 1983; Dreben and Gamoran 1986), perhaps because sociologists examining education have paid little attention to the distinction between opportunities and outcomes. As noted above, absence of direct measures forces a specification of the interaction between opportunities for learning and the student characteristics relevant for how these opportunities are utilized. Such a specification is suggested in Sørensen and Hallinan (1977) allowing an indirect measurement of opportunities for learning from the analysis of growth in academic achievement over time. The full development of that model shall not be repeated here. The basic idea is simple and shall be briefly described.

Assume that the total amount of material presented in some subject, like algebra, is represented by a quantity, v. It will vary among schools, classrooms, and teachers and be a function of curricula, of pacing, and of teacher ability and effort. The quantity v then measures the opportunities for learning the particular subject presented to students in the period. Now, let instruction in the given material start at time t = 0. By time t = t' a student will have learned some fraction of the material and/or utilized some of the opportunities for learning. The amount learned by time t may be denoted as y(t) and measured by an achievement test in the subject. The individual characteristics relevant for the size of y(t) are student ability and effort, assumed measured by a variable s. For the relation between opportunities for learning, student ability and effort, and observed achievement, a very simple mechanism is one where ability, s, determines how much of the new material is learned when presented in a small period of time, or $dy(t) = sdv(t)$. If students know nothing at the start of the instructional period, this implies $y(t) = sv(t)$; if something is already known we obtain $y(t) = y(0) + s[v(t) - v(0)]$.

In Sørensen and Hallinan (1977) a model allowing estimation of v is obtained by specifying the dependence of $v(t)$ on t. This results in a differential equation model. The solution to this model can be used to estimate opportunities for learning or v, using over time observations on $y(t)$ and measures of ability, s. However, the simple argument presented here suffices for making several important inferences.

Estimates of opportunities for learning in different schools (or different parts of schools, such as tracks) can be obtained from estimation of the model in different schools using individual level measures of s in addition to achievement tests (for examples of this see Sørensen (1987), and Sørensen and Hallinan (1986). A likely measurement strategy, given the type of information usually available to sociologists of education, is to take s as a function of measures of ability, family background, and the like. An additive specification of the relation between s and these variables is apt to be chosen and could be justified as a measurement device—the various measured variables are all indicators of the ability of students. It is tempting to extend this strategy and obtain measures of opportunities for learning using school characteristics as indicator variables and again employ an additive specification for how various school characteristics relate to opportunities for learning. If further these two groups of variables measuring ability and opportunities for learning are entered in a linear expression for achievement, we have in fact the model commonly used in research on school effects, including the study that originated this research tradition (Coleman et al. 1966).

An additive specification of the relation between opportunities and ability in producing learning is a serious misspecification of the mechanism suggested above (even though each component ability and opportunity might well be taken to be linearly dependent on measured variables). The multiplicative relation between s and v means that opportunities for learning interact with individual ability—they do not add to the ability variables. Only the multiplicative formulation captures the property that if there are no opportunities for learning no one would learn anything. If school characteristics are shown to have an effect net of measured individual ability variables with the additive specification, these effects probably reflect unmeasured ability variables. Such effects are only genuine school effects if it can be demonstrated that they are effects resulting from changes in the individual learning ability produced by schools.

The simple formulation shows an important property of the interaction between opportunities for learning and ability that produce observed academic achievement. If the opportunities for learning are expressed as a parameter, v, common to a set of students, it follows that $var(y) = s^2 var(s)$. More opportunities for learning mean more inequality in academic achievement for a given distribution of ability. Good schools, meaning schools where there are ample opportunities for learning, result in more inequality in learning outcomes. The simplest way of obtaining equality of achievement is to have schools with few opportunities for learning.

This has an important implication for inequality of opportunity by social origin or family background. There will be a certain correlation between the characteristics of students which are relevant for learning and their family background. The observed association between family background and academic achievement will depend on the opportunities for learning. The more opportunities for learning, the higher the observed association between family background and academic achievement—an association usually interpreted to mean inequality of opportunity. It is however an association not created necessarily by unequal access to opportunities for learning. It is created by unequal ability to utilize opportunities for learning and it will be stronger with the greater number of opportunities.

These implications of the simple formulation are complicated by the possible relationship between opportunities for learning and ability to learn. Presumably what has already been learned is relevant for what may be learned in the future in two ways. One is the development of cognitive strategies that facilitate further learning acquired through learning experiences and development of brain functions. Cognitive psychology has numerous scenarios for how such a development takes place. Further, certain materials are cumulative (for example, mathematical ideas) so that learning has to take place in a certain sequence. There appears to be a great deal of variation in this among subjects with topics like history and literature being less cumulative (though concept development is a cumulative aspect of almost all learning) and the sciences more so. In any event past learning will to some degree be relevant for the development of the aptitude for future learning. This means that more opportunities for learning need not inevitably create more inequality in academic outcomes. If past learning produces more equality in the ability to learn, the predictions do not follow. This assumes that those with the least ability to learn have the most opportunities so that learning compensates for initial deficits in ability. It is of course also possible that those with the most ability receive the greatest number of opportunities so that the relation between opportunities for learning and the variance in academic achievement is magnified. The issue is a classic dilemma in education.

Primary schooling presumably devotes a fair amount of attention to equalizing ability, though through devices such as ability grouping and the like a

positive relation between opportunities for learning and ability is strength-
ened. At the secondary level, U.S. schools have an ambivalent attitude toward equality of educational outcomes. The comprehensive system of secondary education, or the "common school" (Cremin 1951) is a unique American
institution designed to achieve a basic equality of educational outcomes. On
the other hand, much educational policy and practice is legitimized by the
goal of providing each student the opportunity to develop to the maximum of
his potential. The latter implies maximizing inequality in academic achievement, since those with greater ability then should get more opportunities for
learning.

Schools can then affect the distribution of learning outcomes directly by
allocating opportunities for learning differentially among students, and indirectly by affecting the distribution of abilities or aptitudes. Both mechanisms
suggest investigating the allocation of opportunities for learning among students, both over time and cross-sectionally for students at a given age level.
This allocation process is a question of how schools organize instruction.

Instructional groups organize opportunities for learning because teachers
and curricula are assigned to instructional groups. This is perhaps not very
surprising. But, the consequence of it is that identical students in general will
be provided different opportunities for learning in different settings. To see
this, it is necessary to consider what determines the organization of instructional groups and the allocation of teachers and curricula. This is a question of
what outcomes schools desire to produce. These outcomes are rarely defined
as certain scores on achievement tests, but are socially defined labels informing what the graduate is supposed to master, i.e., credentials.

Opportunities for Credentials

Schools and other educational organizations can be characterized as
"loosely coupled" organizations (March and Olsen, 1974). What is meant by
this is that the structure is disconnected from technical (work) activity, and
activity is disconnected from its effects. There is a great deal of evidence that
schools lack close internal coordination and control of their main activity, that
is instruction. This property of schools has been analyzed in detail by Meyer
and Rowan (1978), who argue that while there is loose control in the area of
instruction, there is tight control in such areas as the hiring of teachers, the
assignment of students to classes and topics, and scheduling. Schools are very
much concerned about showing tight control over what constitutes their socially defined outputs as given by the credentials they provide. These credentials are socially standardized while in actual content they may vary enormously, considering the variation in the competency associated with a high
school diploma.

Meyer and Rowan (1978) provide explanations both for the reliance on credentials and standardized classifications in American schools, and for the lack of internal control. The reliance on credentials they attribute to the political consolidation of society and the importance of education for the allocation of people to socioeconomic positions in society. The lack of internal control is attributed to the decentralization of the system of education and the importance of local control over schools. This, in turn, leads to a set of organizational responses producing the decoupling of its "ritual" classification structure from its technical activities and the evaluation of these activities. It is this latter feature of local control that markedly contrasts with highly centralized European educational systems where evaluation of instruction through national examinations are common.

Schools accordingly should be very much concerned about providing the right outputs in terms of degrees and other labels. The actual learning content of these credentials may vary from locale to locale, what matters is that students who obtain given credentials have been taught definite sets of topics by appropriately credentialed teachers.

The opportunities for credentials are then defined locally by decisions about how many and which subjects constitute appropriate credentials. Elementary schools are supposed to cover certain standard curricula in reading, mathematics, social studies and the like. At higher grades in secondary levels of education, increasing curricular differentiation provides opportunities for certain departure credentials—in high schools most commonly vocational oriented tracks, "general" tracks, and academic tracks oriented toward higher education. These curricular paths to educational credentials are defined by school boards, principals, and accreditation boards.

The distribution of credentials by type often has only a modest relationship to the actual competencies and abilities of the student bodies involved. The loose coupling between structure and technical activity in schools means that schools may be able to create a desired output distribution of credentials quite independently of the ability of the student body that receives these credentials. Schools should be expected to be more concerned about providing the proper types of credentials than about the actual competency of those acquiring the credentials provided. Thus the desire for a "proper" distribution of credentials should dominate the concern for student body characteristics when setting up schools, and the credential distribution should only slowly adjust to changes in student body composition, or not adjust at all. For example, schools may maintain a given distribution of credentials where, say, 40 percent are being prepared for college, 30 percent for a specific vocation, and another 30 percent for life in general, even though important changes in student body take place because of neighborhood changes and the like.

Not only will the distribution of credentials be heavily influenced by agencies outside of the school but they represent what state and local authorities find desirable for all schools to do. Once a distribution of credentials is created, it is difficult to change this distribution because it has created the composition and credentials of the teaching staff to which one has employment obligations, the lay-out of buildings, and the availability of in-structional facilities—all things that are very difficult to change in the short run.

This relative independence between the distribution of credentials and the student bodies of schools will be further discussed below. It does have an important implication for the availability of opportunities for credentials. The probability that a person with certain characteristics will obtain a given cre-dential will not only depend on this person's characteristics but also on the characteristics of the student body of which he or she is a member. This is because access to credentials and the instructional groups leading to certain credentials will be based on rankings, as shown below. The consequence is that someone might be able to get a given credential in one locale even though the same amount of ability and effort would not produce the same credential in another locale.

To summarize, schools create a set of educational credentials relevant for the further educational careers and for ultimate positions in society. An indi-vidual with certain characteristics, s_i, will have a certain probability for ob-taining a particular credential, c_j. This probability $p[c_j|s_i]$ will in general vary from locale to locale for given s. In fact, it follows from the argument presented that the variation is such that a distribution of c_j's is maintained even when the distribution of s varies over time or between places for similar types of schools. On the other hand, strong differences between, for example, private and public schools in the distribution of c_j's may exist even though the ability distributions differ little, providing very different opportunities for credentials for identical students. The lack of internal control in schools facilitates this independence between credentials and student characteristics.

The credentials schools provide are obtained by students contingent on participation in certain instructional activities. Schools organize instructional groups to implement decisions about which credentials to provide, though the creation of a certain output distribution is only one of the considerations behind the formation of instructional groups. It is in the decision about which instructional groups to form, and which students to allocate to instructional groups, that a given school establishes a certain match between the individual abilities and competencies of students, the opportunities for learning, and the credentials that are produced. Thus the organization of instructional groups and the process of allocating students to these groups becomes the major process of determining the distribution of educational opportunities in schools and the allocation of these opportunities to individuals with certain ability and aptitudes.

THE FORMATION OF INSTRUCTIONAL GROUPS

It is possible to imagine a system of instruction where each individual student would be taught according to his particular abilities and aptitudes. Such a system of instruction is widely believed to be the one that would allow schools to maximize teaching effectiveness. It would let schools provide opportunities for learning to individual students in such a manner that their ability to take advantage of opportunities would be maximized.

Completely individualized instruction is the exception, though often made the ideal. The property that may be taken as the defining characteristic of schools is that instruction takes place in instructional groups—classrooms, ability groups, tracks, and the like. Opportunities for learning and trajectories to educational credentials are organized by instructional groups, as teachers and curricula are assigned to these groups and not to individual students.

Instruction to groups inevitably involves an element of treating all students in the group as though they were alike. This will reduce teaching effectiveness to the extent that students indeed are different. One main consideration in the formation of instructional groups then is to produce more homogenous groups rather than a purely random partitioning of students. Instructional groups that are believed to differ with respect to a student's ability to learn are important for the distribution of educational opportunities, for such groups necessarily are associated with unequal opportunities. Systems of instructional grouping with this property can be said to be vertically differentiated.

One universal form of vertical differentiation of instructional grouping is age grading. Age is universally believed to be a measure of ability to learn. Perhaps it has become such a popular measure because it is the one indicator of ability to learn that is equally available to everyone. In any event, age is a main criterion for formation of instructional groups believed to be homogenous in ability to learn. Indeed automatic progression between age grades without actual evaluation of whether development is neatly age graded for the individual student is a good example of the loose coupling between structure and technical activity in schools discussed above.

Homogeneity in ability to learn is not the only consideration. There are management concerns that apparently suggest that voluntary cooperation in teaching can be obtained only when instructional groups do not exceed about 30 students. Since ultimately the very reason for having schools with instructional groups presumably is the benefits from economies of scale and division of labor obtained with instruction to groups of students, these groups usually also have some minimum size—classrooms sizes below ten seem rare. If no other concern than management is an issue, then random partitioning of students in classrooms of between 10 and 30 students is the rule.

Finally, the credentials schools provide curricula that justifies the formation of instructional groups. Instructional groups differentiated by subject, but not necessarily by level may be said to be horizontally differentiated. Typically, the concern for credentials results in increasing curricular differentiation of instructional groups the further one advances in the school. The resulting system of groups is one where student preferences may play a role for the organization when a system of elective assignments to groups is used. However, student choice rarely is the deciding factor for the formation of instructional groups, as they usually at most are necessary, but not sufficient for the allocation of a student to a group.

It easily may be accepted that the formation of instructional groups by subjects is strongly influenced by outside agencies and therefore not necessarily strongly dependent on which students attend the school. But, it would seem that the wish to form groups that are homogeneous in student aptitude and preparation should create a vertical organization of instructional groups that closely mirrors student body characteristics with respect to ability to learn. If this were so, then identical students would receive identical opportunities within the same school. Identical students would still receive different opportunities in different schools if schools differ in the number of opportunities they provide.

It is important to note that the degree to which schools provide identical students identical opportunities is not only a question of the organization of instructional groups, but schools presumably will affect to some extent the distribution of ability to learn for a cohort of students. Hence schools may create equal individuals out of initially unequal able individuals. An organization of instructional groups that initially does not match the distribution of student ability, may come to match this distribution better, as students are given equal learning opportunities in an instructional group and eventually become more equal with respect to their ability to learn.

It is however generally the case that identical students rarely will receive identical opportunities within a school. This is because it is difficult for schools to organize instructional groups so that they match the variation of students in their ability to learn. The need to create a distribution of credentials imposed from the outside has already been mentioned. Even when this may be a less salient consideration, organizational constraint may prevent the instructional groups from closely matching the ability distribution. It is here instructive to consider the case of within classroom grouping, where the flexibility in group formation should be greatest.

Within classroom grouping according to ability is common in American primary schools. Its objective is to obtain instructional groups that are homogeneous with respect to ability to learn. This would suggest that teachers should partition the class in such a manner that the within group variation in ability is minimized. Classes varying in their ability distribution should have different ability group systems. It nevertheless empirically is the case that quite independently of the student body, teachers tend to form from three to five groups of roughly equal size (Hallinan and Sørensen 1983). The reason for this is the wish to devote approximately equal time to each group, and the need to manage the classroom. The consequence is that nearly identical students may be assigned to different groups and different opportunities for learning in classrooms with little variation in ability, and that obversely quite unequally able students may be assigned to identical opportunities for learning in heterogeneous classrooms.

The formation of instructional groups at the classroom level is even less flexible than the formation of ability groups within the classroom. For reasons already noted, classroom sizes typically vary within quite narrow limits. The availability of teaching staff and instructional facilities makes it difficult to accommodate specific ability distributions. The need to provide a given distribution of credentials constrains the variation in the size of tracks and related types of educational trajectories defining routes to credentials.

These constraints on the organization of instructional groups means that these groups need not closely mirror the characteristics of student bodies in schools. The organization of instructional groups come to have an independent existence. This has important consequences for the process by which students are allocated to the unequal opportunities for learning associated with different instructional groups, as discussed below.

The match between student body characteristics and the organization of instructional groups should be considered a variable, and there should be some variation by different types of schools. Large schools should have more flexibility in their design of instructional groups than small schools. Growing schools may have more flexibility in teacher staffing than stable or declining schools. Private schools may have stronger constraints on the distribution of credentials than public schools, and the degree of flexibility of public schools may vary with local political factors. We know little about these processes.

Unless schools somehow manage to completely mirror student body characteristics, the instructional grouping system will create unequal opportunities for equal students. The independence between the organization of instructional groups and the characteristics of student bodies which is allocated to these groups has important implications for the type of processes by which students are allocated to instructional groups. The characteristics of this allocation process in turn will be important for the structuring of educational opportunities over the educational career.

THE ALLOCATION OF STUDENTS TO INSTRUCTIONAL GROUPS

The preceding argument—that the system of instructional groups provided by a school generally should be seen as having an existence independent of the students allocated to these groups—implies that instructional groups may be conceived of as providing a set of "empty places," to use an expression coined by Simmel (1908). These places are to be filled by teachers each school-year or term. There are generally three modes of assigning students to the empty places in instructional groups.

Students may be randomly assigned to classrooms. This is common in lower grades where different classrooms at the same grade level have the same curricula. Such assignment will create unequal opportunities depending on the variation in teaching skills of different teachers. But, these inequalities are not distributed in a systematic fashion.

The use of elective assignments is found in higher grades, but such choices are rarely unconstrained at primary and secondary school levels. With elective assignments, a student's choice is usually a necessary, but not a sufficient, condition for assignment to an instructional group when these instructional groups also are vertically differentiated. Further, schools appear to provide subtle manipulation of student choices even when assignment to groups is said to be completely elective (Cicourel and Kitsuse 1963). This is to ensure that no more than the available places in instructional groups are filled and is the result of the constraints on the flexibility in the organization of instructional groups discussed above.

The use of non-elective assignment is the common procedure for allocating students to vertically differentiated instructional groups. One conceivable scenario for how this would be done is one where schools perform tests of aptitudes and abilities of students and then allocate all students within a certain (presumably narrow) range of ability to a classroom. This would ensure homogeneity, but it would not ensure a match between the number of places in the given instructional group and the number of students who would qualify for the assignment to these places. Instead schools almost always rank the candidates for the assignment to verically differentiated instructional groups, and then use the rank order to assign students so that the available places are filled. Rankings always guarantees a match between the number of places and the number of candidates. Indeed, when schools use measures of ability and aptitude with higher metric properties than ordinarily, they commonly convert these measures into percentiles and therefore rankings.

Rankings have important consequences for the relation between student characteristics and opportunities for learning and credentials. Rankings have no metric equivalent for the distances between ranks. They may result in assignments to different level groups of students who differ little in actual ability, if the candidates are alike. Conversely they may assign very unequal students to similar opportunities should the student body be very heterogeneous. Rankings create interdependencies among students so that a student's access to educational opportunities will depend on the characteristics of other students in the school. This is well known by everyone who has been to school. But it is a feature that is largely neglected in sociological research on educational processes. The consequence for student effort has been noted in the so-called "frog pond" effect (Davis 1966).

The use of ranking has another important consequence for the allocation of educational opportunities. Rankings are presumably done with the goal of assigning students to groups where they can be expected to be able to take advantage of the opportunities for learning provided. This means that the prediction of future performance is the issue. Teachers, like employers in other organizations performing ranking in hiring and promotion decisions, will use information on past performance and educational credentials obtained in the past to predict future performance. Past courses taken are thought to be relevant for ability to perform in future courses, past performance to be the best indicator of future performance. Rankings therefore create strong effects of past assignments to instructional groups on future assignments. This is often formalized in secondary levels of education in the form of explicitly defined tracks. However, even when such explicitly defined tracks are not defined, schools heavily rely on past circumstances to decide about the future. Eder (1979) shows how information and rankings from kindergarten teachers provide the main criterion used in the assignment of students to ability groups in the first grade, and the first grade assignments were provided to the second grade teacher for her assignments.

The dependence of future assignments on past assignments means that schools, through their organization of instructional groups, create educational trajectories that establish the match between initial student characteristics at the time of entry into the school and eventual educational outcomes. These trajectories and the instructional groups involved can be characterized by how *closed* they are. This concept (for a further elaboration see Sørensen 1983) refers to how easy it is for a student in one educational trajectory to get access to another trajectory. At one extreme, students are early on channelled into educational trajectories that inevitably lead to a distinct patterns of opportunities for learning and certain educational credentials at the exclusion of other credentials. At the other extreme we may conceive of schools where trajectories are difficult to identify and students are reassigned to instructional group at different levels in response to their differential development.

Very closed educational trajectories are a characteristic of the very stratified European systems of education. Open and diffusable educational trajectories represent a traditional ideal of American schools. There are mechanisms to reduce closure typical of American schools, such as the use of different teachers at different grade levels and the use of elective assignments. However, even with these mechanisms, schools are unlikely to provide very open trajectories.

The inflexible size distribution of instructional groups produces important constraints on mobility among these groups end therefore among the educational trajectories involved. Movement in one direction must be compensated with movement in the other direction to keep the size distribution intact. Even when the size distribution should be most flexible, as with within classroom ability grouping, very little mobility takes place (Hallinan and Sørensen 1983). Constraints on mobility created by differences in curricula only adds to the need to keep the size distribution intact. The very reluctance to evaluate instruction and the heavy reliance on classification and credentials created by past assignments reduces the possibility of discovering differential individual development. Closure of educational trajectories results.

In summary, the processes of formation of instructional groups and the use of rankings in the assignment of students to these groups create educational trajectories that will tend to be closed. This has important implications for the distribution of educational opportunities within and between schools and for the degree of inequality of opportunity to be observed. These implications are discussed next.

THE DISTRIBUTION OF EDUCATIONAL OPPORTUNITIES

The analysis of the distribution of educational opportunities can be separated into two parts: the distribution within schools and the distribution between schools. There are also two types of opportunities to consider: opportunities for learning and opportunities for credentials. Almost all existing research focuses on differences between schools in actual academic achievement, and rarely employs an explicitly formulated concept of opportunities for learning. This lack of an explicit formulation is also typical of research on tracking and other types of within school variation in opportunities. A recent exception where attention is paid to the courses students actually have attended is provided by Gameron (1987).

The distribution of educational opportunities within schools would be measurable by considering variation in opportunities for learning, and opportunities for credentials over time and across students within a school. Over time very little is known about how opportunities for learning vary in terms of actual mean number of opportunities schools provide students at different grade levels; but presumably schools try to teach more per unit time, the older the student. It seems clear that there is increasing variation in opportunities for learning with age. It is typical of all school systems to produce an increased vertical differentiation of instructional groups with higher grade levels. Higher level groups typically provide more opportunities for learning than lower level groups and usually have more able students assigned to them. The result of this pattern of allocation of opportunities for learning is that in general the more able will be provided the most opportunities resulting in an increasing inequality of academic achievement by grade level. Further this inequality should be stregthened the more opportunities for learning are provided overall.

The proposition that the over-time distribution of opportunities for learning should result in more inequality in actual academic achievement with age should receive strong support, when those who do not continue in schools are included in the samples on which measures of academic achievement are obtained. If only those who remain in school are included, the proposition is less self evident. It may well be that those who remain in school are more equal in terms of ability to learn and this may counteract a tendency toward more inequality in academic achievement produced by more opportunities for learning by grade level. This sample selection problem certainly should be the likely pattern in traditional European systems where vertical differentiation is strongly related to the school leaving ages. In comprehensive American schools, the school leaving age affects the ability distribution less. It is still possible that the tendency toward more unequal outcomes is counteracted by teaching affecting the distribution of the ability to learn, though such equalization probably primarily occurs at lower grade levels. It should be noted that empirical evidence about any of this is difficult to establish, given the practice of standardizing tests by age level.

The overall distribution of opportunities for learning within schools is associated with vertically differentiated instructional groups. As discussed above, only if this vertical organization of instructional groups closely mirrors the student body with respect to ability to learn, will it be likely that equally able students are guaranteed equal opportunities for learning within a school. For many reasons this is unlikely to be the case. The extensive use of rankings in the allocation of students to vertically differentiated instructional groups may cause initially very similar students to be assigned to different level groups and hence be exposed to different opportunities for learning. This in turn is determined by the degree to which educational trajectories are closed.

It is an important complication for the analysis of the equality of opportunities for learning within schools that teaching may make students equal in ability who started out unequal. For this reason it is important when assessing the extent to which equal students receive equal opportunities within a school to compare opportunities for learning over the educational career for students who were equal at entry into the school. This evidently is difficult. However, the danger with short term comparison is that the ability distribution used to assess the degree of inequality of opportunity for learning will be partly endogenous to these opportunities.

It does seem a safe prediction that the more closed the educational trajectories of schools are, the greater the consequences for academic achievement and educational attainment of the possible inequality in opportunities for learning within the school for identical or almost identical students. Closed educational trajectories preserve initial inequalities, even though learning in such trajectories eventually may result in students becoming equally able in the end, so that equal students appear to be allocated equal learning opportunities.

Schools provide a well defined set of credentials and there is usually not much variation in how and when such credentials can be obtained. The main issue for the analysis of within-school opportunities for credentials is the degree to which these opportunities are unequally allocated to equal students. Such inequality in the opportunities for credentials results from the association between educational trajectories and credentials. Credentials will be unequally allocated to identical students to the extent that the organization of instructional groups is independent of student characteristics and the associated educational trajectories are closed. As with opportunities for learning, the possibility for inequality of opportunities for initially identical students within the schools will depend on how much mobility there is between educational trajectories and the instructional groups associated with these trajectories.

Openness of educational trajectories should reduce the degree of inequality of opportunity within a school because it allows for reassignment that responds to individual development and the discovery of earlier assignment errors. However, as discussed above, there are strong constraints on how open a system of educational trajectories can be because of the need to control the distribution of instructional groups, curricula, and organizational constraints. In particular it is very difficult to conceive of a system which avoids the use of ranking to vertically differentiated instructional groups. Rankings, because they do not provide information about distance between ranks always makes it possible that very similar students will receive very unequal credentials.

Between schools, differences in opportunities for learning and credentials result from differences among schools in credential distributions and curricula, in the ability and effort of teachers, in instructional facilities, and so forth. The general proposition that follows from the discussion here is that schools providing more opportunities for learning should provide higher levels of academic achievement. Further, schools providing more opportunities for learning should produce more inequality in academic achievement for given distribution of ability.

School differences in opportunities for learning would be minimal if instruction were adjusted to individual aptitude, and instructions had identical objectives with respect to desired learning outcomes; only the within-schools allocation of opportunities would then be a concern. The conclusion most have drawn about the main results of the school effects study is that all schools treat students pretty much alike. This is not necessarily the correct conclusion.

The conclusion about the similarity of schools are drawn from models additive in measures of individual characteristics as well as in measures of school's characteristics that are estimated on cross-sectional samples or short term longitudinal studies with measures of verbal ability and mathematics achievement as the dependent variables. It is difficult to draw believable conclusions with this research design.

First consider the dependent variable. A measure is needed that can be compared across schools. However, the strong local control of schools and the lack of internal control of teaching means that schools do not cover exactly the same curricula and therefore cannot be compared in national studies with respect to what they teach. What actually seems to be obtained are measures of aptitudes, if not ability, that only reflect opportunities for learning to the extent that teaching has changed the ability distribution of students. But if schools do affect aptitude distributions then cross-sectional or short term studies cannot identify the opportunity effects. This is simply because independent variables measuring student characteristics relevant for aptitude will be endogenous to independent variables measuring school characteristics. Schools effects reflecting differences in what schools teach are more likely to be found using outcome measures relating to what they teach.

With respect to the specification of the independent variables, the conventional additive specification suggests that schools add to the abilities of individuals in producing academic achievement, not that they provide opportunities for these individual characteristics to act on. As noted above, opportunity effects of schools should be detected as interaction effects using over time data. With these specifications, meaningful effects of opportunities for learning can in fact be established (see Sørensen and Hallinan 1977). The additive specification suggests that a certain level of academic achievement can be obtained even when schools teach nothing. This makes little sense.

Finally, as noted above, the ideal design for a study showing the relevance of school differences in opportunities for learning would be one that compared schooling inputs, in terms of initial ability at entry, to final educational outcomes across schools. Only such a comparison will allow unambiguous assessment of the cumulative impact of opportunities for learning as they directly affect academic outcomes through the provision of materials to learn, and indirectly by changing abilities to learn. The latter effect of opportunities cannot be differentiated from initial ability differences unless these differences are known. This design is not likely to be ever completely realized; though long term longitudinal studies exist, measurement problems are a serious obstacle.

There are good reasons to believe that differences among schools can be established with properly designed studies. In fact, the simplest interpretation of the difference between private and public schools reported by Coleman et al. (1982) is that private schools try to teach more than public schools, though a model properly designed to capture opportunity effects was not used in this research. The sector differences are greatly reduced when track is controlled for (Alexander and Pallas 1983), but this only proves the point since the main way private schools can provide more opportunities for learning would be to assign more students to tracks where they are taught more.

The organization of the opportunities for learning in educational trajectories has very important implications for the extent to which identical students are provided with different opportunities for learning. Even when schools provide completely identical opportunities overall, they may provide very unequal opportunities for individual students. This is because a student's access to opportunities for learning will depend on which other students he or she is competing with for this access. The degree to which a student's access to opportunities depends on the composition of the student body he belongs to, is a question of the degree to which educational trajectories are closed. The more closed the educational trajectories of a set of schools, the more inequalities in opportunities will be created by differences in student body composition, even if all schools are trying to create the same credentials, employ the same staff, and organize instruction identically.

The openness of educational trajectories in schools is then very important for what can be called inequality of educational opportunity by locale. Closed trajectories not only produce inequalities in opportunities for learning by locale, they also produce inequality of opportunities for credentials. As suggested above, it is in fact likely that schools are even more unresponsive to student body characteristics with respect to credentials than with respect to learning, so that the inequalities by locale could be greater with respect to credentials than with respect to learning. Such inequalities can be maintained because of the decoupling between structure and technical activity discussed above. In fact the decoupling allows schools to diffuse the degree of inequality of opportunity by locale. This may be a reason for its existence.

There is almost no direct evidence on the degree of inequality of opportunity by locale. The school effects studies do not address the issue in an interpretable manner for reasons discussed above. Closure of educational trajectories is not a variable that has been measured in research, though a beginning has been made (Rosenfeld and Sørensen 1987). When inequality of opportunity is studied by sociologists, it is inequality of opportunity by social origin.

As noted above the distribution of educational opportunities is important for the degree of inequality of opportunity by social origin. In given distribution of ability, the more opportunities for learning there are, the more inequality of opportunity for learning will be observed. Schools may of course try to change the distribution of ability in such a manner that the association between origin and ability is reduced, countering the impact of opportunities on inequality of opportunity. That the pattern still comes through, at least in higher grades, is shown in Sørensen (1987).

Inequality of opportunity by locale interacts with inequality of opportunity by origin. For example, it can be shown that both with respect to assignment to high ability groups in primary grades and with respect to assignment to academic tracks in High School, black students appear to be advantaged over white students. Net of ability, blacks seem to have a greater probability to be assigned to the instructional groups that should provide the most opportunities for learning (Sørensen and Hallinan 1983; Sørensen 1987). This is not because of reverse discrimination. The race effects appear when controls are introduced for the organization of the instructional groups, in particular the relative sizes of different level groups. High level instructional groups are simply relatively larger in schools black students attend.

It is likely, that inequality of opportunity by locale in general reduces inequality of opportunity by social origin also for other origin variables than race, but further research is clearly needed to establish the point. The general mechanism is that residential segregation increases the probability that students from lower origins will be assigned to educational trajectories providing better opportunities for learning. We know that there is no consistent effect of socioeconomic background on assignment to academic track net of ability (Heyns 1974; Alexander and McDill 1976). This result is surprising. In other contexts, such as promotion decisions, where rankings based on some prediction of future performance are used, there is an inclination to use ascriptive characteristics believed to convey information. It is quite possible that an origin bias in assignment of students to vertically differentiated instructional groups is counteracted by the different opportunity structures of the schools attended by students from different origins.

In terms of opportunity structures, the existence of inequality of opportunity by locale suggests that social segregation helps to reduce inequality of opportunity by origin. However, this will reduce the association between origin and academic achievement outcomes only if educational trajectories in different schools are closed and if schools with different student bodies provide the same opportunities for learning to students in similar trajectories. The provision of actual opportunities for learning is unlikely to be independent of the degree of segregation.

CONCLUSION

This chapter has emphasized the concept of educational opportunity as a key one for the sociological study of educational processes. It has proposed that major educational outcomes of interest to research should be seen as the result of individuals utilizing opportunities for learning and for credentials provided by schools. Schools affect educational outcomes by determining the number and kinds of opportunities provided and by structuring access to these opportunities. The organization of instructional groups and the process of assigning students to these groups have been shown to structure access to opportunities. It has been argued that of particular relevance is the degree to which the organization of instructional groups creates closed educational trajectories, because this will determine the degree to which students' access to educational opportunities depends on who they study with.

The measurement of opportunity differences within and between schools should be done by comparing educational outcomes for equally able students. It has been argued that most existing sociological research on the educational process is ill equipped to detect such variations in opportunities because of the specification of the models employed and the use of cross-sectional data. However, even when proper models and longitudinal data are employed, the variation in opportunities may be underestimated. Opportunities for learning provided at one point in time may be relevant for the distribution of abilities later on. Ideally, school variation in opportunities should be measured over long stretches of time; otherwise the ability distribution controlled for when measuring opportunities will be endogenous to the opportunity structure.

Much educational research in sociology has addressed the issue of inequality of opportunity by social origin, but little research has addressed systematically the concept of opportunity and the types of inequality of opportunity generated by the unequal allocation of opportunities to equally able students. While inequalities of opportunity within and among schools have received little attention, the discussion here nevertheless suggests that such inequalities are important for the existence of school effects and that the resulting inequalities of opportunity by locale is very relevant also for the degree of inequality of opportunity by social origin that has occupied research so much.

REFERENCES.

Alexander, K. L. and E. L. McDill 1976. "Selection and Allocation Within Schools: Some Causes and Consequences of Curriculum Placement". *American Sociological Review* 41:963–980.

Alexander, K. L. and A. M. Pallas 1983. "Private Schools and Public Policy: New Evidence on Cognitive Achievement in Public and Private Schools". *Sociology of Education* 56:(4) 170–181.

Barr, R. and R. Dreeben 1983. *How Schools Work*. Chicago: Chicago University Press.

Bidwell, C. E. and N. E. Friedkin 1987. "The Sociology of Education". *The Handbook of Sociology,* edited by Neil Smelser. New York: Sage Publications.

Cicourel, A. V. and John I. K. 1963. *The Educational Decision Makers*. Indianapolis: BobbsMerrill.

Coleman, J. S., E. Q. Campbell, C. J. Hobson, J. McPartland, A. Mood, F. D. Weinfeld and R. L. York 1966. *Equality of Educational Opportunity*. Washington, D.C.: U.S. Government Printing Office.

Coleman, J. S. and T. Hoffer 1987. *Public and Private Schools:—The Impact of Communities*. New York: Basic Books.

Coleman, J. S, T. Hoffer and S. Kilgore 1982. *High School Achievement*. New York: Basic Books.

Cremin, L. A. 1951. *The American Common School*. New York: Knopf.

Davis, J. S. 1966. "The Campus as a Frog Pond: An Application of the Theory of Relative Deprivation to the Career Decisions of College Men". *American Journal of Sociology* 72:17–31.

Dreeben, R. and A. Gamoran 1986. "Race, Instruction and Learning". *American Sociological Review*. 51:(5) 660–669.

Eder, D. J. 1979. *Stratification Within the Classroom*. Madison, Wisconsin: University of Wisconsin.

Gamoran, A. 1987. "The Stratification of High School Learning Opportunities". *Sociology of Education* 60:(3) 135–155.

Goldberger, A. S. and G. G. Cain 1982. "The Causal Analysis of Cognitive Outcomes in the Coleman, Hoffer and Kilgore Report". *Sociology of Education* 55:(2–3) 103–122.

Hallinan, M. T. and A. B. Sørensen 1983. "The Formation and Stability of Instructional Groups". *American Sociological Review* 48:(6) 838–851.

Heyns, B. 1974. "Social Selection and Stratification in Schools". *American Journal of Sociology* 79: 1434–1451.

March, J. G. and J. P. Olsen 1976. *Ambiguity and Choice in Organizations.* Bergen: Universitetsforlaget.

Meyer, J. W. and B. Rowan 1978. "The Structure of Educational Organizations". Pp. 78–109 in *Environments and Organizations,* edited by Marshall W. Meyer. San Francisco: Jossey-Bass.

Rosenfeld, R. A. and A. B. Sørensen 1987. "The Determinants of High School Tracking". Paper Presented at the 1987 Meeting of the American Sociological Association, Chicago.

Simmel, G. 1908. Soziologie. Leipzig: Duncker and C. Humblot.

Sørensen, A. B. 1983. "Processes of Allocation to Open and Closed Position in Social Structure". *Zeitschrift fuer Soziologie,* 12: 203–224.

―――1987. "The Organizational Differentiation of Students as an Opportunity Structure". Pp. 103–130 *The Social Organization of Schooling,* edited by Maureen T. Hallinan. New York: Plenum Press.

Sørensen, A. B. and M. T. Hallinan 1977. "A Reconceptualization of School Effects". *Sociology of Education* 50:(4) 522–535.

―――1983. "Race Effects on the Assignment to Ability Groups". Pp. 85–103 *The Social Context of Instruction,* edited by Louise Wilkenson Penelope Peterson and Maureen T. Hallinan. New York: Academic.

―――1986. "Effects of Ability Grouping on Growth in Academic Achievement". *American Educational Research Journal* 23:(4) 519–542.

EARLY SCHOOLING AS A "CRITICAL PERIOD" PHENOMENON

Doris R. Entwisle and Karl L. Alexander

Well into the present century, Americans believed schooling was the chief remedy for inequalities in social and economic opportunity. Over the last two decades, however, leaders and laypersons alike are increasingly disturbed by the failure of children from low socioeconomic groups (roughly the bottom 15 percent of the population in terms of income) to secure an education that will boost their life chances. Schools do not compensate for inequality in other spheres of life.

The facts as presently known are disquieting. Several independent lines of research indicate that secondary schools in the United States do not moderate to any appreciable degree cognitive or affective differences among youth, and

Research in the Sociology of Education and Socialization,
Volume 8, pages 27–55.
Copyright © 1989 by JAI Press Inc.
All rights of reproduction in any form reserved.
ISBN: 0-89232-929-7

that members of disadvantaged groups underachieve in school (Coleman et al. 1966; Hauser 1971; Jencks et al. 1972; Mosteller and Moynihan 1972). Whether evidence comes from large national surveys or from single class-rooms, the conclusion is the same: Blacks, Spanish-Americans, Chicanos, and American Indians do not profit as much from school as majority group students do. In a country dedicated to equality of opportunity, these facts are unsettling.

The fact that secondary schools appear to make little or no difference in terms of youths' relative achievements is hard for many people to accept. Null findings in general are psychologically unsettling, and, of course, ultimately unverifiable. Too, this particular "dismal conclusion" flies in the face of widely held beliefs in the American ethos that schools are, or at least can be, a potent force for good. So despite the evidence, seasoned investigators have continued to search for differential effects that secondary schools "should exert." And there are several reasons why differential effects of schools might not have been given proper credit in this literature: (1) Schools are the wrong unit of analysis; schooling effects are more pronounced within class-rooms where instruction actually takes place; these differences cancel out and are obscured when instructional groups or classes are combined in studies cast at the school level (Barr and Dreeben 1983; McPartland 1968; Alexander, McPartland, and Cook 1981). (2) School effects are confounded with large family effects that obscure school effects (Heyns 1978), and since schooling now is near univeral, it is difficult, if not impossible, to assess the effects of schooling per se. (3) Dynamic models may be needed to assess school effects; models used in practically all studies to date may be of the wrong functional form and so may fail to capture school effects (Sorensen and Hallinan 1977). (4) Models for explaining secondary (or later) attainment omit earlier attain-ment levels, so the contribution of home or background factors is spuriously inflated and overshadows school effects (Cook and Alexander 1981). (5) Longitudinal data that span many years are required to assess changes in school outputs net of intake variables, and a broader spectrum of outputs, including variation in behavioral problems and delinquency, should be exam-ined (Rutter 1970). All these explanations probably have some kernel of truth. None, however, gives reason to anticipate *large* school effects at the second-ary level through technical improvements in either research design or analysis plan.

The purpose of this chapter is to offer a new hypothesis and suggest a different arena for study: its thesis is that schooling is a "critical period" phenomenon. We suggest that schools do affect children differentially, but mainly *early* in their school careers when they are learning basic skills and their academic self-images are first taking form. It holds that in making the transition from home to full-time schooling, children develop different patterns of learning and different patterns of reliance on significant others to support that learning. One consequence of these patterns is that early in their school careers children enter achievement trajectories that place boundaries on their attainment thereafter. Another consequence is that the patterns of learning and of social relations established during this period tend to persist.

Curiously, the beginning school transition, which is closely linked to the critical period notion, has no label. No doubt in part because of this oversight, this transition has attracted remarkably little attention from researchers who take a life course perspective or from sociologists of education. However, the reader will see that considering this transition along with the critical period hypothesis organizes and integrates a diverse literature.

Beginning School as a Critical Period

The beginning school transition, like other major life transitions, implies that notions of the self change and that the person's role set is redefined by some new non-familial authority (see Elder 1968, p.4). When children begin school, they acquire a new definition of self—the academic self—and add a new role, that of student. This new role is a fundamental one, furthermore. Children are no longer wholly dependent on the family, and their work is evaluated by teachers, classmates, and ultimately by society as a whole. At this stage, too, because their social horizons suddenly expand, children discover that some people react to them according to physical appearance, social class, ethnic background, or level in school. They become ''social beings'' with an identity distinct from that of their familial group, and they begin to be seen in terms of long-range life goals.

The beginning school transition fits the usual definition of a critical period because it offers opportunities for development that coincide with key cognitive changes within the individual. The onset of formal schooling occurs at around the time children move from pre-operational to operational modes of thinking, and the first few years of school are designed to capitalize on these emergent cognitive capacities. The aim is to make children competent in terms of literacy, numeracy, and the other basic skills needed to function in modern industrial society. Furthermore, because these basic skills support all the schooling that will follow, if they are not laid down solidly at this time, the student finds it virtually impossible to attain a high level of schooling. Beginning school also triggers the start of a cumulative written dossier in which children's attributes, actions, and aptitudes are documented in great detail. This written record, which follows the individual for a long time, provides data for all to see, and by this means the reputations children earn during the first few years of school can directly help or hinder them for many years to come.

What kind of evidence is needed to support the critical period hypothesis? The most direct evidence would be that rates of children's growth vary more over this period than they do at other times and that differences among children established during this period persist. Less direct evidence would be that children's growth rates co-vary significantly in line with the resources or stimulation offered them during this period. To be more specific, some elementary schools have more resources than others, and if this period in life is indeed critical, then schools with more resources should stimulate more growth—we should see differences among the effectiveness of elementary schools.

To assess the idea of a critical period, we require two lines of evidence. The first would document individual or group differences in how, or how successfully, children negotiate the transition to full-time schooling. The second would demonstrate that how children negotiate this transition has long-lasting effects. The word ''critical'' implies the potential for failure—children who do not negotiate the transition as well as others are left more or less permanently behind.

REASONS FOR A CRITICAL PERIOD

Why would there be a ''critical period'' at the beginning of elementary school? A general reason, already stated, is that some important internal changes coincide with a profound change in the child's social status and social relations when formal schooling begins. More particular reasons, spelled out in what follows, have to do with children's psychological make-up, particularly their receptivity to schooling in the early years; with the nature of learning and the curriculum in the primary school years; and, perhaps most important, with the interaction between the child and the social character of the particular elementary school the child attends—the child's fit into the social niche provided by the school. We will discuss these in turn.

Children's Makeup

Prominent among the psychological characteristics that typify latency (age 6 to 8) children is *receptiveness to school experience*. Some first graders are eager to go to ''big school,'' happy to have a new pool of friends, and ready to embark on a new life adventure, while others are frightened and miserable. But happy or sad, first graders are not bored by school or the daily routine. They are learning about important everyday activities—how to make change, select lunch, tell time, or read signs. They need to know about the things they are learning, and the curriculum makes sense to them and to their parents. For this reason elementary students are very much in tune with the goals of the school. Virtually all parents and students are seriously concerned with basics of learning at this stage: literacy, numeracy, and good citizenship.

And there is considerable evidence of young elementary students' greater receptiveness to learning as compared to older students. For example, academic achievement on many standardized tests begins to level off in the upper elementary grades in the familiar sigmoid fashion. Schneider (1980) found that students' yearly gains decreased from the third through the seventh grades, both in terms of vocabulary and Iowa Tests of reading and math concepts. Similarly, in a random sample of Baltimore school children, we find diminishing gains in verbal achievement (California Achievement Test Levels 11, 12, 13, and 14) as children progressed from first through fourth grade. Children gained 56 units in verbal achievement over grade 1, 43 units over grade 2, 30 units over grade 3, and 35 units over grade 4.

Actually, this sort of decelerating cognitive growth pattern as children mature has been documented for a long time though it has seldom attracted comment. For example, the same decelerating trends appear in 1916 data pertaining to speed in silent reading and in 1944 Stanford Achievement Test scores (Stephens 1956, pp. 162–163). And in the recent debate as to whether private secondary schools are more effective than public in fostering cognitive growth, at least one commentator (Jencks 1985) has directed attention to the quite small average gains registered altogether during the last two years of high school in both public and private schools. The "diminishing returns" idea is certainly not novel as applied to school learning, but its implications for school effectiveness are generally overlooked. If increments in test scores are many points greater in the lower than in the higher grades, there is obviously more room for individual variability in performance in the lower grades. This in consistent with the requirements for a "critical period."

Another notable fact about the psychological makeup of children ages 6 to 8, in contrast to older students (Coleman 1961), is the positive connotation of being a "good" student. Young students like to have their work posted on the class bulletin board; they carry home papers for their parents to praise; they are not afraid to be "the best" or "the first" in anything, and genuinely admire others who achieve that status. Because of this zest and enthusiasm for learning, young students tend to be closely engaged with the schooling process. By contrast, at higher grade levels, high dropout rates, repeated acts of vandalism, widespread disaffection with school, and students' general disengagement from school all attest to the limited nature of this "honeymoon" period, at least for many youngsters.

Young school children also possess a pervasive optimism about their own abilities. The majority of first graders have high expectations for their own success, whether they are rich or poor, white or black (Entwisle and Hayduk 1982; Entwisle et al. 1987), so whatever the level of their ability or the task at hand, they approach the classroom in a positive frame of mind. Over the years some children revise their attitudes in a downward direction, but their prevailing initial optimism undoubtedly increases their receptivity to school influence in the early years. This contrast in students' self-images between the early and the later school years is not well understood (Entwisle et al. 1987), but children's self-esteem does diminish the further they go in school (Morse 1964). Older children rate themselves as less smart, less good, and less hardworking than do younger children (Blumenfeld et al. 1986), and they are less likely to perceive themselves as able (Blumenfeld et al. 1982). Given the positive relation between a favorable self-image and learning (Brookover et al. 1967; Bachman et al. 1978), we would expect that younger children would be especially responsive to schooling.

One reason children's academic self-images erode as they progress in school could be that until then children are compared mainly with themselves at an earlier age. Before children start formal schooling, they are growing bigger, learning more, and gaining better control over themselves, just through physical maturation with the passage of time, so there is a positive valence attached to ipsative comparisons. Being compared with a group of peers is another matter, however, because all are growing and maturing, but at different rates. Those who are taller or get their permanent teeth sooner are awarded higher status by their peers even though physical characteristics have little to do with schooling. Another reason children's self-images erode is because they become more realistic about rating themselves as their cognitive capabilities increase. Certainly by second grade children engage in self-comparison (Markus and Nurius 1984), and no one is likely to measure up favorably against thirty other classmates on all dimensions. In the class as a whole, since only one child can be "best" in any given activity, all others experience some loss of prestige. And children do not spare each other's feelings—it is crystal clear who is chosen last to play or to eat lunch with. In fact, children sometimes find it hard to learn not to voice invidious comparisons or comment on others' perceived weaknesses.

Still another reason for young children's psychological receptiveness pertains to teacher-student relations. Primary children tend to be emotionally attached to their teachers, often perceiving them as parent surrogates, and many elementary teachers reciprocate their pupils' feelings. Frequently teachers in the early grades have selected this level of education because of their own needs to nurture, and because they believe that teachers can make a critical difference in the sensitive early years. The teacher's positive or negative expectations do seem to matter more for young children than they do for older ones (Brophy and Good 1974; Mendels and Flanders 1973; Seaver 1973), and certainly the teacher as an authority figure is more impressive to younger than to older children if only because more social distance separates the two.

Nature of School Learning

The nature of learning in the early school years also is relevant to the "critical period" notion as it applies to this stage of schooling. There is a dearth of comparative information on how the nature of school learning may change with age, but we do know that younger children are more receptive to rewards, especially extrinsic ones. They are also surprisingly sensitive to minor nuances in the teacher's tone of voice (Kashinsky and Weiner 1969) and to non-verbal communication of either a visual or auditory nature (Hall 1984). It seems likely that the reward system of the school may be much more effective for young children than it is for older children.

Another circumstance that may promote unusually effective learning at the elementary level is that the school curriculum *is* concretely and clearly defined, most often consisting of individual instructional units in a mastery-oriented sequence with daily tasks matched to individual pupils' skill levels. Commonly there are at least three reading or math groups in a class with a clear hierarchy in terms of competence. In Balitmore City, for example, each instructional unit is followed by a competency test, but even in less structured curricula the daily checking of papers and homework, frequent demands for recitation, and the like, keep students closely on task with materials matched to their skill level. Teachers know exactly where each student stands, and because of this, resources are likely to be deployed more effectively than at higher grade levels, where such individualization is impractical.

Early schooling, especially in the first two grades, is also very intense in focus. Reading and mathematics dominate the day. Students spend all or most of their time with one or two teachers and the same set of classmates, even in open-space schools. Children who are doing well can make great strides, but those who are not doing well, perhaps because of a personality clash with the teacher or because of differences in pupil-teacher background (Alexander, Entwisle, and Thompson 1987), remain day after day in an uncongenial environment. This intensity and concentratedness of the instructional setting must increase interindividual variability in performance or produce a Matthew effect. Children who are doing better tend to move even faster, while those who are less competent fall further and further behind.

Children's learning in elementary school is also cumulative and vertical in a way that later learning is not, and this should serve to magnify individual differences. In reading, for example, children acquire function words ("and," "if," "of") and are drilled on them. Thus, they gradually accumulate a sight vocabulary that they use every day. Similarly in arithmetic, children learn to add 2 and 2 and then use this fact almost daily as a base to support more learning. A child who misses learning one or two "number facts" must make up the lack, but "making it up" is not always easy. Falling behind also triggers affective fallout, undermining the child's confidence or other people's expectations for the child.[1]

Perhaps most critical for early learning is that beginning pupils have to develop a cognitive map to guide themselves through the labyrinth of knowledge they are asked to master. They try to figure out the frames of reference teachers employ and the symbols of evaluation teachers use (White 1968) even though this may be a difficult or even an impossible task. On standard report cards children may be graded on thirty or more topics, and it is hard to imagine how a teacher can rate thirty youngsters reliably on thirty criteria. We found in an earlier study, for example, that first grade teachers had no consistent frame of reference for "language," even though it was a topic for which they assigned marks on report cards (Entwisle and Hayduk 1978). But however unrealistic or unreliable, children must deal with such systems, and once they make assumptions about the schooling process there may be little incentive or opportunity to change. For example, a child who tries hard in reading for one marking period may see no results—perhaps he/she went from a "low B" to a "high B" or perhaps the teacher gave everybody a "B." What the child sees, however, is that extra effort had no pay-off. The point is that outcomes of schooling for elementary students cover much more than the subject matter because they learn how to meet the demands of the school, discover how to deal with adults in authority, construct cognitive schema by which to understand how classrooms work, and develop strategies to deal with the bureaucracy of the school. These strategies or assumptions may be misguided but there is no guarantee that they will change. Particularly striking evidence of this is that children from low SES schools continue to have high expectations for marks even when they have received low marks on several successive report cards (Entwisle and Hayduk 1982). Such unrealistic expectations must provide a weak basis for effective self-regulation of behavior.

Fit Between Student and School

It is during this period that children must first accommodate to a bureaucratically organized institution, and this too contributes to its "critical" character.

Although it tends to be largely overlooked, in the first year or two of school children are sorted and categorized by the school in ways that have great bearing on their long-term fate in the educational system. Within-class ability grouping for instruction in reading and math has received considerable research attention in this regard (Felmlee and Eder 1983; Haller and Davis 1981; Eder 1981; Rowan and Miracle 1983; Hallinan and Sorensen 1987), but there are many other aspects of "sorting and selecting" that have gone largely unnoticed and, in fact, are obscured in the typical research design. For example, decisions are made to provide children special services, to place them in classes for slow learners, to hold them back, or to take other administrative actions, and many of these decisions can have permanent consequences. Researchers tend to overlook this early triage-like sorting because they do not focus on birth cohorts but focus rather on "sixth graders" or "junior high students," or some other group defined by the school. This focus, though, is on *survivors* of a birth cohort—those who remain after much of the critical sorting has occurred. With school grades as sampling units, not birth cohorts, the great variability that characterizes children during the critical period is disguised because many of those who started school at the same time have been reassigned or redirected. The largest part of this redirection occurs in the first year or two.

In the Beginning School Study, for example, which is comprised of a random sample of 825 Baltimore first graders in 1982, we found that fully 16 percent were held back at the end of the first grade, 22 percent had received various kinds of special services, and 11 percent had been placed in special education classes. In year two, an additional 8 percent were retained in grade, and 11 percent received special services. By the end of year two 13 percent of all children who started first grade in 1982 had been assigned to special education classes. Clearly, the first year or two is a critical period for sorting and labeling students, and these labels, once applied, are usually there to stay. The research literature on grade retention suggests that its effects on cognitive and affective outcomes generally are deleterious, at least in the short term (Harvard Educational Letter 1986; Jackson 1975), and virtually nothing is known about the consequences for youngsters of other administrative classifications that might be imposed on them. We do know, however, labeling of a child as "difficult" or "retarded," once established, seems very hard to dislodge (Sameroff 1975; Sameroff and Chandler 1975).

One direct consequence of this severe sorting process is the social identity that children acquire, and such social constructions of student identity could either help or hinder schooling. A child with a "good" reputation is well aware of it and works hard to live up to that image. A child with a "bad" reputation, on the other hand, also may try to live up to it, or may have little

opportunity to change it. The importance of "reputation" is hard to exaggerate. In an elementary school, for example, if a teacher knows older sibs of a
first grader, she sets her expectations accordingly (Seaver 1973). Teachers
also know which children come from solo parent homes and adjust their
expectations downward (Epstein 1984). The school reacts strongly to children's "reputations" because the elementary school community is small and
closely connected. The child in elementary school is rather like the village
resident whose state of health, family problems, financial status, job history,
and religious affiliation are public knowledge, all taken into account if he/she
applies for a loan from the local bank. Teachers build strong expectations for
children in the first two grades that *follow* them into the next grade (Entwisle
and Hayduk 1982).

The fit between student and school also tends to be tight in elementary
school because schools are relatively small and their catchment areas match
residential neighborhoods. In many parts of the country, even in large cities,
elementary schools are placed so students can walk to school. Middle class
students go to "middle class" schools, and working class or minority students go to schools where their classmates tend to be like themselves. This
close matching between the home and the school leads to larger between-
school variation and smaller within-school variation in terms of student characteristics in the primary grades than at higher grade levels. Rosenberg (1979)
reports, for example, that for a random sample of children in Baltimore, 47
percent of those eight to eleven years old attended schools where the within-
school variation in class was less than .7 on the Hollingshead Index, whereas
for children fifteen or over in the same random sample, only 20 percent
attended schools where within-school variation was this small. The greater
between-school variability in home background for children in Maryland
elementary schools is also noted in a statewide accountability survey (1976)
showing that among elementary schools in Baltimore the median education of
children's mothers ranged from 8.1 years to 12.4 years, whereas among
secondary schools the range in median mother's education was less, 8.8 to
11.4 years. A close fit between home and school would be expected to
potentiate effects of schools on students, whether positive or negative.

Elementary schools look highly similar because their curricula and clientele
are perceived as similar, yet, because these schools are small and scattered all
over school districts, they differ enormously in terms of the facilities they
offer and the kinds of students they enroll. In fact, we believe elementary
schools are much *more* heterogeneous in terms of their facilities and student
bodies than secondary schools (Alwin and Otto 1977, p. 270, make this same
point).

Direct evidence of the greater variability of elementary as compared to secondary schools is available for individual states. For example, both the number and variety of elementary schools in Maryland school districts consistently exceeds the number and variety of secondary schools. In Baltimore City the majority of schools offering instruction in the first six grades enroll students from kindergarten through grade 6. But there are some 14 other organizational patterns (K–3; K–4; K–5; K,4–6; K–9; K–12; P–2; 5–6; P–3; P–4; P–6; 2–3; 2–6; 3–6; 4–6; 5–6) that exist in 30 other Baltimore elementary schools. By contrast, Baltimore City secondary schools are 9–12 with only three exceptions (K–12; 7–12; 8–12). The greater variability in structure at the elementary level would be expected to lead to greater variability in performance.

Details aside, there are many reasons to suggest why youngsters may be especially sensitive to school in the first few years, reasons why the period could be critical. In what follows we will assemble research evidence consistent with differences in school effectiveness that could impinge on students over this critical period.

DIFFERENCES AMONG ELEMENTARY SCHOOLS

As mentioned, indirect evidence in favor of the critical period hypothesis would be that children progress at markedly different rates in primary or elementary schools. If the period is "critical," then some schools or programs or curricula or teachers should have stronger effects than others. At the beginning of this chapter we pointed out that there are only small differences in schooling effects at the secondary level. The critical period hypothesis says, in effect, that secondary school is the wrong level to search for such effects, or that larger inter-school differences would occur at the elementary level. There is considerable evidence to marshall in support of this proposition.

Evidence of this cropped up in the very early surveys related to school effectiveness, for example. In the Plowden Report (1967), with respect to teachers' salaries, non-teaching staff and wages, proportion of oversize classes, expenditures for fuel and the like, all coefficients of variation for primary schools exceeded the coefficients for equivalent indices of secondary schools.

Also in the Coleman Report (1966), the proportion of variance accounted for by between-school variation is greater at the elementary than at the secondary level. Table 3.21.2, p. 293, cites percentages of school-to-school variation (in relation to total achievement) as follows: nonverbal ability 18 percent and 17 percent at grades 1 and 3 compared to 14 percent at grades 9 and 12; verbal ability 18 percent and 22 percent at grades 1 and 3 compared to

16 percent and 17 percent at grades 9 and 12. Elementary schools are likely to be less closely regulated than secondary schools so variance in school facilities is more readily tolerated at the elementary level. Whereas 62 percent of elementary schools were known to be accredited by the state at the time of the Coleman Report, 93 percent of secondary schools were known to be accredited.

Cross-National Research

Cross-national research in third world countries provides another kind of evidence that elementary schools have differential effects. Heyneman and Loxley (1983) compared primary schools across countries in Africa, Asia, Latin America, and the Middle East. They found effects of school and/or effects of teacher quality on academic achievement in primary schools to be comparatively greater in countries with the lowest incomes. Likewise, Madaus, Airasian, and Kellaghan (1980), in their review of IEA projects in 21 countries, noted that the proportion of variance in achievement accounted for by differences between schools is much higher in underdeveloped than in developed countries. In fact, Inkeles (1977) believes that the most important evidence produced by the IEA studies is their demonstration that the ''quality'' of schooling children receive plays a substantial role in determining the scores they obtain on standardized tests.

One interpretation of the strongest school effects being found in the least developed countries hinges on the idea that there is greater variability in school facilities in less than in more developed countries. Whereas wealthy countries can put a high floor under the minimal standards for teacher certification, for instance, poor countries may not have any floor, no matter how little training teachers have, because that would disqualify too many teachers. For this reason the range in teacher quality is likely to be greater in less developed than in more developed countries. With a greater range in teacher quality, associations between school characteristics and student outcomes will be stronger. Put another way, by restricting variance on an independent variable (quality of teachers), one thereby attenuates statistical associations of that variable with others, like pupil achievement. Another interpretation is that with population socioeconomic levels strongly skewed toward the low end in poor countries, there is more opportunity for school influence to manifest itself and not overlap home influence. In support of this line of reasoning, research on secondary schooling in Israel has found that contextual effects on both achievement and aspirations are especially strong in ungrouped schools, i.e. those that are highly variable in student body composition (Shavit and Williams 1985).

Evidence of Differential Effects of U.S. Elementary Schools[2]

A number of studies in the U.S. document differential effects of elementary schools or classrooms. Those reviewed below were selected because of their variety as well as because of the quality of their evidence.

Brookover et al. (1979) surveyed fourth and fifth graders in a random sample of 91 Michigan elementary schools and found considerable inter-school variability in achievement associated with the socio-psychological climate and the role definitions that characterized a school's social system. Net of effects of socioeconomic background and racial composition, the increment in between-school variance in students' average achievement in reading and math explained by social climate varied from 4 percent in the total statewide sample to 36 percent in the black portion of that sample. A complementary analysis (p. 58) suggests that about 6 percent of the variance in average achievement between schools in unique to climate in the statewide sample.

School climate explained even more between-school variance in students' self concept of ability (a minimum of 58 percent after socioeconomic status and racial composition were taken into account). Differences among school climates were defined in terms of students' sense of academic futility, students' perceptions of teacher expectations, student academic norms, and the like.

The Brookover group also directly observed pairs of schools with contrasting levels of achievement matched for low socioeconomic level and racial composition. In the higher achieving schools, where staff had high expectations for students and were committed to seeing that mathematics and reading were learned, teachers assumed that it was possible for students to learn and that students would learn if provided appropriate instruction. In the lower achieving schools, "slow" students were often totally left out of instructional activities.

To see whether school resources affected the cognitive achievement of black inner-city children in New Haven, Murnane (1975) studied children's reading and arithmetic performance in the second and third grades longitudinally. He concluded (p. 77) that there are important differences in the amount of learning that takes place in different classrooms, and that "these differences consist both of differences among classrooms within the same school and *differences among schools*" (italics ours). Teachers in some schools were more successful in raising the cognitive skills of their students than in other schools. In other words, average quality of teachers differed across schools.

With a randomly selected sample of public school students in Philadelphia, Summers and Wolfe (1977) found several kinds of convincing differences among schools. They examined how differences in school resources affected gains from the third to the sixth grade on the Iowa Test of Basic Skills (Composite). They distinguished between teacher quality and other school measures such as class size and minority representation. Teachers with degrees from higher rated colleges had students whose learning rates were greater, especially if the student came from a lower income family. Summers and Wolfe also found that low achieving students did worse in larger classes (more than 28 students), while high achieving students did better. Smaller schools appeared to be better for all students but especially black students. All students did better in racially balanced (40% to 60% black) rather than in segregated schools.

So far in this section the main focus has been on inter-school differences in students' standardized test scores as a function of various kinds of school resources. Entwisle and Hayduk (1982) studied mainly processual differences from one elementary school to another. They followed several cohorts of children who began first grade between 1971 and 1976 in three Baltimore elementary schools that differed strongly in social class and ethnic composition. Using a model that included parent, teacher, and peer ratings, they traced youngsters' expectations for achievement and their marks in reading and arithmetic over a three-year period. Children in the two working class schools consistently expected marks much higher than those they received and did not modify their expectations downward in light of the low marks that actually appeared time after time on their report cards, as noted earlier. Children in the middle class school, on the other hand, not only expected marks close to the level of marks they received, but raised or lowered their expectations in accordance with the marks they saw on their report cards. The children's process of expectation regulation was thus not the same from one school to another.

Entwisle and Hayduk found in addition that teachers' marks were less persistent from one semester to the next in the middle class as compared to the two working class schools. (Structural coefficients representing the persistence in children's marks from one grade to the next in reading and math were typically three times as large in the integrated working class school as in the white middle class school.) One implication of strong persistence in teachers' marks is that pupil change was less possible or, put another way, that the schooling process was less open in the working class as compared to the middle class school. In this sense students exercised less influence over what happened to them in the working class schools.

Also, parents in the working class schools exercised less influence. Parents in all three schools had significant influence on their children's very first marks in first grade, but only in the middle class school did parents' expectations and their estimates of their children's general ability continue to affect the children's performance later on. In one school, then, home influences continued strong, while in other schools they faded.

These results have important implications we believe: studies that are far removed from the day to day experiences of youngsters risk missing much of what is important in the schooling process, as do studies which consider only the "snapshot of the moment." Critical period experiences most likely are grounded in the details of classroom and interpersonal dynamics, not in gross features of the school as a collectivity. It is equally certain that they reflect a cumulation of experience that expresses itself over time. Evidence on this last point is reviewed next.

LASTING EFFECTS OF EARLY SCHOOLING

A key aspect of the "critical period" hypothesis is evidence for long-term effects of early schooling. To be critical, a period must have implications that carry on into the future, so that inter-person differences established during that period bear on students' life chances. Some research, although not a great deal, can be assembled that documents long-lasting effects of early schooling on later schooling or on life outcomes more generally.

Some evidence for lasting effects of early schooling comes from 11 experiments, conducted by 11 different research teams during the 1960s, reviewed in a monograph by Lazar and Darlington (1982). In a follow-up conducted when children in the original studies were 9 to 19 years old, experimental group children were less likely to be assigned to special education (58 percent or less) or to be retained in grade (38 percent or less) than control children.[3] These more positive outcomes occurred regardless of the child's sex, ethnic background, or initial ability level. Furthermore, some of these long-lasting effects of the experimental programs differed from school to school. For example, the proportion of students who later ended up in special education classes or who were retained in grade differed across schools within programs. In these experiments both the achievement related attitudes of the child and the mother's attitudes toward the child's school performance were also affected over the long run.[4]

Other evidence consistent with long-lasting effects of early schooling comes from a research project of "unconventional methodology and unusually long duration" in a disadvantaged urban neighborhood. Pedersen, Faucher, and Eaton (1978) examined how different first grade teachers affected their students' status when children reached adulthood. There was a positive correlation between having one first grade teacher (Miss A) and youngsters' later success. When Miss A's pupils were between 13 and 30 years old, they surpassed other pupils from the same school in that 57 percent of them had completed ten grades or more compared with 42 percent for pupils of other first grade teachers. Adults who had been in Miss A's class had better homes, paid more rent, had better looking homes, themselves were better looking, and held more prestigious jobs than did adults who had Misses B or C in first grade.

Although these findings could stem from unknown selective factors that gave members of Miss A's class some advantage from the start, number of sibs, father's occupational status, and the family's welfare status were controlled in the path model used in the evaluation. This study thus provides data consistent with the critical period hypothesis because differences in children's early school experiences appeared to have long-lasting and important effects.

Entwisle and Hayduk (1988) found substantial long-term effects of the processual differences they noted among three Baltimore elementary schools. In a follow-up of children identified in their three-school study cited earlier, they found that some of the differences in children's school performance observed in the first three grades that were attributable to parents or teachers persisted over the long term. For example, children who attended the middle class school continued to respond to early parent influences four to nine years later. The parent's estimate of the child's ability in third grade was a strong predictor of these youngsters' English/reading scores (explained variance increased by over 16 percent with *cognitive ability controlled*). In the other two schools which were in working class neighborhoods where teachers' expectations had had substantial effects in the early grades, Entwisle and Hayduk found that teacher expectations measured in grades 1 and 2 significantly predicted youngsters' English and math scores four to nine years later (current cognitive ability controlled). Thus, depending on the school the children had attended during their early years, their achievement later on continued to reflect either parent *or* teacher expectations measured many years earlier. (It is noteworthy that teachers' influence persisted for working class students because this is consistent with Heyns's [1978] conclusion that schooling helps compensate for the dearth of intellectual resources in disadvantaged households or communities). Furthermore, these long-lasting effects are robust in that they are consistent across two kinds of tests (California Achievement Tests and Iowa Tests of Basic Skills) in both English/reading and math, and hold up when the child's *later* cognitive ability is controlled.[5]

Stevenson and Newman's (1986) study in Minneapolis agrees with that of Entwisle and Hayduk, for they found children's grade 10 standardized test scores in reading and math were significantly affected by teachers' ratings made in grades 2 and 5. Likewise, Hess et al. (1984) found that maternal expectations for the child's achievement in preschool predicted achievement in grade 6.

There are thus convincing links in a number of studies between early social influences and children's achievement much later in that students' standardized achievement scores in English and mathematics continued to respond many years later to teacher or parent influences experienced in the critical period. How could this come about? We hypothesize the following sequence. In making the transition from home to school, students need emotional support. As they build an academic self-image, learn what is important to do, and discover ways to deal with a potentially threatening and frightening environment, students come to depend on *particular* significant others who enable them to cope early in their school careers. Getting off to a good start gives these students a competitive advantage from that point on.

The precise mechanisms involved in explaining the long-term effects observed by Entwisle and Hayduk are debatable, but with later cognitive ability controlled, as it was, persistence in cognitive traits cannot be the answer. Although teachers could resemble each other at the earlier and later points in time, it seems unlikely that any resemblance between a first or second grade teacher and the youngster's later teachers would be strong enough to produce effects of the size observed. What seems more likely is that teachers prompted a superior performance in some students in elementary school. Children for whom teachers have high expectations are held to stricter standards, called upon more, and are more often pressed for answers (Brophy and Good 1974). The favorable teacher expectations would promote more learning in the early grades, and help in establishing high achievement levels. In other words, teachers in the primary grades helped some of these children cope in the critical period. Not only does a high level of performance in one year facilitate a high level in the next, but a ''paper person'' is created that follows the child from grade to grade. These cumulative records that follow children through school could support high performance in the later grades by affecting subsequent teachers' expectations.

Whatever the actual mechanisms involved, these data and other similar data suggest that continuity in achievement over substantial time periods can be linked to social resources in children's early environments. The social context of early schooling accounted for persistence in children's achievement trajectories quite apart from any persistence that can be ascribed to stability in the children's cognitive characteristics.

These findings support a proposition easily stated but seldom tested, namely, that children's development is embedded in social life, so that to understand it one must take account of the social system in which children function. The children in Entwisle and Hayduk's sample appeared to develop ''distinctive intellectual adaptations to the special demands of their environment'' (see Ginsburg 1986, p. 186). Some relied more on parents than on teachers, while others relied more on teachers than on parents. And the follow-up suggests that children's achievement responded *for a long time* to the social influences they experienced during the critical period.

Finally, there is direct evidence of differences in effects of elementary schools on standardized test performance in the 7th through 12th grades (Alexander, McPartland, and Cook 1981). In the Educational Testing Service Study of Academic Prediction and Growth, which is based upon 17 communities scattered throughout the United States, biennial surveys were made of 27 high schools and their junior high and elementary feeder schools from 1961 to 1969. The criteria considered are individual students' standardized test scores in 7th, 9th, 11th and 12th grade. In the ETS data there are appreciable differences in effects of elementary schools on standardized test performance in both the verbal and quantitative domains at every later test point. These differences, associated with net standardized regression coefficients in the 0.1–0.2 range at 7th grade, diminish in size with the passage of time but remain significant (in the 0.1 range) even in 12th grade.

To sum up: There are lasting effects of early schooling when we examine later school performance in terms of grade retention or achievement scores. There also appear to be lasting effects of the social determinants of learning in the critical period, in that exposure to particular kinds of teachers or parents in the crucible years leaves an indelible imprint. Although the exact mechanisms to explain these milieu effects are not altogether clear, the evidence itself is impressive because it comes from several sources.

NEGOTIATION OF THE TRANSITION TO FULL-TIME SCHOOLING

Finally, direct evidence in support of the critical period hypothesis consists of data showing that some children are more successful in negotiating the transition into full-time schooling than others and that this success is related to social background. We can present some limited evidence of this sort from our ongoing panel study of cognitive and affective development over the primary and middle school years.

In 1982, as mentioned earlier, we began to follow a stratified random sample of Baltimore school children of whom about half are white, and half black. This project has been designated the Beginning School Study (BSS). When the cognitive growth of these children is plotted in relation to the yearly calendar, so as to separate growth during the school year from growth over the summer, we see first that attending school has a strong equalizing effect. Table 1 shows that, over the first two grades, children who come from the least favorable home backgrounds, if they are white, grow at a faster rate in

Table 1. Changes in CAT Scores in the Verbal and Math Domains by Parent Education Level and Minority/Majority Status[a]

	Verbal			Math		
	Black	White	Difference W-B	Black	White	Difference W-B
School year, first grade						
Parent education						
Less than 12	48.80	58.89	10	39.49	48.11	9
12	61.75	65.00	3	48.12	51.22	3
More than 12	51.46	47.83	−4	42.31	36.25	−6
Summer after first grade						
Parent education						
Less than 12	−2.24	−0.24	2	3.40	−0.83	−4
12	−4.40	1.66	6	−0.14	0.50	1
More than 12	4.54	19.88	15	2.44	16.71	14
School year, second grade						
Parent education						
Less than 12	45.04	48.55	4	40.16	45.97	6
12	44.33	40.08	−4	41.30	40.96	0
More than 12	39.87	35.54	−4	44.55	37.23	−7

[a]The 534 children in this sample are those for whom all data were present on measures in Table 1 and who were 6.90 years or less in age as of December 1982. There are no significant differences in test scores between this sample and the full sample for whom we have fall scores in 1982 (N = 770 for verbal, N = for 769 for math).

terms of standardized verbal and math achievement than do children who come from the most favorable backgrounds. And black children do as well as, or better than, white children if their parents are high school graduates or better. Black children who come from less favorable backgrounds do not do as well, however, even though the personal resources they brought with them—beginning test scores, personal maturity level, and the like—and their home backgrounds, look similar to those of the white children. The less advantaged black children profited significantly less from instruction in both first grade and second grade than did the comparable white children.

It bears emphasis that in this study, black children and white children were almost exactly equivalent in terms of their backgrounds and personal resources. Average verbal CAT scores in October of first grade were 280 for blacks and 281 for whites; their math scores showed only a small difference (269 for blacks versus 274 for whites). Yet, the blacks' growth did not follow the pattern of the whites' in grade one because better off black children gained more than their white counterparts in grade 1, while blacks whose parents' education was limited to high school graduation or less gained less than their white counterparts (Table 1). Over the second year the relative gains of blacks improved for those whose parents had at least a high school education, but white children from the least advantaged homes continued to outpace blacks from similar family circumstances. Summarizing these trends from the beginning of first grade to the end of second grade reveals small or no lags for blacks *except* for blacks from homes where parents are not high school graduates—by then they lagged 16 points (about half a standard deviation) in the verbal domain and 10 points (about a third of a standard deviation) in math. The grade 1 shortfall persisted into grade 2, and in grade 2 the rate of growth for relatively less well off blacks continued at a slower pace than that of comparable whites. Thus, blacks from lower parent education backgrounds had more difficulty making the transition into full-time schooling than did whites, and these differences persisted.

Elsewhere (Entwisle and Alexander in preparation) we have devoted considerable attention to modeling this phenomenon, and its roots appear to be in school more than in home experience. Black parents have about the same expectations for their children's deportment in school as do white parents, and differences in behavior standards between home and school are not a source of difficulty for children in this sample (Alexander, Entwisle, Cadigan, and Pallas 1987). Although more black children than white children came from solo parent homes, this is not linked to the differential growth over the first two grades (Thompson, Alexander, and Entwisle in press). Nor is there evidence that TV watching is a factor.

We do see, however, that black children received lower marks from the very start of first grade than white children did, with many other variables controlled (Entwisle and Alexander 1988) and that a low mark is more likely to persist for a black child than for a white child. The reasons for this pattern are not entirely clear (see Alexander and Entwisle in press for some of the possibilities), but when combined with the fact that blacks recieve lower marks than whites as early as the first marking period of first grade (despite having near equivalent fall testing averages), its implications are sobering.

Our investigations also have revealed that teachers' own social origins exercise a strong influence in how they react to the status attributes of their students (Alexander, Entwisle, and Thompson 1987). In particular, low status and minority pupils experience difficulty in the classes of high status teachers. They are evaluated by their teachers as less mature, their teachers hold lower expectations for them, and their year-end marks and test scores are depressed by these indicators of social distance. The black children from homes where parents have less than a high school education are both low status and minority—the ones for whom teacher disaffection is the greatest. And the consequences of this likely are both magnified and especially long lasting under such circumstances. Such youth, more so than others, depend on the resources and experiences of schooling for their cognitive development (Heyns 1978), *and* they are more sensitive than others to variations in such resources and experiences (Coleman et al. 1966; St. John 1971), yet the interpersonal climate of their early school experiences often is distant and rejecting rather than close and supportive. For many such youth the critical period experiences of the early school years serve only to set the stage for an all too common pattern of chronic underachievement.

That early performance indicators should anticipate later ones is not at all surprising, but the fact that early shortfalls appear for blacks is disturbing, for it indicates that minority youngsters will have to "bounce back" from academic difficulties that may be peculiar to this primary school transition period. If the early achievements of such youth are in fact depressed owing to more severe "transition shock," then the present analysis is cause for concern for it could signal reverberations which continue long after the "temporary adjustment problems" have been resolved.

More research is needed on the social resources that support the transition into full-time schooling, but the research reviewed above lends credence to the notion of a critical period. Furthermore, the differences in transition shock that we observe between blacks and whites who are judged to be in other respects comparable, line up with the extensive data showing that black and minority children generally do not achieve in school at levels comparable to those of majority students. The gap in achievement associated with minority status, long a source of perplexity, may have its origins in the failure of social supports or lack of social resources over a critical period.

COMMENTARY

If a critical period does exist, why has it attracted so little attention? There are several possible reasons, not necessarily mutually exclusive.

1. A latency period. The imagery of a latency period in middle childhood, originating with Freud, is pervasive and carries with it some subtle assumptions. Over the past 20 years there has been an explosion in research on the cognitive functioning of school-age children (Collins 1984), much of it starting from a Piagetian perspective. That perspective, despite its strengths, nevertheless downplays individual differences and/or social contexts of learning so that researchers in this tradition have sought out commonalities among

children, not differences. Most research over the past two decades that has focused on children's attainment in the early grades takes a perspective biased away from searching out differential effects.

2. Historical accident. The modern wave of research on schools, which began with the Coleman Report (1966), was triggered by issues in social stratification, specifically, how schools may contribute to, or diminish, the inheritance of social status. Sociologists who studied educational attainment were interested in social stratification, not schooling per se. Accordingly, they tried to explain social inequality or differential occupational attainment of adults, and research on *early* educational growth was of little interest.

Simultaneously, educational psychologists by the 1960s had become disillusioned with trying to understand schooling because without computers and large data sets, they could not prove that promotion policies, or a progressive versus a traditional curriculum, or any other administrative arrangement, affected school outcomes (See Stephens 1956, esp. Chapter 15). After 30 years of effort, in the 1960s they had turned to other topics, even though the consensus of their research on schooling anticipated the major findings of the Coleman Report. Thus it happened that sociologists, and not education researchers, took over research on schooling at the very time when technological advances made the precise study of schooling effects at the elementary level a possibility. Sociologists' interests, however, centered on adults, not on children, and the most salient concerns in this agenda were those that bore upon the high school to college transition or the transition from school to work. Almost completely neglected was the transition that sets the stage for these subsequent branching points, the transition from home to school.

3. Research on Headstart. Not long after the Coleman Report, several credible (at the time) evaluations of Headstart and other preschool programs concluded that such programs had at best only fleeting effects. The fact that these conclusions agreed with Coleman et al. (1966) and others at the time made them credible in a way they might not otherwise have been. Lately, of course, the Lazar-Darlington (1982) monograph cited earlier and similar work show that preschools do have long-term effects. This recent research has attracted relatively little attention, however, for one thing because the current political climate favors fewer rather than more social programs.

4. Assumptions about elementary schools. Instead of seeing elementary schools as heterogeneous, it is easy to conclude the opposite because they all cover the same curriculum and enroll students around age 6. These similarities tend to camouflage the wide variety in social climate, personnel, facilities, and resources for learning among elementary schools. Also, because most educational research uses grades and not birth cohorts as sampling units, the critical role schools play very early in allocating students to various

slots or "niches" is lost sight of. A student who fails first grade or who is shunted into a program for "exceptional children" very rarely rejoins the mainstream. Those who disappear from view are separated into special programs very early. Schools have a vested interest in directing attention away from children who fail to negotiate the transition successfully. It is widely suggested, for example, that in many instances school promotion practices are driven more by the pursuit of politically acceptable grade level testing averages than by sound pedagogical considerations.

5. Practical obstacles. Children of the "critical period" age are hard to study in large numbers. They cannot write answers to questionnaires, be asked how far their parents have gone in school, or what their parents' attitudes are. Children of this age do have more ability to provide data than they have been credited with, but survey methods and personality tests suitable for research with children beginning school are underdeveloped. These problems make it expensive, risky, time-consuming, and difficult to study large groups of children younger than 9, let alone to follow them for a period of several years.

OVERVIEW

This chapter offers a new perspective on effects of early schooling. Consideration of youngsters' psychological characteristics, of the nature of school learning, and of the tight fit between clients and schools at the primary level all make the hypothesis of a critical period attractive. Although these considerations have not prompted much research so far, we nevertheless could assemble a variety of findings—cross national studies, input-output studies in the economic tradition, follow-up studies from the war on poverty, and an increasing number of studies in the socio/psychological/educational literature—that do document differential effects of elementary schools. We could also assemble a limited number of longitudinal studies suggesting that differential effects of elementary schools persist into high school. We are also encouraged that structure and process in the social organization of schooling in the primary grades has begun to be studied from several vantage points: the balancing of ascription and achievement (Davis and Haller 1981; Leiter and Brown 1985); ability grouping as a facet of organizational differentiation (Felmlee and Eder 1983; Haller and Davis 1981; Eder 1981; Rowan and Miracle 1983; Hallinan and Sorensen 1987); various aspects of classroom management and teacher effectiveness (Barr and Dreeben 1983; Bossert 1979); and classroom or school climate effects (Brookover et al. 1978; St. John 1971). Our own study, the BSS project, is intended to illuminate how the transition to full-time schooling takes place and who has trouble negotiating it. As seen above, some of its evidence already has helped buttress the argument for thinking of the early years of schooling in "critical period" terms. As we continue to monitor the school experiences of this group of youngsters into their middle school years we expect to muster additional evidence on the lasting effects of experiences during this transition period.

For policy purposes as well as for scientific understanding, more research is needed on how early schooling shapes the course of human development. We know that achievement trajectories take form early and are thought to be highly stable thereafter, but there may be considerable variability in individual growth curves. We also know that ideas about one's academic self coalesce during this time, as do attitudes and habits relevant to school deportment and commitment. The disposition to learn may be preserved or destroyed in these formative years. If early schooling does constitute a critical period, then actions taken at this point are of particular import as their consequences potentially will echo for many years. This potentially long time frame should be kept in mind by people planning programs for the first few grades.

ACKNOWLEDGMENTS

This research was supported by National Institute of Child Health and Development Grants *1 RO1 HD16302* and *1 RO1 HD21044-01,* and by the W. T. Grant Foundation Grant *83-0796-82.* Preparation of this report was made possible by the National Science Foundation Grant *SES-8510535.* We thank the children, parents, and teachers who helped us with this research. We also thank Dr. Thomas Foster, Dr. Lewis Richardson, and Ms. Alice Pinderhughes, Superintendent, Baltimore City Public Schools.

NOTES

1.   The carefully prescribed order of the curriculum, the concentration on math and reading, and the mainly self-contained classroom, it should be noted, all contribute to a situation outside the student's control. Elementary students have few options: they rarely can change teachers or schools; they cannot select subjects of study other than math or reading. If they are being terrorized by the school bully or being picked on by the teacher, they cannot escape. School for children at this age is almost a total institution.

2.   We do not see the body of research on effective schools (see e.g., Lipsitz 1984), at least now, as a challenge to the conclusion that secondary schools have negligible differential effects. Although identifying effective schools is sometimes seen as a "breakthrough in applied research on schools" (Mackenzie 1981, p. 5) and as evidence that differences among schools do make a

difference in achievement of poor and minority children, current research on effective schools has several "conceptual and methodological shortcomings that call into question its utility both as a model for future research and as a source of findings" (Rowan, Bossert, and Dwyer 1983, p. 25) (see also Edmonds 1983; Good and Weinstein 1986; Purkey and Smith 1983). For one thing, effective school research does not provide a scientific model for the evaluation of educational programs (see Ralph and Fennessey 1983). For another thing, major technical problems plague assessments in terms of instructional outcomes, the criteria used so far. Furthermore, as commonly occurs in studying extreme groups of any kind, at least part of the deviation of an outstanding school is owing to regression effects or random factors. To use research of this genre to draw conclusions about differences among schools at present, we think, is at least premature.

3. In one of these preschool programs, the Perry Preschool Project (Berrueta-Clement et al. 1984), low income participants at age 19 were more likely to have graduated from high school, enrolled in post-secondary education, more likely to be employed, and less likely to be arrested or on welfare than a comparable group who had not taken part in the program.

4. In further analyses of their published data, we find additional evidence of differential effectiveness by school, which is consistent with conclusions in the previous section. Since Lazar and Darlington were not interested in school differences, they did not themselves explore this. In their Table 5, however, which reports program effects on placement of children in special education classes, chi-squares associated with program/control differences are 0.23, 0.55, 3.55, 5.10, 8.07, 8.16 when listed in increasing order of magnitude. Testing these X^2 differences shows that the third program (3.55) significantly exceeds the two lowest programs (0.23, 0.55), the fourth program (5.10) also exceeds the two lowest programs, and the fifth and sixth programs (8.07 and 8.16) exceed all four of the other programs. Thus, of 15 possible contrasts among preschool programs in terms of children's later placement in special education, 12 contrasts are significant. Similarly, for ordered contrasts among the eight programs listed in their Table 8, which reports program effects on students retained in grade, 12 of 28 (43 percent) of the possible comparisons among preschool programs are significant. In their Table 7, which tallies program effects on either special education or grade retention, 18 of 28 possible ordered comparisons are significant. We conclude, therefore, that there were differences in effectiveness from one school to another because (1) some of the schools produced significant effects while others did not and also (2) there are significant differences *among* the various experimental programs in the proportion of students later placed in special education classes or retained in grade.

Lazar and Darlington's Tables 8 to 11 also cite t-statistics for regression coefficients that measure program effects net of background variables and pretest IQ scores. For Table 8, which like Table 5 measures the later placement of children in special education classes, 3 of 15 (20 percent) of the possible differences among regression coefficients are significant. For Table 9, which like Table 6 measures retention in grade, only one of 21 possible differences is significant (chance level). For Table 10, which like Table 7 combines placement in special education and grade retention, 3 of 21 (12 percent) comparisons of regression coefficients are significant. Altogether, 12 percent of the differences between regression coefficients exceed the 5 percent level. Conclusions from Tables 8 to 10 are thus not as strong as those based on the reanalysis of Tables 5 to 7, but the data point in the same direction.

The data reviewed above are actually stronger than they appear, however. Each t-statistic represents the significance of a difference between regression coefficients measuring the magnitude of an experimental vs. a control treatment(s). In comparing these coefficients we are underestimating actual differences *among* preschools because we are asking only whether *effective* experimental preschools differ from other effective and ineffective experimental preschools. Any effective experimental preschool obviously differs from its own control, and the "control treatment'' in many of the experiments included an alternative kind of schooling. Effective experimental preschool programs can also differ not only from the control treatment to which they were compared, but from other control treatments in other places to which they were not compared although we cannot investigate this possibility with Lazar and Darlington's published information. Nevertheless, our secondary analysis of their published data on long-term effects of preschools indicates that these schools had a number of differential effects that persisted over the long run, as listed above.

5. In this study there is further evidence of differences across schools. When metric coefficients for key variables in third grade (parents' ability estimate and teachers' marks) are compared two at a time, seven out of 13 possible differences between schools are significant at the 5 percent level. Furthermore, these differences are consistent across outcomes in both English and mathematics for both the California and Iowa tests.

REFERENCES

Alexander, K. L., and Entwisle, D. R. In press. *Achievement in the First Two Years of School: Patterns and Processes. Monographs of the Society for Research in Child Development.*

Alexander, K. L., Entwisle, D. R., Cadigan, D., and Pallas, A. 1987. ''Getting Ready for First Grade: Standards of Deportment in Home and School.'' *Social Forces* 66:57–84.

Alexander, K. L., Entwisle, D. R., and Thompson, M. 1987. ''School Performance, Status Relations, and the Structure of Sentiment: Bringing the Teacher Back In.'' *American Sociological Review* 52:665–682.

Alexander, K. L., McPartland, J. M., and Cook, M. A. 1981. ''Using Standardized Test Performance in School Effects Research.'' *Research in Sociology of Education and Socialization* 2:1–33.

Alwin, D. F., and Otto, L. B. 1977. ''High School Context Effects on Aspirations.'' *Sociology of Education* 50:259–73.

Bachman, J. G., O'Malley, P. M., and Johnston, J. 1978. *Adolescence to Adulthood: Change and Stability in the Lives of Young Men.* Ann Arbor, Mich: Institute for Social Research.

Barr, R. and Dreeben, R. 1983. *How Schools Work.* Chicago: University of Chicago Press.

Berrueta-Clement, J. R., Schweinhart, L. J., Barnett, W. S., Eptstein, A. S., and Weikart, D. P. 1984. *Changed Lives: The Effect of the Perry Preschool Program on Youths Through Age 19.* Monographs of the High/Scope Educational Research Foundation. Ypsilanti, MI: High/Scope Press.

Blumenfeld, P. C., Pintrich, P. R., and Hamilton, V. L. 1986. ''Children's Concepts of Ability, Effort, and Conduct.'' *American Educational Research Journal* 23:95–104.

Blemenfeld, P. C., Pintrich, P. R., Meece, J., and Wessels, K. 1982. ''The Formation and Role of Self Perceptions of Ability in Elementary Classrooms.'' *The Elementary School Journal* 82:401–420.

Bossert, S. T. 1979. *Tasks and Social Relationships in Classrooms.* Cambridge: Cambridge University Press.

Brookover, W. B., Schweitzer, J. H., Schneider, J. M., Beady, C. H., Flood, P. K., and Wisenbaker, J. M. 1978. ''Elementary School Social Climate and School Achievement.'' *American Educational Research Journal* 15:301–18.

Brookover, W., Beady, C., Flood, P., Schweitzer, J., and Wisenbaker, J. 1979. *School Social Systems and Student Achievement.* New York: Praeger.

Brookover, W. B., Erickson, E. L., and Joiner, L. M. 1967. *Self-Concept of Ability and School Achievement.* USDE Cooperative Research Project No. 1-E-107.

Brophy, J., and Good, T. 1974. *Teacher-Student Relationships.* New York: Holt, Rinehart, and Winston.

Coleman, J. S. 1961. *The Adolescent Society.* Glencoe, Ill.: Free Press.

Coleman, J. S., Campbell, E. Q., Hobson, C. J., McPartland, J. Mood, A., Weinfeld, F. D., and York, R. L. 1966. *Equality of Educational Opportunity.* Washington, D.C.: U.S. Government Printing Office.

Collins, W. A. 1984. "Conclusion: The Status of Basic Research on Middle Childhood." Edited by W. A. Collins *Development During Middle Childhood.* Washington, D.C.: National Academy Press.

Cook, M. A., and Alexander, K. L. 1981. "Design and Substance in Educational Research: A Case in Point." *Sociology of Education* 53:187–202.

Davis, S. A., and Haller, E. J. 1981. "Tracking, Ability, and SES: Further Evidence on the 'Revisionist-Meritocratic' Debate." *American Journal of Education* 89:283–303.

Eder, D. 1981. "Ability Grouping as a Self-fulfilling Prophecy: A Micro-analysis of Teacher-Student Interaction." *Sociology of Education* 54:151–162.

Edmonds, R. R. 1983. *Search for Effective Schools: The Identification and Analysis of City Schools That are Instructionally Effective for Poor Children* (Final Report). East Lansing: Michigan State University.

Elder, G. H. 1968. *Adolescent Socialization and Personality Development.* Chicago: Rand-McNally.

Entwisle, D. R., and Alexander, K. L. In preparation. *Children's Transition into Full Time Schooling.*

Entwisle, D. R., and Alexander, K. L. 1988. "Factors Affecting Achievement Test Scores and Marks Received by Black and White First Graders." *Elementary School Journal* 88: 449–471.

Entwisle, D. R., Alexander, K. L., Pallas, A. M., and Cadigan, D. 1987. "The Emergent Academic Self-Image of First Graders: Its Response to Social Structure." *Child Development* 58:1190–1206.

Entwisle, D. R., and Hayduk, L. A. 1978. *Too Great Expectations.* Baltimore: The Johns Hopkins Press.

Entwisle, D. R., and Hayduk, L. A. 1982. *Early Schooling.* Baltimore: The Johns Hopkins Press.

Entwisle, D. R., and Hayduk, L. A. 1988. "Lasting Effects of Elementary School." *Sociology of Education* 61: 147–159.

Epstein, J. L. 1984. *Single Parents and the Schools: The Effect of Marital Status on Parent and Teacher Evaluations.* Baltimore: The Johns Hopkins University, Center for Social Organization of Schools, Report No. 353.

Felmlee, D., and Eder, D. 1983. "Contextual Effects in the Classroom: The Impact of Ability Group on Student Attention." *Sociology of Education* 56:77–87.

Ginsburg, H. P. 1986. "The Myth of the Deprived Child: New Thoughts on Poor Children." Edited by U. Neisser. *The School Achievement of Minority Children.* Hillsdale, N.J.: Erlbaum.

Good, T. L., and Weinstein, R. S. 1986. "Schools Make a Difference: Evidence, Criticisms, and New Directions." *American Psychologist* 41:1090–1097.

Hall, J. S. 1984. *Nonverbal Sex Difference.* Baltimore: Johns Hopkins Press.

Haller, E. J., and Davis, S. A. 1981. "Teacher Perceptions, Parental Social Status and Grouping for Reading Instruction." *Sociology of Education* 54:162–174.

Hallinan, M. T., and Sorensen, A. B. 1987. "Ability Grouping and Sex Differences in Mathematics Achievement." *Sociology of Education* 60:63–72.

Harvard Educational Letter. 1986. *Repeating a Grade: Does It Help?* Harvard Educational Letter Vol. II, No. 2, March.

Hauser, R. M. 1971. *Socioeconomic Background and Educational Performance.* The Arnold M. and Caroline Rose Monograph Series. Washington, D.C.: American Sociological Association.

Hess, R. D., Holloway, S. D. Dickson, W. P., and Price, G. G. 1984. "Maternal Variables as Predictors of Children's School Readiness and Later Achievement in Vocabulary and Mathematics in Sixth Grade." *Child Development* 55:1902–1912.

Heyneman, S. P., and Loxley, W. A. 1983. "The Effect of Primary School Quality on Academic Achievement across Twenty-Nine High- and Low-Income Countries." *American Journal of Sociology* 88:1162–1194.

Heyns, B. 1978. *Summer Learning.* New York: Academic Press.

Inkeles, A. 1977. "Review of International Studies in Evaluation." (9 volumes). *Proceedings of the National Academy of Education* 4:139–200.

Jackson, G. B. 1975. "The Research Evidence on the Effect of Grade Retention." *Review of Educational Research* 45:438–460.

Jencks, C. 1985. "How Much Do High School Students Learn?" *Sociology of Education* 58:128–135.

Jencks, C. S., Smith, M., Acland, H., Bane, M. J., Cohen, D., Gintis, H., Heyns, B., and Michelson, S. 1972. *Inequality: A Reassessment of the Effect of Family and Schooling in America.* New York: Basic.

Kashinsky, M., and Wiener, M. 1969. "Tone in Communication and the Performance of Children from 2 Socioeconomic Groups." *Child Development* 40:1193–1202.

Lazar, I., and Darlington, R. 1982. "Lasting Effects of Early Education: A Report from the Consortium for Longitudinal Studies." *Monographs of the SRCD.* Serial No. 195, Vol. 47, Nos. 2–3.

Leiter, J., and Brown, J. S. 1985. "Determinants of Elementary School Grading." *Sociology of Education* 58:166–180.

Lipsitz, J. 1984. *Successful Schools for Young Adolescents.* New Brunswick, N.J.: Transaction.

MacKenzie, D. E. 1981. *Leadership for Learning.* Washington, D.C.: National School Boards Association.

Madaus, G. F., Airasian, P. W., Kellaghan, T. 1980. *School Effectiveness: A Reassessment of the Evidence.* New York: McGraw-Hill.

Markus, H. J., and Nurius, P. S. 1984. "Self-Understanding and Self-Regulation in Middle Childhood." Edited by W. A. Collins. *Development During Middle Childhood.* Washington, D.C.: National Academy Press.

Maryland State Department of Education. 1976. *Maryland Accountability Program Report Year II.*

Mendels, G. E., and Flanders, J. P. 1973. "Teachers' Expectations and Pupil Performance." *American Educational Research Journal* 10:203–12.

Morse, W. C. 1964. "Self-Concept in the School Setting." *Childhood Education* 41:195–98.

Mosteller, F., and Moynihan, D. P. 1972. *On Equality of Educational Opportunity.* New York: Vintage.

Murnane, R. J. 1975. *The Impact of School Resources on the Learning of Inner City Children.* Cambridge: Ballinger.

Pedersen, E., Faucher, T. A., and Eaton, W. W. 1978. "A New Perspective on the Effects of First-Grade Teachers on Children's Subsequent Adult Status." *Harvard Educational Review* 48:1–31.

Plowden Report. 1967. Pp. 618–19 in *Children and Their Primary Schools,* Vol. II. London: Her Majesty's Stationery Office.

Purkey, S. C., and Smith, M. S. 1983. "Effective Schools: A Review." *Elementary School Journal* 83:427–452.

Ralph, J., and Fennessey, J. 1983. "Science or Reform: Some Questions about the Effective Schools Model." *Phi Delta Kappan* 64:689–694.

Rosenberg, M. 1979. *Conceiving the Self.* New York: Basic.

Rowan, B., and Miracle, A. W. 1983. "Systems of Ability Grouping and the Stratification of Achievement in Elementary Schools." *Sociology of Education* 56:133–149.

Rowan, B., Bossert, S. T., and Dwyer, D. C. 1983. "Research on Effective Schools: A Cautionary Note." *Educational Researcher* 12:24–31.

Rutter, M. 1970. "Psychological Development—Predictions from Infancy." *Journal of Child Psychology and Psychiatry* 11:49–62.

St. John, N. 1971. "Thirty-six Teachers: Their Characteristics and Outcomes for Black and White Pupils." *American Educational Research Journal* 8:635–648.

Sameroff, A. 1975. "Transactional Models of Early Social Relations." *Human Development* 18:65–79.

Sameroff, A., and Chandler, M. J. 1975. "Reproductive Risk and the Continuum of Caretaking Causality." Edited by R. D. Horowitz. *Review of Child Development Research,* Vol. 4. Chicago: University of Chicago Press.

Schneider, B. L. 1980. *Production Analysis of Gains in Achievement.* Paper presented at meetings of the American Educational Research Association, Boston, Mass.

Seaver, W. B. 1973. "Effects of Naturally-Induced Teacher Expectancies." *Journal of Personality and Social Psychology* 28:333–42.

Shavit, Y., and Williams, R. A. 1985. "Ability Grouping and Contextual Determinants of Educational Expectations in Israel." *American Sociological Review* 50:62–73.

Sorensen, A. B., and Hallinan, M. T. 1977. "A Reconceptualization of School Effects." *Sociology of Education* 50:273–289.

Stephens, J. M. 1956. *Educational Psychology.* New York: Holt, Rinehart and Winston.

Stevenson, H. W., and Newman, R. S. 1986. "Long-Term Prediction of·Achievement and Attitudes in Mathematics and Reading." *Child Development* 57:646–659.

Summers, A. A., and Wolfe, B. L. 1977. "Do Schools Make a Difference?" *American Economic Review* 65(4):639–52.

Thompson, M. S., Alexander, K. L., and Entwisle, D. R. In press. "*Household Composition, Parental Expectations, and School Achievement.*" *Social Forces.*

White, M. A. 1968. "The View from the Pupil's Desk." *Urban Review* 2:5–7.

COMPARING INDIVIDUAL AND STRUCTURAL LEVELS OF ANALYSIS

Hubert M. Blalock, Jr.

Two complementary objectives of the growing body of literature on school effects are readily apparent. The one is to explain a number of individual-level dependent variables, such as performances on standardized tests, educational attainment levels, educational and occupational aspirations and expectations, or curriculum choices. The other is to examine social organizations as units of analysis and to assess the effectiveness of schools, school systems, or schooling processes, as for example those that occur within the classroom.

The first objective refers to the micro or individual level but may involve macro-level explanatory variables as contextual or compositional influences. The second refers to macro units such as classrooms, schools, school districts,

Research in the Sociology of Education and Socialization,
Volume 8, pages 57–86.
Copyright © 1989 by JAI Press Inc.
All rights of reproduction in any form reserved.
ISBN: 0-89232-929-7

or perhaps even entire school systems, as for example that of the United States as compared with that of England or Japan. But the dependent variables, or outcomes, for these macro analyses may consist of aggregated performance measures of individual students, as for example test scores or attainment levels. In both instances, then, it may be necessary to utilize data and theoretical assumptions that pertain to levels of analysis other than the one which is the direct focus of attention. For simplicity, I shall refer to analyses of these types under the general heading of cross-level analyses, with the recognition that there may be several distinct levels nested within one another: students in classrooms, within schools, within districts, within larger statewide or even national educational systems.

The quality of the *methodological* discussions of such cross-level analyses in educational research is excellent, in my judgment. A number of very critical issues have been raised, formulated in relatively technical terms, and then applied to major data sets. The *empirical* findings, however, have been both disappointing and ambiguous, except perhaps in terms of the negative conclusions they have suggested. The explanatory power of most if not all micro-level analyses has been weak, at least in terms of an explained variance criterion, implying that there is still much to be learned about the impact of the schooling process on student learning and performance. At the macro level it is easier to ''explain'' a higher percentage of the variance, but often because of artifacts of aggregation and the confounding of the variables of interest with unmeasured self-selection mechanisms and other extra-school factors.

Perhaps it is because of the weak and controversial negative findings at the micro level that methodological discussions have been relatively rich and enlightening in this area. But there remains the obvious need to translate these excellent insights into sets of findings that are more fruitful from the standpoint of improving our basic understanding of educational processes and outcomes.

Ever since the so-called Coleman Report (Coleman et al 1966) appeared over two decades ago, there seems to be a general consensus that ''school quality'' must be assessed in terms of student outcome variables, rather than school input criteria such as per capita expenditures, teacher salaries, student-faculty ratios, or physical facilities. The major finding of the Coleman Report, namely that school input factors were extremely weakly related to student performance scores once family and peer characteristics had been controlled, has been replicated on numerous occasions though exceptions have been noted and conclusions disputed and methodological objections raised.[1]

There does appear to be general agreement on one major point that is important for our own subsequent discussion. Student outcomes are basically micro-level phenomena, do not involve highly coordinated behaviors on the part of organized student groups, and are at least partially attributed to individual differences in innate abilities, as well as idiosyncratic experiences that occur sometimes within school contexts and sometimes outside. This means that such individual-level outcomes are only partly the result of schooling processes. Therefore in assessing school quality or effectiveness it is ideally necessary to control for such extraneous causal factors, insofar as they can be identified and measured. As we shall note below, this implies that out*comes,* as dependent variables, need to be distinguished from school out*puts* or the actual contributions made by schooling variables, net of outside or exogenous causal factors.

Unfortunately, many of these latter factors operate in conjunction with those that occur within the schools themselves. Peers interact within the classroom, on the playground, on the bus, and within the home and neighborhood. Parents may or may not reinforce teacher expectations regarding homework. Thus a clearcut distinction between causal factors attributable to schools and those claimed to be "extra-school" often cannot be made. If one could be assured that the latter in effect cancel out in the aggregation process, school effects could be more easily inferred. But reality is far more complex than this. As we shall see, such extra-school factors may, indeed, be further confounded with school effects as a result of improper aggregating decisions.

In order to come to grips with these and other problems, in the next section we shall briefly discuss some of the major methodological issues that have been raised in this connection, as well as summarizing some important basic principles that have been established. Before doing so, however, it will be helpful to illustrate in terms of a specific debate in which several important points have emerged.

A Debate Over School District Effects on Student Achievement

Bidwell and Kasarda (1975, 1976) have argued that organizational factors at the school district level help to explain differences in average district-level student achievement scores in reading and mathematics. Although their specific findings apply to districts as units of analysis, the issues raised by their study, as well as the subsequent debate, are equally relevant to analyses at the school level or to any macro unit, including school classrooms. Using a path diagram involving only variables actually measured and used in the analysis, Bidwell and Kasarda attempt to sort out the impacts of certain environmental conditions (such as school district size, average parental educational levels, and percent nonwhite) and of organizational attributes (such as pupil-teacher ratios, staff quality, and administrative intensity) on student achievement outcomes, aggregated by districts. Using *standardized* partial regression coefficients they conclude that the organizational variables at the district level have moderately strong direct effects on the outcome variables, net of the impact of the exogenous environmental variables contained in the model. They then argue that district-level factors are important in accounting for student performance levels.

Alexander and Griffin (1976) and Hannan, Freeman, and Meyer (1976) sharply criticize the Bidwell-Kasarda study on several grounds that highlight a number of important methodological issues. Both sets of critics point out that the study did not control for *student* input variables crucial to the interpretation that outcome variables were actually the result of school (or district) factors, and thus could be referred to as outputs of school factors alone. Alexander and Griffen supply a set of nearly comparable data from another state, for which input performance measures were available, showing that the explanatory power of the Bidwell-Kasarda type model is substantially reduced when the student inputs are introduced. The important issue being addressed in this connection is that of possible self-selection, in this instance of students and their families into neighborhoods and school districts, a self-selection process that is only imperfectly "controlled" by the use of variables such as average parental education and racial composition.[2]

Hannan, Freeman and Meyer raise two additional issues. First, they point to the improper use of standardized measures in an instance where aggregation would be expected to inflate one's measures of association. But beyond this is the problem of using aggregated data (here by districts) in an instance where the dependent variable, as well as the underlying substantive theory, applies to the individual student as the unit of analysis. Given the probable self-selection involved, grouping by districts (an areal unit) will ordinarily tend to *amplify,* rather than control for, any specification error biases that may exist in the micro theory, even had Bidwell and Kasarda used unstandardized rather than standardized regression coefficients.

Given that the appropriate theory is at the individual or micro level, the implication is that the proper unit of analysis should also be at that level, but perhaps with macro-level contextual variables (such as classroom size or teacher qualifications) added as independent variables. As we shall see in the next section, however, the existence of certain kinds of contextual variables in a micro model may make it impossible to achieve "consistency" between macro and micro-level formulations.

The obvious reply to these criticisms is that, for purposes of macro analysis of school systems, it *is* both sensible and legitimate to evaluate quality in terms of output variables that may involve average student achievement levels, or perhaps student averages on such things as job or educational aspirations, work habits, reasoning ability, motivation, adaptability, appreciation for cultural differences, or any number of other individual-type variables in terms of which organizational objectives have been formulated. In brief, the "products" of schools (or school systems) are individual students having certain desired or undesired characteristics, just as the products of General Motors are automobiles with desired characteristics.

We see here the two general kinds of purposes alluded to in the opening paragraph. Ideally, one would want theoretical explanations at the two (or more) levels to be compatible or complementary. In terms of policy analysis, one may wish to focus on variables that are manipulable at the district, school or classroom level, with some assurance that changes in these variables will actually produce desired changes in student outcomes. But the tangle of causally interrelated variables and possible methodological artifacts, combined with very rudimentary theoretical explanations at each level of analysis, has made this task extremely difficult, at best, and conducive to inconclusive debates and overly simplistic policy recommendations, at worst.

SOME METHODOLOGICAL ISSUES

If one has theories at several different levels, say with the first being appropriate to individual students and a second pertaining to schools as units, a common sense observation would be that in the ideal both theories should be as well specified as possible. Furthermore, since biases will inevitably occur in any theoretically based data analysis owing to a variety of causes, the seriousness of such biases will be a function of the specification errors at either level. Whichever theory is better specified should have the smallest biases. It turns out that these rather obvious intuitive observations are sound as far as they go, but it becomes necessary to be much more specific about the kinds of biases that are likely to arise in both micro and macro formulations and then to apply the principles discovered to the special case at hand.

Let us begin with a "consistency" criterion developed in the econometrics literature and exposited by Hannan (1971) and by Hannan and Burstein (1974). Such a criterion presupposes that we have theoretical formulations at two levels, with each formulation involving the "same" variables in exactly the same causal roles. At the micro level we might take a dependent variable Y, say a child's performance level, as a function of several micro-level explanatory variables X_i, say ability, motivation, confidence, and knowledge. We then construct a comparable macro-level equation by aggregating these individuals, say according to the schools they attend. We use the identical kind of equation to explain the aggregated Y variable in terms of the aggregated X_i. Finally, we need to specify the nature of the aggregating function, as for example one which uses group means for all variables.

We thus have three functions: a micro-level equation, a macro-level counterpart, and a set of aggregation equations. "Consistency" across levels is then defined in the following way. There are two methods of obtaining the macro-level dependent variable. One may use the micro equation to obtain the micro Y value for each individual, and then use the aggregating function for Y to obtain the macro Y value. Or one may first use the aggregating functions on each of the micro independent and dependent variables to obtain macro-level counterparts of each micro variable and then use the *macro* equation to obtain the macro dependent variable. Consistency across levels obtains if and only if these two procedures yield the same scores on the macro dependent variable.

As Hannan and Burstein point out, it is unlikely in realistic social science models that one's micro and macro theories will indeed contain exactly the same variables playing identical roles, and we shall return to this matter shortly. As a standard by which to assess aggregation and specification biases, however, it is important to indicate the conditions under which consistency holds. It turns out that these conditions are indeed strict: both the micro and macro-level equations need to be linear in form—with constant coefficients—*and* the aggregating functions also need to be linear. This last condition is of course satisfied if one uses either group means or proportions as the aggregating functions, but it would not hold for dispersion measures such as the variances of the X_i. Fortunately, the aggregation operations with which we are usually concerned do involve this linearity condition.

Let us suppose we have the micro equation

$$Y_{ij} = \alpha + \beta_1 X_{1ij} + \beta_2 X_{2ij} + \cdots + \beta_k X_{kij} + \epsilon_{ij} \tag{1}$$

and a corresponding macro equation

$$\bar{Y}_j = \alpha' + \beta_1' \bar{X}_{1j} + \beta_2' \bar{X}_{2j} + \cdots + \beta_k' \bar{X}_{kj} + \bar{\epsilon}_j'$$

where we assume that the two disturbance terms are uncorrelated with the independent variables in their respective equations. Ordinary least squares (OLS) then provides unbiased estimates in both instances, and we shall refer to each equation as being correctly specified.

So where do our problems lie? First, it should be noted that a micro model may involve one or more macro variables, as for example group means inserted to represent contextual effects. Firebaugh (1978) notes that whenever a group mean appears in an equation for Y, net of the effects of the corresponding micro variable, aggregation biases will be produced. Furthermore, as has been noted by several authors (Przeworski 1974; Irwin and Lichtman 1978; Blalock and Wilken (1979), an additive contextual effect term in a micro equation will be totally confounded with the corresponding individual-level variable in situations where only the aggregate data are available. For example suppose we have the simple micro equation for the ith individual in the jth group:

$$Y_{ij} = \alpha + \beta_1 X_{ij} + \beta_2 \bar{X}_j + \epsilon_{ij} \qquad (3)$$

If we aggregate to obtain group means for the j groups we will get

$$\bar{Y}_j = \alpha + (\beta_1 + \beta_2) \bar{X}_j + \bar{\epsilon}_j \qquad (4)$$

Only if $\beta_2 = 0$, meaning no contextual effect, will the macro estimate of $\bar{X}_j$'s coefficient correspond to the coefficient of X_{ij} in the micro equation.[3] Practically speaking, this means that such contextual-effect models will produce biases in aggregate-level estimates of the corresponding micro parameters, implying that at least additive-type contextual-effects models of this special type will produce a lack of correspondence between macro- and micro-level systems.

Those who wish to include contextual effects of this type in their micro theories therefore cannot hope to extract information about their impacts unless data have been disaggregated to the micro-level of concern. For example, the micro unit might be the individual classroom, with average classroom levels serving as school-level contextual variables for the classrooms. If data were provided at the school but not the classroom level, such contextual effects could not be separated from those of the corresponding classroom variables.

Aggregation biases also depend on the *nature* of the aggregating criterion, as for example a spatial or organizational one. The reason for this is that additional specification errors at the macro level, over and above those that are almost inevitable at the micro level, will be created. There will be a confounding, at the macro level, of variables contained in the disturbance term $\bar{\epsilon}_j$ with independent variables in a macro equation such as equation (2), thus producing biases in the OLS estimates at the macro level. Such a confounding will occur if the grouping criterion, say schools, is either a dependent variable or correlated with the micro-level dependent variable and one or more micro independent variables. In effect, if the grouping criterion belongs in the equation for the micro dependent variable Y, net of the explicitly included independent variables, there will be aggregation biases created in estimates of unstandardized regression coefficients. If, for example, parents select neighborhoods or schools on some basis, then the schools in which their children are enrolled (and appear in the aggregated measures) will be *dependent* on these choices, and perhaps the ability levels of the students themselves. Let us examine this possibility more closely.

If one aggregates individuals either randomly or according to their scores on one or more included *independent* variables, no biases will be created in estimates of unstandardized regression coefficients. But if one groups by levels on the *dependent* variable Y, putting together students with the highest Y values, those with the next highest levels, and so forth, then omitted causes of Y will become positively correlated with X's operating in the same direction. If there are only two causes of Y, say X and an omitted variable Z represented by the disturbance term, and if both causal relationships are positive, then even though, at the micro level, X and Z may be uncorrelated, it will take high values on *both* X and Z to produce very high values of Y, and similarly for very low values of Y. Thus, for the aggregated data involving group means, $\bar{X}$ and $\bar{Z}$ will be confounded, producing biases in ordinary least squares estimates of the unstandardized regression coefficient of $\bar{X}$ whenever $\bar{Z}$ has been omitted and has thus become part of the disturbance term $\bar{\epsilon}$. A similar porperty holds in the multivariate case and also in instances where the grouping criterion is a common cause of both X and Y, or even a correlate of both.

Standardized coefficients, such as path coefficients and correlations, will be further inflated unless the criterion for grouping is totally unrelated to both X and Y, as would be true for completely random groupings. Practically speaking, of course, random groupings of human actors rarely occur, implying that the grouping criterion will be associated with either X or Y, or both. The critical point is that if the grouping criterion—which we shall call A following Hannan (1971)—belongs in the micro equation for Y (with X controlled), aggregation biases will result.

As noted by Hannan and Burstein (1974), and also by Langbein and Lichtman (1978), there are therefore two sources of bias. There may be specification errors at the micro level, which produce "specification biases." These occur when the true micro disturbance term is correlated with one or more of the explicitly included independent variables because of measurement errors in independent variables, omitted causes that are correlated with included independent variables, or incorrectly specified equational forms. Secondly, at the macro level, there may be "aggregation biases" due either to the failure to take certain kinds of contextual effects into account or to the fact that one has grouped either by the dependent variable or a variable that would belong in the correctly specified micro equation. The total bias at the macro level is thus an additive combination of specification biases at the micro level and aggregation biases.

It is possible for these two sources of bias to offset one another, if they are of opposite sign and approximately equal magnitude. If so, there may be an actual aggregation *gain,* in the sense that the estimated coefficients at the macro level may have smaller biases than estimates based on the micro data. If, for example, there are strictly random measurement errors in micro independent variables, these may be substantially reduced through aggregation, producing superior estimates at that level. As noted by Irwin and Lichtman (1976) and Langbein and Lichtman (1978), the critical question to ask is, "Which model is better specified, the micro or macro-level one?" In the kinds of models we have been examining, for which the "same" variables are included at both levels, if we assume no substantial measurement errors it will generally turn out that the grouping process will produce aggregation biases operating in the same direction as micro-level specification biases, thus *amplifying* any biases that may exist at that level.[4]

If both models are perfectly specified, meaning that the grouping criterion does not actually belong in the micro equation for Y, then both will yield unbiased estimates. But this will never occur in realistic data analyses, nor will it usually be possible to invoke the Langbein-Lichtman criterion involving the relative magnitudes of specification errors at the two levels. Where data are only available at the macro level, one will also be in the unfortunate position of lacking the information necessary to apply Firebaugh's $\bar{X}$ rule, as well. In a later article, Burstein (1978) compares the relative merits of this $\bar{X}$ rule and the Hannan-Burstein criterion for assessing aggregation biases, giving a slight edge to the $\bar{X}$ rule.

For our purposes, the most important implications of these methodological discussions are as follows:

1. Where feasible, use micro-level data so as to examine the possibility that contextual-effect variables may belong in the equations for micro-level dependent variables. Where such contextual variables must be represented by group means for included independent micro variables, and where these are simply added to micro-level independent variables, as in equation (3), one may expect such contextual-effect terms to be confounded with their corresponding individual-level variables whenever data are only available at the macro level.

2. Pay careful attention to the specification of models at *both* levels, making such specifications as complete as possible. At the macro level this will require a theory relating the grouping or aggregating criterion (e.g., classroom or school) to the other variables in the model. If the grouping criterion A actually belongs in the equation for the micro dependent variable, but has been omitted from the data analysis, aggregation biases will usually operate to produce greater total biases in the macro model than in the micro-level counterpart. Given that measurement errors may be more substantial in the micro model and that macro data on additional variables may be available, however, it will not always be the case that micro-level formulations produce smaller biases.

3. At both levels it is essential to state one's assumptions about the

behaviors of omitted variables and the implications of random and nonrandom measurement errors, so that readers may judge the adequacy of specifications at each level. Contrary to conventional practice (including that of Bidwell and Kasarda), causal diagrams representing the respective models at both levels should contain omitted variables in all instances where these would be relevant to specification and aggregation biases. This includes omitted variables correlated with included variables, as well as the relationship of the aggregating criterion to both independent and dependent variables at the macro level.

4.   Possible self-selection mechanisms should be specified at both levels, but are especially critical where they impact on the aggregating criterion, as for example schools or classrooms. Even where proper controls for such self selection cannot be introduced, as for example measures of students' prior levels of ability, their implications for possible amplifying aggregation biases should be noted.

5.   Since "consistency" across levels depends heavily on the linearity of the equations at both levels, it is critical that one not aggregate over non-homogeneous kinds of individuals for whom there are different regression coefficients. If, for example, there are two types of individuals characterized by different slopes, then the regression coefficients are not really constants. The problem is discussed in some detail by Hannan (1971) and was emphasized in an earlier formulation by Goodman (1959). It should also be noted that self-selection processes may vary by type of individual, so that relative aggregation biases may also differ.

6.   In instances where contextual or compositional effects are suspected, careful attention needs to be paid to the specification of the appropriate unit boundaries, and to contextual units such as classrooms that may have been neglected because of the use of too high levels of aggregation (e.g., schools rather than classrooms).

There is a very extensive body of literature on contextual effects that I have summarized elsewhere (Blalock 1984). Those contextual-effect issues that are relevant to the present discussion will be developed in the subsequent section. The main point to emphasize here is that contextual-effect models introduce further complications whenever one is attempting to compare theoretical explanations at two or more levels of analysis. I would prefer to think of contextual-effect models as "belonging" to micro-level theories designed to explain micro dependent variables. Whenever such effects are minor or of no theoretical importance, cross-level comparisons will thereby be simplified. But this must be established in terms of theoretical specifications at the *micro* level and then evaluated using data at both levels. It does not seem appropriate merely to assume them away at the macro level where, as we have seen, they are likely to be confounded with micro variables in the aggregation process.

There is a further major point that is suggested by the debate stemming from the Bidwell-Kasarda study. Decisions regarding the *measurement* of macro variables often depend upon a well specified micro theory. For instance, it was noted that one cannot legitimately equate aggregated student performance levels, such as test scores, with organizational out*puts*. Instead, these should be conceptualized as out*comes* of a combination of organizational or schooling processes *and* input variables that need to be controlled. Unfortunately, in the case of schooling processes, many of these input factors impact on students during the entire duration of the learning process, rather than solely at the time of school entry.

This is in contrast with conventional input-output analyses in economics, where it is more reasonable to assume that input qualities (such as the properties of the steel that has been supplied) can be measured at the outset of the production process and that they remain constant during the relevant time period. In such an instance, once the inputs are supplied, the system is assumed closed to outside influences, so that outputs can be measured by in effect controlling for these input variables. In the case of schools, however, parental and peer influences continue to interact with in-school processes in a confusing way.

THE SPECIFICATION OF MICRO MODELS

The dependent variables of interest in most micro models that have come to my attention are internal states of students: such things as the accumulation of factual knowledge, reasoning or thinking abilities, motivation, academic self-esteem, aspirations and expectations, and perhaps the learning of social skills and an appreciation of cultural differences. There are also "objective" factors such as educational attainment, grades, and performances on standarized tests, with the latter two kinds of variables being taken as indicators of abilities or knowledge. Outcome variables in macro models are often aggregated values of these same variables, particularly test scores and average educational attainment levels.

If we focus on performance measures as indicators or as representing samples of student capabilities in action, I suspect that most of us would agree that if a complete listing and perfect measurement of all relevant internal states were available, such performances could be completely explained and predicted by a combination of such internal states and *contemporary* stimuli affecting the responses. Such things as the nature of the examination questions, their "fit" with the student's knowledge base and reasoning abilities, any extraneous distracting factors in the testing environment, the student's motivation, interest, fatigue, self-esteem and anxiety levels, expectations regarding the consequences of doing well or poorly, and perhaps several other contemporaneous external or internal factors might completely account for performance levels. There would be no need to invoke the past or to bring in so-called "contextual variables" that may have earlier affected the student's learning, motivation, or expectation levels. Psychological theories would suffice to account for the behaviors in question, provided that such theories were sufficiently broad to encompass contemporaneous factors operating in the immediate social setting.

As soon as we wish to explain how the student got that way, however, we need to invoke a long series of behavioral sequences, including the reactions of others to previous student behaviors. How did the teacher respond to the student's questions, classroom recitations, or performance on homework assignments? How did significant peers behave when he or she bungled a recitation or showed them an A paper or a gold star on a math homework assignment? Did the teacher place the student in a slow or fast reading group, tolerate or even praise a very inadequate performance, or sanction other students for ridiculing an embarrassing performance? Did the parents encourage more careful attention to homework after a failing exam? Did they obtain accurate feedback from the teacher concerning strengths and weaknesses? Was the student's prior record and reputation simply passed along from one teacher to the next? Was he or she encouraged to select the more demanding of two math or English courses?

It is here that so-called contextual factors, as variously defined, may enter into the explanatory model. Such variables can be thought of as indirect causes of contemporary "intervening" variables, namely those internal states (such as knowledge, self-esteem, and expectations) that, in turn, affect behavioral performance levels. If we take the student performance levels as Y_i, the student's internal states as X_j, and the contextual variables as Z_k, we might diagram the prototypic model of this type as in Figure 1.

Alternatively, one could formulate a dynamic model in which contemporaneous variables at time t are functions of combinations of earlier internal states, behaviors, and responses patterns. These could then be aggregated,

Figure 1.

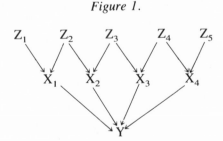

though using differential weights to allow for relatively greater impact of more recent events. I will present several illustrative models of this sort toward the end of the section. The essential point to note, however, is that such dynamic models may also allow for the impact not only of other significant actors within and outside the school setting, but for feedback processes through which the *student's* prior behaviors have influenced teachers, parents, and peers.

Such a theory would allow for a *set* of autonomous actors, including the particular student of concern, each of whom is influencing the others over a period of time, culminating in some "final" performance level, as for example performance on an SAT or other standardized examination. This is in contrast to the explanatory models used in all of the studies I have examined, which have used single-equation approaches in which student behaviors have been taken as dependent variables that do not influence any of the independent variables.

Contextual-Effect Models

As noted, there have been a number of excellent methodological discussions of contextual effects in school settings. Yet, the empirical findings have been disappointing and there remain considerable ambiguities regarding the relative importance of contexts as contrasted with individual-level variables, the mechanisms through which the former operate, the appropriateness of different contextual units, and the kinds of variables to be subsumed under the label "contextual affects." There have also been substantial data gaps and a high degree of collinearity among contextual variables, making it all the more difficult to agree on the overall value of contextual-effect models of any kind.

As noted by Hauser (1974), in response to a paper by Farkas (1974), one of the issues involved is the stage at which contextual variables should be introduced into an explanatory model. If one has used only one or two individual-level explanatory variables, say "ability" X_1 and race X_2, one can hardly expect to account for a high percentage of explained variance in, say, test performance Y. There will most certainly be additional explanatory X_i, some of which will be correlated with X_1 and X_2, which if omitted from the model will produce specification errors in such a very simplistic micro model.

If one then introduces group means on the two independent variables to represent, say, average peer abilities and percent black, these contextual variables may be correlated with omitted X_i and thus represent proxies for them, rather than true "contextual effects" of the peers themselves. Or they may represent contextual influences of very different kinds, as for example teacher expectation levels or the curriculum to which the student is exposed. This may indeed be an illustration of Firebaugh's (1978) point that group

mean variables may have different meanings than their individual-level counterparts in that they may indirectly tap another variable that is difficult to
measure. If one of the individual-level variables, say X_1, has been measured
with random error, perhaps the group mean on X_1 will pick up some of the
measurement error involved and appear to have an impact even where there
has been no true contextual peer influence.

One problem in this connection is that the methodological literature on
contextual effects stems from more narrowly focused arguments in which the
contextual variables have been linked with the actor's peers or near equals.
Empirically, the levels of variables for these peers have been measured as
group means, with these group means (or proportions) then being used either
as categorical control variables in the earlier formulations of Blau (1960) and
Davis, Spaeth, and Huson (1961), or inserted as $\bar{X}$'s into regression equations. Other kinds of contextual variables, such as so-called "global" group
characteristics, supervisor behaviors, or reactions of subordinates or clients,
have then been omitted from methodological discussions.

Thus although group means for peers have been recognized as only one set
of possible contextual variables, it has been these variables that have dominated our methodological discussions. For instance, Firebaugh's $\bar{X}$ criterion
for deciding whether or not micro-models and their macro counterparts will be
"consistent" may be technically correct in that consistency cannot be expected if $\bar{X}$ "stands for" or is correlated with omitted macro variables that
belong in the micro equation. But the $\bar{X}$ criterion, itself, clearly places the
emphasis on the group mean, rather than these other possible explanatory
variables.

There have also been efforts to distinguish the effects of so-called "compositional" effects of entire schools (say, percent black or average parental
educational level) from "contextual effects" in smaller groupings, as for
example, the subset of friends named by the respondent. (See Karweit et al
1978). Here one encounters severe multicollinearity problems which, combined with unknown measurement errors, may make it virtually impossible to
separate out the these "compositional effects," which may affect teacher
expectations or curriculum mixes, from the more immediate impacts of a
student's closest friends. Similarly, Alexander et al. (1979) discovered that it
was almost impossible to distinguish "true" peer effects from those of a
school's composition.

Erbring and Young (1979) are sharply critical of those who construct contextual-effect models containing group means on *independent* variables such
as ability or motivational levels. How can a given student's behaviors be
affected by others' *abilities,* for example? Their *behaviors,* including previous test performances, would seem more likely candidates for inclusion,

meaning that a model designed to explain, say, an individual's test performance Y might contain the group mean on that same variable! Of course a properly specified model would require the introduction of lags, since it would be their *past* performances that could affect the given student's performance, or perhaps his or her mental states and prior learning. This might occur either as a result of positive normative influences or frog-pond effects (Davis 1966; Firebaugh 1980) through which the student comes to believe that he or she is bright or dumb according to the performance levels of others in the class. Unfortunately, since group means on many of the X's will tend to be highly correlated with group means on the dependent Y's—even where individual-level correlations are much weaker—collinearity problems may make it exceedingly difficult to distinguish between $\bar{X}$-type and $\bar{Y}$-type contexts.

As already implied, there may also be multiple contexts, some nested within others but some that partially overlap one another. A child's classroom peers may not coincide with his or her best friends or neighborhood playmates. As one moves up a nested hierarchy, rules or other group properties at the higher level may constrain variables at the lower level, as for example peer or teacher reactions. (Eulau 1969). Thus student-teacher ratios may affect the average amount of attention and feedback each teacher may give to individual students. Grading and curriculum policies may also constrain the teacher. Therefore district-level policies may have indirect impacts on the schooling process through such constraining variables.

If we assume that students are most directly affected by their immediate classroom environments, however, these more remote indirect effects may be relatively minor in terms of their impacts on the explained variance of *individual* student behaviors, though their explained variance effects on between-school or between-district differences may be more substantial. Thus a multilevel contextual-effects model may be appropriate in many instances, though serious practical problems involving ambiguous or overlapping boundaries, other types of specification errors, and multicollinearity may prevent us from obtaining definitive results using such more complex models.

Finally, as already suggested, it will be necessary to identify and then assess various kinds of self-selective mechanisms at each level. Parents may select neighborhoods, and thus school systems and in some cases individual schools, and they sometimes do so precisely because of average past performance levels of students within them. Children may be sorted into classrooms, reading groups, or tracks on the basis of their own previous performance levels as perceived by possibly biased teachers. Peers may be selected partly in terms of residential location, age and sex, and compatibility on a number of psychological dimensions, which may or may not include academic abilities or interests. Some peers may "influence" a given student, where-as others may be selected out because of their similarities on already existing attitudes and behaviors.

Thus assumptions about the "grouping criterion" are just as critical in contextual-effect models as they are in assessing consistency between micro and macro-level formulations. The question of whether it is legitimate first to introduce controls for individual-level X_i and only then introduce group means or other indicators of contextual effects, or to proceed in the opposite order, depends upon one's causal assumptions and information about possible self-selective mechanisms. Yet the critical information is seldom available.

The general implication of these and other criticisms of efforts to handle contextual effects merely by inserting group means or global variables into micro equations is that considerably more information will be needed if one wishes to interpret such contextual effects in a straightforward manner. There are practically always too few supplementary data upon which to base such interpretations and therefore no effective way to eliminate plausible rival alternative explanations.

As a substitute approach, an interdependent set of equations will be recom-mended below. The essential feature of this equation system is the treatment of parents, teachers, peers, and individual students as autonomous actors responding to each others' behaviors. Ideally, we would like to specify dy-namic models that allow for lags in responses, as well as cumulative impacts of past behaviors. Considerable exploratory research involving a combination of observational data, structured and unstructured interviews, and question-naires may be necessary before it becomes possible to specify sets of dynamic equations that approximate the interactive processes that actually occur. I have not encountered any serious efforts to construct such theories, however, nor do I believe that researchers have given adequate attention to investigating such responses of other significant parties. The major empirical investigations that I have examined have focused almost entirely on performance of students as *dependent* variables, rather than as causal determinants of other actors' responses.[5]

Toward Dynamic Equation Systems Involving Interdependent Actors

As noted, our assumption is that although student behaviors may be directly affected only by a combination of contemporaneous stimuli and internal states such as abilities, knowledge, and motivation, one must also attempt to explain how the student got that way. The presumption is that there has been a long series of behaviors and reactions on the part of other persons that have culminated in the internal states that the individual brings into the testing situation, job interview, or first day at work.

Clearly, our models must simplify these past histories and aggregate together the past actions of similar significant actors in the student's environment: teachers, important peers, parents, and perhaps a few others. For illustrative purposes let us assume that there have been four kinds of autonomous actors: the individual student of concern, teachers, parents, and other students in the role of peers. This may require us to aggregate over teachers if the period of study has been such that several teachers have been involved. If we believed such teachers (or parents) to differ significantly in terms of their reactions, we should distinguish among them and perhaps use two sets of teachers or treat the mother and father separately. The same applies to sets of peers.

Notice that we are distinguishing between individual students, as performers, and sets of other students acting in their roles as peers. Johnny thus enters the system in two capacities: as test taker or evaluated performer, and as a peer who reacts to the performances of other students. He may also react to the teachers who are attempting to respond to or sanction whichever fellow student has performed publically, as for example in an oral recital, in which case the teacher equation may need to include one or more terms taking into account the "peer" reactions to the teacher's prior behaviors.

In an interdependent system of equations we do not take the individual student's performance as a single dependent variable, but rather we treat it as an independent variable as well. Ideally, if our data were adequate it might be possible to specify the appropriate lag periods so that the equation system could be made recursive by using lagged endogenous variables for various time periods t, t-1, t-2, . . . , t-k. Johnny's response at, say, t-5 may have influenced the teacher's and peers' responses at t-4, which in turn affected Johnny's behavior at t-3, which affected the others' responses at t-2, and so on. By distinguishing Y_{t-5} from Y_{t-3} from Y_{t-1}, all of which involved Johnny's behaviors, we could retain the recursive format, though autocorrelated disturbance terms could create estimation problems. Collinearity among these three variables might also be high.

In spite of these expected complications, it is important to examine a series of alternative dynamic formulations of this type to see what they imply for data collection and analysis. It will obviously be impossible to take Johnny and his parents, teachers, and peers back over his entire learning career, but as we shall see, it may possible to impose some reasonable simplifying assumptions that may enable us to obtain parameter estimates by using only a small number of points in time. As always, the fewer such observations we actually have, the stronger and less realistic these simplifying assumptions will have to be. It is critical, however, to attempt to specify our models *in advance* of data collection so as to guide the research designs.

Let Y_t represent the behavior of a particular student at time t, and X_t be the behavior of the teacher, parent(s), or fellow students as peers. Assume that we have already written an equation for the student's behavior Y_t as a function of whatever additional variables we wish to use as explanatory factors, as well as prior values of X's representing the influences of the teacher, parents, and peers. The explanatory system does not contain any $\bar{X}$-type variables to represent contextual effects, however, since these are represented directly by the behaviors of these other actors. We could also write a separate equation for each autonomous actor, with the understanding that some actors, such as peers, may be aggregated for reasons of parsimony.

We now focus our attention, not on the equation for the student's behavior Y_t, but on the equation for one of these other actors. For the sake of specificity, let us assume this to be the response X_t of the teacher to an act of the student that has very recently occurred, say an incorrect response to the teacher's question. Similar equations might be written for other students, who may giggle or snicker or perhaps play a supportive role on that particular occasion. We assume that all these responses are nearly instantaneous, so that we may use the same temporal subscript t to represent them. Actors will have memories, however, so that their responses may be influenced by their own or other parties' prior responses at t-1, t-2, and so forth.

We shall introduce three illustrative models, which of course should be motivated by prior exploratory research. In the first, the teacher's response X_t is a simple function of the most immediate behavior Y_t of the student and the teacher's most recent prior response X_{t-1} (which, in turn, would be a function of still prior responses). We introduce a parameter lambda$_1$ to represent the relative weights given to these two terms, with $0 \le \lambda_1 \le 1$. Thus

$$X_t = \alpha_1 + \lambda_1 X_{t-1} + (1 - \lambda_1)\beta\, Y_t + \epsilon_t \qquad (5)$$

where the constant term represents the effects of all omitted exogenous factors, and where the disturbance term is assumed to have a zero mean and to be uncorrelated with the included variables.

The first equation, then, does not force us to go back in time more than one period and could be estimated if we knew the teacher's prior response and the current behavior of the student in question. In effect, we assume that the teacher (or parent or peers) merely adjusts his or her prior behavior somewhat to take into account the most recent student behavior. If lambda were unity, the teacher would provide exactly the same response, ignoring completely the student's behavior Y_t. In contrast, if lambda were zero, the teacher would respond (without prior memory) only to the current value of Y. Intermediate values of the lambda parameter therefore indicate the degree to which the teacher relies primarily on his or her own prior responses versus the contemporary student performance level.

In the second model the teacher responds not to his or her own prior response levels but to a long sequence of behaviors by the student in question, namely at times t, t-1, t-2, . . . , t-k, where k may be a relatively large number. Practically, of course, neither the teacher nor the researcher will be able to "recapture" all of these past events, so that it will be necessary to simplify the model in some manner. Suppose we represent the model as follows:

$$X_t = \alpha_2 + \beta_0 Y_t + \beta_1 Y_{t-1} + \beta_2 Y_{t-2} + \cdots + \beta_k Y_{t-k} + \epsilon_t \qquad (6)$$

where we assume that the beta coefficients diminish in value, and in some lawlike fashion, as we go backwards in time, so that the student's most recent behaviors carry the most weight. We can model this by letting

$$\beta_k = \lambda_2^k \beta_o, \quad 0 \le \lambda_2 \le 1$$

giving us

$$X_t = \alpha_2 + \beta_0 Y_t + \lambda_2 \beta_0 Y_{t-1} + \lambda_2^k \beta_0 Y_{t-2} + \cdots + \lambda_2^k \beta_0 Y_{t-k} + \epsilon_t \quad (7)$$

where once more the lambda value, here λ_2, is between zero and one. Again, when lambda is zero the teacher relies totally on the student's most recent behavior and, in effect, ignores the past. In contrast, when lambda is unity, all previous and current behaviors count equally. Here, then, lambda represents a memory decay factor that, as a parameter, may require theoretical explanation.

In order to see the relationship between equations (5) and (7) we may proceed as follows. We lag equation (7) by one time period, rewriting it in terms of X_{t-1} instead of X_t, getting

$$X_{t-1} = \alpha_2 + \beta_0 Y_{t-1} + \lambda_2 \beta_0 Y_{t-2} + \cdots + \lambda_2^k \beta_0 Y_{t-k-1} + \epsilon_{t-1} \qquad (7a)$$

If we now multiply this last equation by $lambda_2$ and subtract it from (7) we find that most of the intermediate terms cancel out. Furthermore, unless lambda is close to unity (a case we shall later examine), then if k is at all large, the final term in (7a) will be negligible, so that we may write

$$X_t - \lambda_2 X_{t-1} = \alpha_2 (1 - \lambda_2) + \beta_0 Y_t + (\epsilon_t - \lambda_2 \epsilon_{t-1})$$

or $$X_t = \alpha_2(1 - \lambda_2) + \lambda_2 X_{t-1} + \beta_0 Y_t + (\epsilon_t - \lambda_2 \epsilon_{t-1}) \qquad (8)$$

Thus the teacher response at time t is again a function of his or her own response at t-1 and the student's behavior at t. Indeed, the two equations (5) and (8) are equivalent, as can be seen by setting

$$\alpha_1 = \alpha_2(1 - \lambda_2), \quad \lambda_1 = \lambda_2, \quad \text{and} \quad \beta_0 = (1 - \lambda_1)\beta$$

We must remember that equation (8) is inexact, however, since in taking differences we dropped a final term involving lambda raised to the kth power. If the two lambdas are both zero, the teacher relies only on the student's most recent behavior in both models. Where the lambdas are both small, the two models will correspond very closely, but as $lambda_2$ begins to approach its upper limit of unity, it is no longer reasonable to neglect the final term in equation (7a), and when $\lambda_2 = 1$, we would get on subtraction the result

$$X_t = X_{t-1} + \beta_0(Y_t - Y_{t-k-1}) + (\epsilon_t - \epsilon_{t-1}) \qquad (9)$$

and therefore the teacher's behavior is a function of the *difference* or change in the student's behaviors between the initially recalled level and the most current one. The two models diverge, then, whenever lambda is large or k is relatively small.

One final illustrative model can be suggested. Suppose the teacher (or parents or peers) compares a relatively recent *set* of behaviors, perhaps performances on the last three exams, with an average of earlier performance levels. This would be a reasonable assumption if we presume that any single performance might be interpreted as idiosyncratic or as a result of either good or bad luck or perhaps due to the student's having a "bad day." But if the student began performing consistently better, say after a vacation period or the introduction of a new subject, this overall improvement might be taken more seriously. Or a student might be able to convince his or her peers or parents that a single poor (or good) performance was unlikely to be repeated, whereas a series of poor scores could not so easily be explained away.

In such an instance, an additional parameter would be the size of the set of behaviors to be compared with previous ones. The teacher might react not to Y_t alone, but to an average of $Y_t, Y_{t-1}, \ldots, Y_{t-j}$, which would be compared with an average of behaviors at times t-j-1, t-j-2, ... t-k. If, for simplicity, we ignored the memory decay factor we might then write

$$X_t = \alpha_3 + \frac{\beta_0}{j+1}(Y_t + Y_{t-1} + \ldots + Y_{t-j}) - \qquad (10)$$

$$\frac{\beta_0}{k-j-1}(Y_{t-j-1} + \ldots + Y_{t-k}) + \epsilon_t$$

where I have omitted the term representing the teacher's own previous behavior. This model in one sense represents a generalization of equation (9), which contained only the most recent and the very earliest of the student behaviors.

Obviously, there are many additional types of dynamic equations that could be used to represent the teacher's behaviors, and a selection among them would require considerable preliminary exploration involving the systematic observation of teachers in classroom settings, as well as interviews designed to elicit from teachers their perceptions as to their own causal working theories, how best to motivate particular students, and their memory recalls. Also, it is very likely that the particular dynamic models selected to represent the *teacher's* response patterns will be different in form from those used to explain peer reactions. Perhaps the teachers have longer memories. The relative magnitudes of the peers' lambda coefficients may shift as students mature, with very young students reacting primarily in terms of most recent behaviors and older ones in terms of their own earlier response patterns or to a more long-term averaging process. Parental response patterns may be very different from those of either peers or teachers.

Once a set of equations has been formulated for each kind of autonomous actor, the entire set should then be treated as an explanatory system, there being no single dependent variable that does not feed back to affect the others. If one must stop short of such a dynamic system, the next best bet would be to use a set of *simultaneous* though static equations that do not involve the time dimension in an essential way. One could, for instance, write one static equation for the student, another for the teacher, a third for peers, and a fourth for the parents. Such a set of equations for four endogenous "dependent" variables would be underidentified, containing too many unknowns for solution. But by introducing additional predetermined exogenous variables, and making the assumption that such variables do *not* directly affect all of the endogenous variables, the simultaneous system could be identified.

In sum, the essential point is that models that take the individual student's behaviors as strictly dependent, without allowing for the impacts of prior student behaviors on any of the other actors, are likely to be incorrectly specified. If one inserts group means as representations of peer influences, for example, one is ignoring the impacts of each student on these peers, including a self-selection among peers according to prior performance levels. One is also ignoring the effects of student performances on teacher expectation levels, as well as their behavioral responses. And parents are presumed to be uninfluenced by their own children! Such assumptions are not only unrealistic, but they may also tend to inhibit the theorist from attempting to understand the dynamics of the schooling process.

MACRO ANALYSES OF SCHOOLS, DISTRICTS, OR SYSTEMS

It is certainly a legitimate scientific objective to focus entirely on macro units, such as schools, school districts, or even larger school systems. A variety of explanatory variables may be used to account for variations among these larger units, including exogenous variables associated with still larger ones. The methodological and practical problems one encounters at these levels are, in some instances, basically the same as those we have discussed in connection with micro analyses: multicollinearity, selectivity, contextual effects, and the necessity of pinning down temporal processes. But the problem on which we shall focus is the central concern of the exchange over the Bidwell-Kasarda study: that of disentangling school effects from those in the environment, given that the latter continue to operate throughout the schooling process.

The basic issue is that of isolating and measuring the actual contributions of schools, in this case to average student performance levels or other individual characteristics. As we have argued, one cannot simply use out*come* variables, such as average test scores, as though they were school out*puts* unless one is willing to make some very strong assumptions about environmental influences. As noted, the most straightforward "solution" to this problem is to control for student inputs on measures that are, on the face of it, highly similar to those used to measure final outcomes. One might have before measures on reading and mathematics tests and then use the gain or net change values as measures of the "value added" by the schools. Or one could obtain process variables appropriate to schools as units of analysis, using the initial scores as control variables in assessing the impacts of these school variables on the ultimate dependent variables. Coleman et al. (1982) attempted to make an analysis similar to that of Bidwell and Kasarda by using demographic variables as proxies for these "input" factors. They were criticized, however, for implying that self-selective mechanisms had then been "controlled" (Alexander and Pallas 1983).

As I suggested earlier the basic problem is much more difficult, even were it possible to obtain perfect measures of student "inputs" at the time of school entry. This is over and above measurement problems we would encounter in comparing, say, "ability" scores of six year olds and those of eleven year olds, or of 9th and 12th graders. The difficulty stems from the fact that students are exposed to mixtures of in-school and out-of-school factors that combine to affect their ultimate performance levels. Unfortunately, the latter cannot be assumed to be equal across schools except under very unusual circumstances.

In a nutshell, the fundamental problem is that the measurement (and thus control) of input variables at the macro level requires a *micro theory*. To assess school quality, or actual outputs, it is necessary to have a much better understanding of micro processes than we presently have. To base policy recommendations on outcome variables, for example, is to mislead one's audience to the degree that the micro theory has been misspecified. In part, the difficulties stem from selection biases that lead to grouping or aggregation biases that in turn amplify misspecifications at the micro level. But another part of the problem lies in our inability to disentangle school and environmental impacts *during* the interval that schooling is occurring, and regardless of any initial self-selection that has taken place. In general, then, the more we know about micro-level processes, the more justified we can be in making the simplifying assumptions necessary at the macro level to justify data analyses at that level.

Ideally this implies that we should work upwards to increasingly macro levels, rather than downwards from macro to micro. The need to make policy recommendations at the former level, however, not only creates an understandable tension among scholars but may also encourage vested interests in holding onto totally unrealistic assumptions that are conveniently hidden from view. The assumption that out-of-school factors are either constant across schools or have influences only at points of entry is one such assumption.

Yet there may be advantages to aggregating, as we have already noted. Clearly, out-of-school influences will have relatively more impact on some students than others, and there may be nonadditive joint effects of the two kinds of factors that, at the micro level, may contribute to specification errors in simple additive models. With luck, some of these factors may cancel out in the aggregation process in a manner similar to that which reduces random measurement errors. Coleman (1972), for example, noted that measures of objective school facilities, such as library books or science equipment per capita, do not tell us which students actually *use* and therefore benefit from these facilities. But aggregated student usage levels may be a simpler function of facility levels, so that such per capita measures may be relatively better indicators of average use levels. *Perhaps* the same applies to average parental expectation levels, which may be a more predictable function of average SES levels than individual expectation levels are of individual parental SES. In a sense, our micro-level models might have to be more sophisticated in these regards than a "corresponding" macro model.

"Frog-pond" effects may be a case in point. Some students may respond very well to higher levels of competition brought about when their classmates have high abilities and strong motivations. Others may have the opposite reaction, however, perhaps because they perceive themselves to have relatively lower ability levels or because they are motivated to compete only when they are close to the top of the class. The two kinds of students *may* tend to cancel each other out in terms of contributing to average performance levels, say on standardized exams. At the micro level, one would want to introduce terms allowing one to assess such frog-pond effects, as for example a series of group means on the relevant variables. But at the macro level, and in terms of policy implications, such frog-pond effects may not be considered important. In selecting among schools, individual parents may wish to take them into consideration, especially if they know their own children's tendencies. But school administrators can perhaps afford to ignore them in instituting policies designed to raise average performance levels.

Or can they? Certainly, one cannot always count on factors such as these to average out. The crucial point is that there will always be assumptions required, and these may either be explicit or implicit. My argument is that, even where our micro theories are weak, it is preferable to make such assumptions explicit and then to examine the resulting models for their implications. This at least has the advantage of facilitating informed debate about the merits of each specific assumption and of pointing to needed micro-level research so as to assess its plausibility. The problem of self-selection and its impact on aggregation biases is merely one example of this general point.

Let me illustrate in terms of a very simple recursive causal model formulated at the level of the classroom, where we are concerned with the impact of two teacher variables, amount of homework assigned X_1 and toughness of grading X_2. For simplicity, assume these two variables to be uncorrelated, and that X_1 but not X_2 is affected by the average performance level Y_{t_1} of students at the time they entered the class. Let Y_{t_2} represent their average performance level at some later time t_2. Assume, also, that earlier performance levels directly affect later performance levels and that some parental variable Z, say parental supervision of or assistance with homework, has

Figure 1.

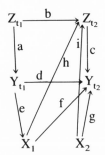

operated in the past so as to affect Y_{t_1} but also continues to operate so as to affect Y_{t_2}. But the teacher's behaviors X_1 and X_2 also affect the parental behaviors at t_2, and shortly beforehand, but not prior to the students' entry at t_1. Perhaps the students have entered a far more demanding school or class than they had previously experienced.

We might represent such a very simple model as in Figure 2, in which we have also drawn in an arrow between Z at time 1 and itself at time 2. This means that although parental behaviors may change in response to the teacher's behavior, they will also have a tendency to persist over time, for whatever reasons, perhaps because of a constant parental interest in their children's education. For simplicity, I have labeled the (standardized) path coefficients among the variables as a,b,c, . . . , i.

Suppose our interest is focused on the schooling effects of the two teacher behaviors X_1 and X_2 on average student learning within the classroom. We would obviously want to control or adjust for their initial test levels, and if we were able to do so perfectly, this would remove the coefficients a, d, and e from further consideration. Notice that, without any controls at all, the correlations between the two X variables and performance at time 2 (ignoring sampling errors) would be:

$$r_{X_1 Y_{t_2}} = f + de + hc + eabc \tag{11}$$

and

$$r_{X_1 Y_{t_2}} = g + ic \tag{12}$$

A control for Y_{t_1} would mean that, if we ignored the parental variable Z_{t_1}, we could in effect set $a = d = e = 0$ and our estimates of the two teacher effects would be $f + hc$ and $g + ic$, respectively, rather than f and g, the simple direct effects of the teacher behaviors on average performance levels. Is this what we want?

In a sense, it is, given our model. We are assuming that the teacher's homework assignments and grading practices are affecting the parents, so that there are both direct and indirect effects of the teacher on average student behaviors. But should these impacts be attributed to the *school?* What if a teacher, in another school, employed exactly the same practices but was unable to influence the parents, so that $h = i = 0$? Or what if the parents were unable to influence their own children, so that $c = 0$? Our estimates of the "teacher effects" would differ, and rightly so given the model. But assuming all coefficients in the first instance to be positive, so that parental behaviors reinforced those of the teacher, that teacher would appear more "effective" than the corresponding one in the second school, even though both teachers had behaved in exactly the same way!

Before returning to the basic problems here, let us examine a few more possibilities. With an imperfect measure of average student performance levels at time 1, and thus an imperfect control for their real prior performance levels (or abilities), we would not completely wipe out d and e but, since they are standardized coefficients, we would reduce them toward zero to the degree that we were successful in taking out random measurement errors in the measured Y_{t_1}. Aggregation would probably be helpful in this regard.

Next suppose we were able to control for certain average parental characteristics, say SES W_1 and percent black W_2. If these latter variables, at the micro level, were causes of the parental behavior Z, then at the aggregate level we might be able to produce a reasonably decent control on the average Z level at time 1. This might nearly wipe out the coefficients a and b, and substantially reduce the variance in the average Z at time 2. But we are assuming that the teacher's behavior also influences Z_{t_2}, so that h and i, being standardized coefficients, might also increase because of the fact that certain of Z's other causes had been controlled. Whether or not c also decreased would depend on the remaining variance in Z at time 2 and of the partially controlled Y_{t_1}'s influence on later average performance levels. How these changes in numerical values would impact on the explanatory power of the teacher's behaviors might be difficult to assess without additional information.

We see in this instance the disadvantage of working with standardized measures, such as path coefficients. But the more critical issue is that of how we would evaluate the "quality" of the schooling, given that it is also influenced by parental factors. I have assumed that teachers' behaviors affect parents, whereas it might be more reasonable to assume reciprocal causation. If parents do not insist on their children's working on homework assignments, teachers' expectations may be lowered, as may their grading standards. If parents also insist on their children receiving good grades, or being automatically passed regardless of performance, the influence of parents on teachers may be much greater than in the reverse direction. Therefore a more realistic model would be nonrecursive, and ideally one that allowed for time lags of the type discussed in the previous section.

All this implies that "schooling quality" is very much bound to out-of-school factors. Even teacher performance (and by implication a principal's performance as well) cannot be dissociated from these outside factors unless one is willing to assume a highly simplistic explanatory model (e.g., one in which both h and i are zero or c is zero). With an adequate model the *direct* effects of teacher behaviors on student performance could be assessed, and perhaps it is these effects, alone, that ought to be used in deciding which teachers are to be rewarded or let go. But perhaps not, if we wish to take into account the teacher's ability to deal with parents, including getting them to reinforce in-school learning patterns. Or perhaps it might be argued that both teachers and principals should be impervious to parental pressures, whether positive or negative!

CONCLUDING REMARKS

It has been strongly emphasized that, although it is desirable to conduct analyses at several distinct levels, it is also critical that such analyses be compatible in some sense. Simple "consistency," as technically used in econometrics, may not be expected. Nevertheless, to the degree that models at any given level can be well specified, this will serve to justify theoretical assumptions needed at other levels. In particular, where macro dependent variables are considered to be "outcomes" involving aggregated scores of individual students, micro theories will be needed to justify *measurement* decisions at the macro level. Also, as a general rule, it is critical to understand how the aggregating criterion (e.g., classrooms, schools) enters into one's theory so as to assess whether or not aggregation biases will be substantial and whether they will operate in the same or the opposite direction from that of one's micro-level specification errors.

This suggests that micro-level research needs to proceed more rapidly and much more systematically, with macro-level formulations following somewhat behind. For example, we have noted the problem created by the entanglement of in-school and out-of-school factors in assessing school input variables in macro models. It also implies that policy recommendations based on school or district-level analyses need to be made with extreme caution. In particular, school "quality" should not be equated with outcome levels, even where several "input" variables have been introduced as crude controls.

In terms of the causal processes involved, it seems reasonable to assume that student performance levels or other student characteristics are most directly affected by factors in their immediate environments: the classroom, home, and peer groups. This does not mean, of course, that more macro factors do not, in turn, impact on some of these more immediate causes, as for example teacher-student interactions. It does suggest, however, that at the *micro* level these more remote variables are unlikely to explain more additional variance over and above that explained by a well specified micro model. I have argued that the latter should allow for interdependencies among students, teachers, and parents, rather than simply taking individual student performance levels as single dependent variables. Given a model based either on lagged or simultaneous interdependent equations, I also suggested that it may become possible to avoid "contextual effect" terms involving group means.

Finally, I believe that there are important implications in terms of the ways we are organized to conduct research. Studies need to be much more carefully coordinated if we are to achieve genuine cumulative knowledge. Ultimately, we shall require very large-scale data collection efforts that permit the analyst to combine longitudinal data for individual students with those for their teachers, parents, and peers. Supplementary data for nested (and possibly overlapping) contextual units would also need to be collected in such a manner that individual-level data can be properly aggregated to provide intervening and dependent variables needed for macro analyses. But if we rush, prematurely, to develop macro theories that are not adequately based on our understanding of the micro processes involved, we are at risk of producing a series of highly misleading policy recommendations and, possibly, another "backlash" reaction among the general public.

NOTES

1. See especially Cain and Watts (1970) and the series of critiques in Mosteller and Moynihan (1972).

2. See Alexander and Pallas' (1983) critique of Coleman et al. (1982) for their failure to control adequately for selection factors in comparing public and private schools.

3. If there is an interactive term involving the product $X_{ij}\bar{X}_j$, however, aggregation will produce a squared term $\bar{X}_j^2$, which permits identification. See Przeworski (1974).

4. For more technical discussions see Hannan (1971), Hannan and Burstein (1974), and Langbein and Lichtman (1978). For a direct application to schools, see also Langbein (1977).

5. There are, of course, a number of smaller-scale studies of alternative teaching strategies, student-student interaction patterns, and teacher expectations. See especially Bossert (1979), Slavin (1977, 1980), and a review of the effective schools literature by Purkey and Smith (1983). To my knowledge, however, theories of teacher responses to student behaviors have not been tested in large-scale, quantitative studies, nor have simultaneous-equation models of the type under discussion been formulated or systematically tested.

REFERENCES

Alexander, K. L., J. Fennessey, E. L. McDill, and R. J. D'Amico. 1979. "School SES Influences—Composition or Context?" *Sociology of Education* 52: 222–37.

Alexander, K. L., and L. J. Griffin. 1976. "School District Effects on Academic Achievement: A Reconsideration." *American Sociological Review* 41: 144–52.

Alexander, K. L., and A. M. Pallas. 1983. "Private Schools and Public Policy: New Evidence on Cognitive Achievement in Public and Private Schools." *Sociology of Education* 56: 170–82.

Bidwell, C. E., and J. D. Kasarda. 1975. "School District Organization and Student Achievement." *American Sociological Review* 40: 55–70.

————. 1976. "Reply to Hannan, Freeman, and Meyer, and Alexander and Griffin." *American Sociological Review* 41: 152–60.

Blalock, H. M. 1984. "Contextual Effects Models: Theoretical and Methodological Issues." Edited by Ralph H. Turner and James F. Short. *Annual Review of Sociology, Vol. 10:* 353–72. Palo Alto: Annual Reviews, Inc.

Blalock, H. M., and P. H. Wilken. 1979. *Intergroup Processes: A Micro-Macro Perspective.* New York: Free Press.

Blau, P. M. 1960. "Structural Effects." *American Sociological Review* 25: 178–93.

Bossert, S. T. 1979. *Tasks and Social Relationships in Classrooms.* New York: Cambridge University Press.

Burstein, L. 1978. "Assessing Differences Between Grouped and Individual-Level Regression Coefficients." *Sociological Methods and Research* 7: 5–28.

Cain, G. G., and H. W. Watts. 1970. "Problems in Making Policy Inferences from the Coleman Report." *American Sociological Review* 35: 228–41.

Coleman, J. S. 1972. "The Evaluation of *Equality of Educational Opportunity.*" Edited by Frederick Mosteller and Daniel P. Moynihan. *On Equality of Educational Opportunity.* New York: Vintage Books.

Coleman, J. S., E. Q. Campbell, C. J. Hobson, J. McPartland, A. M. Mood, F. D. Weinfeld, and R. L. York. 1966. *Equality of Educational Opportunity.* Washington: U.S. Dept. of HEW.

Coleman, J. S., T. H. Hoffer, and S. Kilgore. 1982. *High School Achievement: Public, Private, and Catholic Schools Compared.* New York: Basic Books.

Davis, J. A. 1966. "The Campus as a Frog Pond." *American Journal of Sociology* 72: 17–31.

Davis, J. A., J. L. Spaeth, and C. Huson. 1961. "A Technique for Analyzing the Effects of Group Composition." *American Sociological Review* 26: 215–25.

Erbring, L., and A. Young. 1979. "Individuals and Social Structure: Contextual Effects as Endogenous Feedback." *Sociological Methods and Research* 7: 396–430.

Eulau, H. 1969. *Micro-Macro Political Analysis: Accents of Inquiry.* Chicago: Aldine.

Farkas, G. 1974. "Specification, Residuals, and Contextual Effects." *Sociological Methods and Research* 2: 333–63.

Firebaugh, G. 1978. "A Rule for Inferring Individual-Level Relationships from Aggregate Data." *American Sociological Review* 43: 557–72.

————. 1980. "Groups as Contexts and Frog Ponds." *New Directions in Social and Behavioral Science* 6: 43–52.

Goodman, L. A. 1959. "Some Alternatives to Ecological Correlation." *American Journal of Sociology* 64: 610–25.

Hannan, M. T. 1971. *Aggregation and Disaggregation in Sociology.* Lexington, Mass.: Heath-Lexington.

Hannan, M. T., and L. Burstein. 1974. "Estimation from Grouped Observations." *American Sociological Review* 39: 374–92.

Hannan, M. T., J. H. Freeman, and J. W. Meyer. 1976. "Specification of Methods for Organizational Effectiveness: A Comment on Bidwell and Kasarda." *American Sociological Review* 41: 136–43.

Hauser, R. M. 1974. "Contextual Analysis Revisited." *Sociological Methods and Research* 2: 365–75.

Irwin, L., and A. J. Lichtman. 1976. "Across the Great Divide: Inferring Individual Level Behavior from Aggregate Data." *Political Methodology* 3: 411–39.

Karweit, N. L., J. Fennessey, and D. C. Daiger. 1978. "Examining the Credibility of Offsetting Contextual Effects." Center for Social Organization of Schools, No. 250.

Langbein, L. I. 1977. "Schools or Students: Aggregation Problems in the Study of Student Achievement." *Evaluation Studies Review Annual* 2: 270–98.

Langbein, L. I., and A. J. Lichtman. 1978. *Ecological Inference.* Beverly Hills: Sage.

Mosteller, F., and D. P. Moynihan. 1972. *On Equality of Educational Opportunity.* New York: Vintage Books.

Purkey, S. C., and M. S. Smith. 1983. "Effective Schools: A Review." *Elementary School Journal* 83: 427–52.

Przeworski, A. 1974. "Contextual Models of Political Behavior." *Political Methodology* 1: 27–61.

Slavin, R. E. 1977. "Classroom Reward Structure: An Analytical and Practical Review." *Review of Educational Research* 47: 633–50.

―――――. 1980. "Cooperative Learning in Teams: State of the Art." *Educational Psychology* 15: 93–111.

CONCEPTUAL AND MEASUREMENT ISSUES IN THE STUDY OF SCHOOL DROPOUTS

Aaron M. Pallas

INTRODUCTION

Riding the crest of the newest wave of educational reform is the concept of the "at-risk" student. One of the things such children are at risk of is dropping out of high school. There is a widespread belief that far too many young people are leaving school without obtaining a high school diploma. Dropout rates are used like economic indicators to assess the health of the U.S. schooling system as a whole, as well as of individual school districts and school buildings. For the first time in recent memory, powerful constituencies in the education community are promoting head-to-head comparisons of the perfor-

Research in the Sociology of Education and Socialization,
Volume 8, pages 87–116.
Copyright © **1989 by JAI Press Inc.**
All rights of reproduction in any form reserved.
ISBN: 0-89232-929-7

mance of school districts, states, and countries. There is thus a press to develop dropout statistics which can be credibly compared across various jurisdictional boundaries.

With the increased attention to school dropouts, there has been a resurgence of interest in the causes and consequences of dropping out of school. Sociologists of education are striving to understand the social forces that lead to dropping out of school, and the ways in which dropping out constrains socioeconomic success through the life course. From a more pragmatic view, educational policy researchers aim to predict who will drop out of school, and to estimate the economic consequences of dropping out of school, so that they can make recommendations about efficient investments in educational programs.

But in order to count dropouts, and to study them, there first must be agreement on who they are. There currently is no consensus on how to measure the dropout phenomenon, nor even how to conceptualize it. This chapter considers some of the issues in the conceptualization and measurement of school dropouts, as well as the related notion of school completers. I examine both the production of dropout statistics and the research literature on school dropouts. The chapter's recurring theme is that conceptualization and measurement strategies should vary according to the ways in which dropout data are to be used.

DROPOUT STATISTICS

In this section I review some of the issues involved in the production of school dropout statistics. I begin by placing dropping out of school in the context of the educational lifecycle. Then I discuss the relative advantages of common ways of counting dropouts. Next I turn to the construction of dropout rates and the use of period or cohort data. I conclude the section by discussing the use of dropout statistics as education indicators.

The Life Course of Individuals

A useful way to think about school dropout issues is in the context of the educational career. We can think of the educational career as analogous to the occupational career (Spilerman 1977). Like the occupational career, the educational career is embedded in the life course of individuals. Educational career paths represent possible trajectories for the life course (Elder 1985).

Embedded within educational trajectories are transitions, specific events in the life course which represent changes from one state to another, such as enrolled to not enrolled, or college student to college graduate. In addition, there are qualitative variations among nominally similar states, so that we can distinguish among college graduates according to the type of college attended, or among high school graduates according to the type of high school completion credential awarded to an individual.

In an orderly world, it would be easy to map these transitions. In such a world, there would be a single path to high school completion, the regular day high school. This ideal setting also might have a tournament mobility system (Rosenbaum 1976), so that once a student left school he or she could never return. And finally, it would not be possible to advance to the next highest level of schooling without having completed all relevant lower levels of schooling. For instance, it would not be possible to enroll in postsecondary institutions such as two-year and four-year colleges without having graduated from high school.

The imaginary world I have described differs in important ways from the one we live in. First, the contemporary U.S. schooling system is decentralized and highly differentiated, and leaving one school before completion typically does not preclude entering another (Rubinson 1986). Many states offer alternative routes to high school diplomas or "equivalents," in ways that go well beyond traditional day programs. For example, Finn (1987) reports that South Carolina and Virginia awarded 10,000 of their own equivalency credentials in 1985. In that same year, over 400,000 persons were awarded General Educational Development (GED) credentials (GED Testing Service 1986).

Second, in some locales one need not complete a lower level of schooling prior to advancing to higher levels. For instance, in California, all students over the age of 18 are eligible to attend public community colleges, regardless of whether they have completed high school. In California, among high school dropouts from the class of 1983, approximately 13 percent entered community colleges in the fall of 1983 without a high school diploma or equivalent (California Legislature Assembly Office of Research 1985).

The decentralization and differentiation of the U.S. schooling system allows for complex educational trajectories. Figure 1 shows some of the alternative paths that students can follow through secondary school. The initial state for all students is enrolled in secondary school.[1] This initial state can lead to any of three more states. First, if the student fulfills the requirements for a high school diploma, then the student can be a "regular high school graduate," characterized by possession of a regular high school diploma. Second, a student can acquire an alternative equivalency credential directly while still enrolled in a regular day school.[2] Third, a student can leave high school without a high school credential. This latter category conforms most closely to our connotation of a school dropout. It refers to someone who is not enrolled in high school and does not possess a high school diploma of any kind.

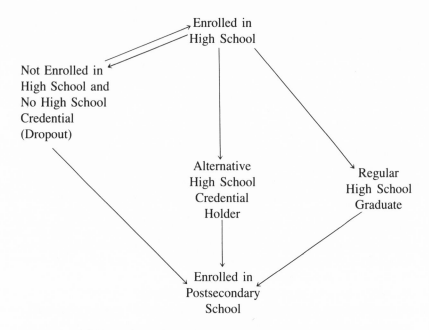

Figure 1. Alternative Educational Trajectories.

Persons who lack a high school diploma and are not enrolled in high school can remain in that state indefinitely. But younger dropouts often re-enroll in high school. It therefore is possible to move from the dropout state back to the initial enrolled state, which is represented by an arrow in the Figure. Some youths repeatedly drop out and re-enroll in school. Once a student has re-enrolled in school, of course, the student may move to any of the states described above: dropout, regular high school graduate, or alternative credential holder.

It is also possible for a school dropout to obtain a high school equivalency credential directly, without re-enrolling in high school. Thus, Figure 1 shows a path reflecting this too. There is no path directly from dropout to regular high school graduate, however, on the assumption that a person must re-enroll in school to obtain a regular high school diploma.

Finally, the lower part of Figure 1 concerns entry into postsecondary schooling. There are paths from each of the dropout, alternative high school credential holder, and regular high school graduate states, indicating that it is possible to enter postsecondary schools from any of these states (although the probability of doing so clearly is lower for the dropout state).

Figure 1 highlights two important points: (1) In general, it is not possible to deduce a person's educational history from his or her current status. The fact that a person is enrolled in college, or may even be a college graduate, does not necessarily imply that that person graduated from high school or acquired an equivalency credential. (2) The concepts of school dropout and high school graduate are not complementary. Eventually, all persons either acquire a high school diploma or equivalent, or they don't. But it is quite possible for a person to be a dropout (not enrolled in school and lacking a high school credential) at one point in time, and a regular high school graduate at a later point. The rate of transition into the dropout state does not in and of itself constrain the rate of transition into the regular high school graduate state.

In contrast to the distinction between dropouts and graduates, regular high school diplomas and alternative equivalency credentials are complementary. The categories are mutually exclusive, in that regular high school graduates are not eligible to acquire alternative credentials. In theory, a person with an equivalency credential could later obtain a regular high school diploma, but such a phenomenon must be exceedingly rare. The next section discusses alternative high school credentials, especially the General Educational Development (GED) test battery.

Alternative High School Credentials

Sociologists of education have been much more attentive to the structural differentiation of higher education than that of secondary education. There has been a great deal of interest in the role of community colleges in the educational and social stratification systems, and much of this work has examined individual trajectories. To date, though, there still are few systematic attempts to take account of the timing and sequencing of post-high school educational events, except as they pertain to family and work events (Featherman and Carter 1976).

It is not surprising that sociologists of education would pay attention to community colleges during a time of relatively rapid expansion and differentiation of this form of higher education. What is perhaps surprising is that there has been no corresponding focus on the expansion and differentiation of secondary education. Most areas now recognize and support alternatives to traditional daytime secondary school programs.

The most well-known alternative to a traditional daytime secondary school diploma is a credential representing a passing score on the General Educational Development (GED) test battery. This test is often thought of as a high school equivalency test. The tests typically are administered through individual states, and states can determine their own criteria for passing scores. The GED tests include tests in writing skills, social studies, science, reading skills, and mathematics. These tests are designed to assess the outcomes of a typical high school curriculum (Patience and Whitney 1982).

Critics of the GED tests have argued that instruction in adult basic education programs and GED classes has supplanted the goal of basic skills acquisition with instruction in how to take the GED tests (Quinn and Haberman 1986). Regardless of whether this is true, there is an important difference between the GED test and a regular day high school. The GED battery is a series of tests, not a school enrollment. A person need not be enrolled in school to take the GED tests. Many, if not most, GED recipients spend less time in the student role than regular high school graduates.

Since many GED recipients obtain their credentials while not enrolled in school, they may share some of the characteristics of other students who have left high school before graduation. We do know quite a bit about the characteristics of students who leave school before graduation (Pallas 1987; Rumberger 1987; Wagenaar 1987). For instance, one study found that GED recipients were less involved in high school activities than traditional high school graduates (Ladner 1986). This seems almost tautological, but participating in high school activities may confer social, psychological and cognitive benefits on participants which may have long-lasting effects on later educational and occupational chances. More generally, the length of time persons spend in school is closely tied to socialization patterns and outcomes. Thus, the fact that GED recipients spend less time in school has important implications for the noncognitive traits learned in school but not reflected in standardized tests.

We know relatively little about the net effects of obtaining a GED credential on the educational and occupational accomplishments of young people. There is a smattering of case studies of single institutions which compare the educational performance of GED holders with that of traditional high school graduates. Most of these have small samples of GED holders, and few are able to control for pre-existing differences between GED holders and traditional graduates which might be relevant to their performance in college. Hence, it is not clear how much faith to put in these studies.

The effects of holding a GED credential on academic performance appear to vary according to the type of post-secondary institution being studied. Several small case studies of two-year institutions have failed to find statistically significant differences between GED holders and traditional high school graduates in their college grade point averages and persistence rates (Wolf 1980; Wilson et al. 1981; Beltzer 1984). Among community college entrants, then, GED holders may not behave very differently than traditional high school graduates. The evidence to date is more suggestive than conclusive.

The available evidence on the relative success of GED recipients and traditional high school graduates in four-year institutions suggests a very different story, though. Quinn and Haberman's (1986) study of GED holders and traditional high school graduates entering the University of Wisconsin at Milwaukee in the late 1970s concludes that entering GED recipients did much worse, on average, than entering students drawn from the bottom half of their high school class, when outcomes such as persistence through four semesters, cumulative GPA and credits earned were examined. In fact, GED holders performed no better than entering high school graduates in the bottom twenty percent of their high school classes.

There are no large-scale studies of the performance of GED recipients at elite colleges and universities, presumably because so few are admitted to these types of institutions. Among new admissions to the University of Wisconsin at Madison, for instance, only .2 percent of the students admitted from fall 1979 to fall 1983 were GED holders (Quinn and Haberman 1986). If obtaining a passing score on the GED test battery represents performance at roughly the thirtieth percentile of high school graduates, it would be surprising indeed to observe many GED holders being admitted to the more elite institutions.

For now, it is an open question whether obtaining a passing score on the GED test battery should be considered commensurate with a regular day high school diploma. The comparability of these two credentials may vary according to the particular educational or occupational outcome of interest. There simply is an inadequate body of evidence to draw firm conclusions about the standing of the GED and other alternative credentials. Some of the unanswered questions include: What are the socioeconomic and academic characteristics of the GED test-taking population? Would these test-takers complete high school in the absence of the GED examination? Does obtaining an equivalency certificate generate the same occupational prestige and income payoffs that accompany a regular high school diploma? How does obtaining an equivalency certificate affect a person's access to, and success in, postsecondary education, relative both to regular high school graduates and persons lacking high school credentials altogether? In many respects these questions directly parallel the community college debate (Dougherty 1987; Karabel 1972; Pincus 1980).

Delineating the differences between alternative credential holders, regular high school graduates, and persons who are not enrolled in school and who lack any high school credential helps to flesh out some of the educational trajectories presented in Figure 1. But it remains to be seen how closely the way we count dropouts maps on to the trajectories in Figure 1. The next section considers the counting of dropouts.

Counting Dropouts

The most important aspect of counting dropouts is that someone is doing the counting. This can be, among others, a school, a school district, a person, or the federal government. Different accounting systems will have different rules for counting dropouts, and different means for coping with the complexity of various educational trajectories. Some of these will conform more closely than others to the imagery drawn in Figure 1.

Already a great deal has been written about the problems of counting dropouts (Morrow 1986; Hammack 1986; Pallas and Verdugo 1986; Barber 1984). Much of this work has been devoted to documenting the myriad ways in which school districts count dropouts and calculate dropout statistics. There is overwhelming evidence that, in general, one cannot compare dropout statistics reported by one local education agency (LEA) with those reported by another LEA. School districts typically differ in their definitions of who is a dropout, what the appropriate base population is, and how to form a dropout "rate." In some cases it may be possible to take account of the discrepant definitions and still make crude comparisons. More typically, though, the differences in conceptualization and measurement are large enough to make comparisons across LEAs meaningless.

There are two major ways to collect data on school dropout and completion: administrative records and household or individual surveys. Schools and school districts typically rely on administrative records for dropout and graduation data, while the federal government uses both administrative records and household surveys. Data gathered by the federal government are discussed later in the chapter.

With sufficient motivation and resources, schools or school districts can keep careful track of who enters and leaves their settings, and with what credentials. Schools can identify who is enrolled in a given school at any point in time, given the local rules for determining enrollment. And, schools can tell when an individual is not enrolled in a given school. Moreover, schools can easily take account of the recipients of regular high school diplomas.

School districts usually can keep track of student mobility across schools in the district. If a student transfers from one school in a district to another, both the sending and receiving school are usually aware of the transaction, and the school district housing those schools can maintain a record of the student's enrollment history. Even if a student leaves a regular day high school for an adult basic education program or GED preparation class run by the school district, the school and district usually manage to track the student successfully.

Where school-based tracking systems fall down is in following students after they have left a given school district. Figure 1 shows that when a person drops out of school, there are several possible patterns. The student can re-enroll in the same school that he or she dropped out of; re-enroll in a different school; or obtain an alternative equivalency credential without ever returning to school. Few schools or school districts count transfers to another school as dropouts. A school can certainly monitor when a person has re-enrolled in that school, but may not be able to judge when a person has enrolled in a different school, or when a person has acquired a high school equivalency credential.

When a student transfers from one school to another, the student drops out of the first school and enrolls in the second. It is a common practice for the receiving school to request the student's records from the sending school. Hence, a request for a student's records is frequently used as a criterion for judging whether a student has dropped out of school or merely transfered to another school. It is conceivable that some schools fail to request entering students' records, or that such requests get lost in transition, but for students transfering to a regular day high school, the odds are pretty good that the receiving school will request the students' records from the sending school, which can then count the student as a transfer rather than a dropout.

A more troubling, and perhaps more common, situation arises when the dropout enters an educational program which has no ties to the school from which the student dropped out. These include adult basic education programs or GED preparation programs that are not sponsored by the school district. There also is no guarantee that a school will be notified if one of its dropouts obtains a passing score on the GED test battery. It is rare for such information to be communicated to schools, and rarer still for schools to know how to store and use that information. In such cases, records indicating that a student has dropped out are usually not updated to reflect a more current, and perhaps more permanent, status.

Identifying dropouts is not a trivial task. The common connotation of a school dropout is someone who is no longer going to school, and who left without finishing school. But laws and administrative practices often specify dropout definitions which diverge substantially from this commonsense notion. In some educational jurisdictions, for example, it is not possible to discharge a person below the compulsory school attendance age as a dropout, even if that person is no longer attending school.

In New York City, for example, only 2.5 percent of the dropouts from the class of 1986 were younger than 17, the compulsory attendance age, at the time they were discharged (New York City Board of Education 1987). New York schools are required by law to carry chronic truants on their school registers. The New York City Board of Education created a new category of student, the Long Term Absentee (LTA), to describe chronic truants. A student is designated an LTA upon being absent from school for 20 consecutive school days.

Average daily attendance figures in New York City schools are calculated both with and without LTAs. Once a student reaches the age of 17, school personnel have some discretion in deciding whether or not to process the paperwork necessary to discharge an LTA as a dropout. Some high schools are much more vigorous in discharging LTAs as dropouts than others. Schools that are conscious of their dropout rates may choose to keep LTAs on their registers rather than discharge them. The social and political pressures associated with a high dropout rate do not carry over to the LTA rate, at least in New York City.

The New York City experience points to the importance of how school dropouts are defined in an educational jurisdiction for determining the number of dropouts and for dropout rates. School districts face real pressures to minimize the seriousness of the dropout problem, owing to local political forces, but also because funding may be allocated on the basis of the number of students on the school register. Because of this disincentive to discharge students as dropouts, many schools and school districts retain students who are de facto dropouts.

The best clue to this phenomenon is the school's attendance rate, indexed by the ratio of the school or district average daily attendance (ADA) to the school or district average daily membership (ADM). The average daily attendance represents the average number of students actually in the school on a given day, while average daily membership refers to the average number of students on the school register. The ratio of ADA to ADM can be thought of as the proportion of the number of school days that students actually attend school. A low attendance rate suggests that there are students being carried on the school register who are not attending school on a regular basis, if at all. There are, however, no common rules of thumb for assessing whether attendance rates are suspiciously high or low. The mean attendance rate is not as informative as the distribution of attendance rates, but the latter is rarely reported.

Dropout Rates

There is considerable confusion over the distinction between rates and ratios in calculating dropout statistics. These terms are grounded in social demography, which makes extensive use of rates and ratios. According to Shryock and Siegel (1976:5), ''the term 'rate' most appropriately applies to the number of demographic events in a given period of time divided by the population at risk. Thus, we may speak of the number of deaths divided by the population as the death rate. The population at risk is usually only approximated.''

Demographers distinguish between crude rates and refined rates. Shryock and Siegel (1976:6) state:

> The adjective 'crude' is especially appropriate in the case of the crude birth rate because obviously men, children, and old people are not at risk of having a baby. . . . In the case of the crude marriage rate, persons who are in the married state throughout the year are likewise not at risk. Various refinements are introduced in the population base in order to obtain a more meaningful rate. These may not only omit that part of the population for which the risk is zero, but they may also take account of the fact that the risk is much greater for some population subgroups than for others. For example, all persons are at risk of dying but the risk is much greater at age 90 than at age 10. Accordingly, we have age-specific rates, for example, the number of deaths during the year to persons aged 20 to 24. . . . Rates may be specific for any other characteristic into which the demographic data are subdivided.

Sometimes the term rate is used to represent a proportion or percentage. Shryock and Siegel (1976:6) state, "The term rate is also loosely used to refer to the ratio between a population subgroup and the total population where the definition of the subgroup reflects a prior event." Thus the "dropout rate" might be simply the proportion of persons in some population of interest who have dropped out of school, without regard to when this event might have occurred. The converse, a "graduation rate," might be the proportion of persons in a population of interest who are classified as having completed high school.

The foregoing discussion has some obvious implications for the way we think about dropout rates. For instance, if we can count the number of dropouts from a school or district in a given school year, and can estimate the total enrollment across all grades in that school or district, it is straightforward to estimate a crude dropout rate (setting aside the problem of persons dropping out more than once in a given school year). In fact, some school districts report dropout rates in this way. It is not surprising that they should do so, since the rates calculated in this way tend to be fairly low. This is because students enrolled in primary grades have a very low risk of dropping out. In some cases, the requirements of compulsory school attendance laws insist that children below a specific age cannot be legally classified as dropouts, even if they are no longer attending school on a regular basis. The inclusion of a large number of persons with a zero or very low risk of dropping out deflates the estimated dropout rate relative to an estimate omitting such persons.

Consider the hypothetical case of Big City School District, which enrolls students from grades one to twelve. Suppose that average enrollments are the same across grades, and that there are different risks of dropping out depending on the grade in which a student is enrolled. Perhaps children in grades one through four have a zero chance of dropping out of school in a given year;

children in grades five through eight have a one percent chance of dropping out in a specific school year, and children in grades nine through twelve are at much greater risk of dropping out of school in a particular school year, say ten percent. The crude dropout rate for Big City School District would be a weighted average of the grade-specific dropout rates. In this hypothetical example, with grades of equal sizes, the crude dropout rate in 3.7 percent. This figure is much lower than the grade-specific dropout rate for ninth through twelfth graders of 10 percent. Little wonder, then, that Big City School District might choose to report a crude dropout rate instead of a grade-specific dropout rate.

Cohort Data Versus Period Data

Social demographers draw a distinction between cohort data and period data. Cohort data pertain to the experiences of a cohort of individuals, defined by having experienced some demographic event in a common period of time. Tracking the experiences of a cohort requires longitudinal data, because different members of a cohort may experience demographic events at different points of time in their lifecycles. In contrast, period data pertain to demographic events occurring in a fixed period of time (frequently a year). Period data provide a brief "snapshot" summarizing the experiences of several cohorts in a period of interest.

Both cohort data and period data are used in the study of school dropouts. Period data are reported more frequently than cohort data at the school or district level, in large part because of the difficulty of collecting and organizing longitudinal data on cohorts of youth. The availability of data, rather than the questions of interest to educational policymakers, tends to drive the reporting of data on school dropouts.

It might be useful to examine some of the common questions asked about dropout data, and to consider which type of data and analysis would be most appropriate to answer those questions.

1.   "How many of this year's ninth graders will eventually graduate from high school?" Students enrolled in the ninth grade this year form a cohort. The best way to answer this question is to track the individual members of this cohort over time, until it is reasonable to assume that anyone who is going to complete high school has already done so. While there might be isolated incidents of individuals finishing high school at age 60, for instance, in most cases following the cohort to about age 30 or 35 is likely to capture virtually all such activity.

A similar logic applies to other grade cohorts (i.e., students entering first grade in 1990), and to birth cohorts (i.e., children born in 1982, or this year's twelve year olds). In all of these cases, a longitudinal approach, tracking the experiences of the cohort over time, is a plausible way to proceed.

2. "What is the 1989–90 dropout rate in Big City High School?" This question pertains to a specific period of time, the 1989–90 school year, and asks about the ratio of dropouts in that time period to total enrollment in that time period, without regard to the specific cohorts from which the dropouts are drawn. For this reason, a period analysis is appropriate.

3. "What is the effect of the school reform movement on the dropout rate?" The appropriate mode of analysis in this case depends on a theory of how the school reform movement might affect students. If the reforms which are put into place are expected to have immediate impacts across all levels of schooling, then comparing dropout rates for different periods would be an appropriate way to gauge the effects of the reform movement. If, on the other hand, the reforms are pitched so that their effects are cumulative, across many years of schooling, then it makes more sense to compare the experiences of cohorts of youngsters who have gone through school after the reforms were implemented with the experiences of cohorts which predate the reforms.

The current school reform movement, following on the heels of the National Commission on Excellence in Education's (1983) report *A Nation at Risk,* involves changes at both the elementary and secondary levels (McDill et al. 1986). Moreover, many of the proposed reforms are being phased in over time, and their effects will not be felt for some years to come. For these reasons, tracking the experiences of cohorts of youngsters who are just now beginning school may prove to be the best evidence of the effects of the school reform movement.

This position is at odds with recent Secretary of Education William Bennett and many others, who were determined to trumpet the effects of the reforms based on the graduation rates of students who finished school before the reforms were even implemented. Pallas et al. (1987) show how the graduation rates reported in the Secretary of Education's Wall Chart have been improperly used to support the prevailing rhetoric about the possible effects of raising standards for performance in schools. The graduation rates in the Wall Chart are being used as education indicators (although in this case it is not a very good use of the data).

Education Indicators

One way to think of dropout statistics is as social indicators. Kaagan and Smith (1985) argue that there are two conditions necessary for a statistic to be an education indicator. First, the statistic should measure something that relates to the health of the education system. Second, to be useful for social policy, an indicator must be placed in a particular context. Let us consider each condition in turn.

Education indicators are predicated on a model of the educational process. Inputs to the educational process are useful as education indicators only to the extent that they have a clear relationship to some specifiable outcomes of the process (Kaagan and Smith 1985). It would be difficult to measure the health of a system without some ideas about what constituted "good health," as opposed to poor performance.

This issue has clear implications for the use of dropout statistics as education indicators. There is no consensus on what makes a secondary education system healthy. The number of students certified as successful completers of high school may be independent of the knowledge, skills and attitudes possessed by such students. In recent years, sociologists of education such as Randall Collins and John Meyer, along with other critics (Berg 1970; Bowles and Gintis 1976), have questioned whether the rapid expansion of U.S. secondary school enrollments and degrees awarded represents an increase in the cognitive skills and abilities held by young people entering the labor force. There is some evidence that the rise in educational credentials may not be directly linked to the personal qualities of individuals certified as successful completers of secondary schooling. For example, the proportion of 17-year olds completing high school rose through the latter part of the 1960s and early 1970s at the same time that the average standardized test scores of such students were falling.

In this example, then, the health of the education system is somewhat ambiguous, depending on which criterion for health is chosen. If the purpose of schooling is to produce individuals with a certain set of cognitive and other skills, then merely counting the number of people who are processed by the school is not enough. Direct evidence of the skills and attitudes which students acquire in school would clearly be preferred. Gathering such data may not be feasible, though, and may have to be inferred from other available information.

It thus is a matter of judgment whether dropout rates or graduation rates can be considered education indicators. If there is reason to believe that the number of students successfully completing a given level of schooling is directly related to the health of the education system, then dropout/graduation figures may be useful indicators. If, on the other hand, counts of dropouts or graduates are merely proxies for other measures of school success, then these statistics may not contribute any unique information.

In spite of the well-known difficulties of counting dropouts from the vantage point of an individual LEA or school district, the problem is not overwhelming. Virtually all school districts have their own internally consistent ways of counting dropouts.[3] A dropout rate is often a single number to which people can easily attach a judgment about the condition of their schools. This is not so for indicators like test scores, where the metrics may be arbitrary and unintelligible to a lay audience.

Educational indicators are placed in context by comparing them to other things. Kaagan and Smith (1985) suggest several possible comparisons. First, an indicator can be compared to some absolute criterion of performance. If a society believes that all young people should graduate from high school, then that creates a standard against which observed proportions can be compared. If there is a universal expectation of high school graduation, and a given society has a graduation rate of 95 percent, that society is quite close to meeting its absolute standard for performance.

Second, an indicator can be contrasted with itself over time. In this way, the direction and magnitude of change in the indicator can imply the direction and magnitude of change in the health of the education system. If the dropout rate is going down over time, and a lower dropout rate implies a healthier education system, then we might claim that the education system is doing better than before.

Third, an indicator can be contrasted with itself over space. This allows for judgments about the relative health of various education systems, based on the relative values of the appropriate education indicators. This sort of logic underlies the Secretary of Education's publication "State Education Statistics," more commonly known as the "Wall Chart," as well as the recent initiative of the Council of Chief State School Officers to create a "report card" which will allow states to be compared on measures of their educational inputs, processes, and outputs. The "Wall Chart," for instance, presents data on high school completion rates for the 50 states and the District of Columbia, and invites direct comparisons among them by ranking them from best to worst.

The Comparability of Education Indicators

The comparability of education indicators over time and across geographic boundaries is jointly a function of the comparability of the measurement procedures and judgments about the comparability of the phenomena being measured. This claim is not new (see for instance, Zelditch 1971), but the specific application of these principles to the study of school dropouts probably warrants some explication.

I have already alluded to the first of these issues earlier. The differences across school districts and schools in the ways dropout and graduation rates are calculated, including the definition of a dropout, the definition of the base population at risk of dropping out, and the time period being measured, make school and district dropout rates problematic as education indicators. There is more agreement on ways to count graduates than there is on ways to count dropouts, because the definition of a high school graduate is more uniform across jurisdictions than is the definition of a dropout.

Those things that can be measured in a comparable way are of necessity fairly simple, and typically fail to represent the complexity of educational trajectories. This is troublesome when educational trajectories change over time, or differ from place to place. I have already mentioned that high school dropouts in California are eligible to enroll in public community colleges upon turning 18 years of age, regardless of whether they have completed high school. Is it therefore meaningful to compare the California high school graduation rate with that of other states, given that a substantial number of California nongraduates are enrolled in college? This presumably hinges on judgments about what it means to be enrolled in a community college without a high school diploma relative to what it means to be a high school graduate.

A similar question arises about the proliferation of alternative high school credentials. In the early 1960s, alternative equivalency credentials like the GED represented less than 3 percent of the total number of high school diplomas awarded annually in the United States, while in recent years alternative credentials have comprised approximately 15 percent of the total number of high school diplomas awarded annually. The comparability of national graduation figures over time depends on judgments about the comparability of alternative credentials and regular day school diplomas. As I have noted earlier, this issue is by no means resolved.

A third instance of comparability issues is the apparent rising age at high school completion. Young people are completing high school at older ages than was true for other post-World War II cohorts, due both to discontinuities in secondary schooling and to age-grade retardation, which has lengthened the course of high school for many youngsters from four years to five years or more. School completion measures which are sensitive to age and timing issues, such as the proportion of 18-year olds who have finished high school, or the proportion of ninth graders in a given year who graduate three school years later, will vary over time because of increasing discontinuities in schooling and age-grade retardation, even if the same proportion of youth eventually finish regular day high school programs. The comparability of such measures over time depends on judgments about the commonalities and differences between uninterrupted, "on-time" schooling and completing high school at older ages and over more school years. There are strong suggestions that these patterns differ in their antecedents and consequences. Featherman and Carter (1976), for instance, report that discontinuities in schooling are related to lower levels of socioeconomic success, and the burgeoning literature on the sociology of the life course, which addresses the timing of events, claims that "off-time" and/or nonnormative life course transitions have negative consequences (Neugarten et al. 1965; Neugarten and Datan 1973; Elder 1975; but see also, Marini et al. 1987).

National Statistics on School Dropout and Completion

Federal statistics on school dropout and completion have been a source of great confusion in recent years. Disparities in rates and proportions reported by different agencies have led many to question the validity of the data collected by the Census Bureau and the U.S. Department of Education (Cooke et al. 1985). Some of this confusion stems from vague terminology (i.e., transposing dropout rates with graduation rates), while some derives from interpretable differences in measurement strategies (Pallas and Verdugo 1986). In fact, until quite recently, the federal government did not routinely report data on school dropouts (Kominski 1987).

The next section reviews some of the federal data on school dropout and completion. I focus on three sources of information: the Bureau of the Census' Current Population Survey, the Department of Education's Common Core of Data, and the Department of Education's High School and Beyond study. I do not try to reconcile statistics generated by these sources of data explicitly, due to space limitations. Other attempts to do this imply that the federal data are not too discrepant when they are measuring similar phenomena (Pallas and Verdugo 1986; Kominski 1987).

Bureau of the Census Dropout and Completion Statistics

The Census Bureau's data on high school dropout and completion are derived mainly from the annual school enrollment supplement to the October Current Population Survey (CPS). The CPS data are based on a household informant's responses to a Census enumerator's questions regarding the school enrollment and attainment of various household members. The CPS surveys approximately 60,000 households each month, which represent about 150,000 household members. The survey provides national estimates for the civilian noninstitutionalized population of the United States.[4]

One relevant datum is the years of school completed by various household members. This measure is based on responses to two questions, "What is the highest grade he/she has ever attended?" and "Did he/she finish this grade?" If the person had ever attended a college, university or other professional school, the Census Bureau categorizes the person as a high school graduate. In addition, persons who are reported to have attended twelfth grade and finished it also are coded high school graduates.

There are at least two potential sources of slippage here. The first is that, in some areas, it is possible to enroll in postsecondary schools without having graduated from high school. Assuming that all postsecondary enrollees are high school graduates may inflate the estimated number of high school graduates relative to its true value.

Second, the responses of the recipients of alternative credentials may be ambiguous. If a student drops out of school in the tenth grade, but later obtains a passing score on the GED examination (or some other equivalency test), it is not clear what the "correct" response should be. With regard to actual school enrollment, such a student neither attended nor completed eleventh and twelfth grades. Many recipients of high school equivalency credentials, however, think of themselves as having completed high school, and would respond that they had both attended and completed twelfth grade.[5]

The Census data on educational attainment indicate that the vast majority of young people today are reported to complete high school. Table 1 shows the proportion of the civilian noninstitutionalized population reported to complete high school, by age, as of October 1985. While only about two-thirds of 18-year-olds are reported to have completed high school, more than 80 percent of 19-year-olds are reported to be high school graduates. Among 20-year-olds, almost 85 percent are reported as high school graduates. And, in 1985, over 87 percent of 31- to 34-year-olds were reported to be high school graduates.

These data have several implications. First, young people are apparently finishing high school at older ages than we are accustomed to recognizing. The CPS figures suggest that substantial numbers of youth are acquiring high

Table 1. Proportion Who Have
Completed High School, by Age,
October 1985

Age	Proportion who have completed high school
18	67.6%
19	81.5
20	84.7
21 to 25	85.4
26 to 30	85.8
31 to 34	87.4

Source: Pallas (1987)

school diplomas of one kind or another after the age of 18. Larger numbers of 18- and 19-year-olds are enrolled in, and completing, high school than was the case in the 1960s and 1970s.

Second, estimates of the magnitude of the high school dropout problem depend on whether one considers 18-year-olds or 30-year-olds. Among 18-year-olds, only about two-thirds are reported to have finished high school, while about six out of every seven 30-year-olds were reported to be high school graduates in 1985.

There are, of course, nonsampling errors in these estimated proportions, and one source of such error is the tendency to exaggerate one's educational accomplishments and those of one's family. It is conceivable that this pressure increases with age, so that there is a greater social stigma attached to not being a high school graduate if one is 30 years old than if one is 19 years old. Still, there is no recent evidence on the extent of overreporting of high school completion, and it is unlikely that this reporting error could adequately account for the pattern of results I have described.

The Census Bureau recently has begun to report a dropout rate based on responses to the October Current Population Survey. The calculation involves the responses to four questions: the highest grade attended, whether that grade was completed, current enrollment status, and enrollment status as of one year ago. A dropout is defined as anyone who is not enrolled as of the October survey date, who has not completed high school, and who was enrolled the previous October.

Kominski (1987) has calculated high school dropout rates for the 1972–73 and 1982–83 school years, based on the October CPS. The rate is formed by dividing the estimated number of dropouts in a given year by an estimate of the total number of persons enrolled in grades 10, 11 and 12 the preceding year. The denominator of this rate is estimated as the number of current enrollees in grades 11 and 12, plus all high school graduates in the past year, plus all estimated dropouts in the past year.

Kominski (1987) shows that the estimated annual national high school dropout rate for persons aged 14 to 24 was 6.3 percent in 1973, and 5.2 percent in 1983, implying a decline in the dropout rate over that ten-year period. This national high school dropout rate is a weighted average of national grade-specific dropout rates for grades 10, 11 and 12. The estimated national grade-specific dropout rates are 3.7 percent for grade 10, 4.5 percent for grade 11, and 7.5 percent for grade 12. These grade-specific rates imply that approximately 15 percent of tenth graders will drop out of school over a three-year period. Curiously, the twelfth grade dropout rate is higher than the eleventh grade rate, and more than double the tenth grade rate, implying that most high school students who drop out of school do so after completing the eleventh grade.

The dropout rates Kominski (1987) reports are based on persons who were reported to have completed at least nine years of school. Thus, the estimated three-year combined rate of 15 percent excludes persons who dropped out prior to completing ninth grade—that is, who dropped out during ninth grade or before. The estimated percentage of persons dropping out of school prior to completing high school is therefore somewhat higher than 15 percent, but how much higher is difficult to say. If negotiating the transition from middle or junior high school is, as many believe, a critical branching point then substantial numbers of youngsters may never even make it to high school, and the estimated cumulative dropout rate would be sharply attenuated. On the other hand, the CPS data suggest that most dropping out of high school occurs during the latter high school years, implying that omitting persons who have not completed ninth grade results in only a modest underestimate of the cumulative dropout rate.

In spite of this ambiguity, Kominski's analysis is a masterful attempt to get as much mileage out of the October CPS school enrollment supplement as possible. The procedures he employs allow for annual estimates of high school dropout rates that are replicable, internally consistent, and comparable over time. As with virtually all of the CPS school enrollment and attainment data, though, there are nagging uncertainties regarding the validity of the household informants' reports. Only studies assessing the concordance of household reports and school records are likely to quell these doubts completely—or exacerbate them.

A more serious problem is the issue of undercount. The CPS is a sample of the Census-enumerable population. But there is evidence that several groups at high risk of dropping out of school are undercounted by the Census. These include youth aged 14–20, blacks and Hispanics, and the very poor (Clogg et al. 1988). Taking the CPS data on school enrollments at face value leads to some wildly implausible results. For instance, the CPS data consistently show higher school enrollment rates for black 16- to 17-year olds than for whites of the same age (Clogg et al. 1988). A possible explanation for this is that the CPS undercounts out-of-school black youth. This kind of differential undercount almost certainly biases CPS estimates of black-white differences in dropout rates, and may also bias estimates of the national dropout rate to some unknown degree. The larger the undercount of population subgroups at high risk of dropping out, the more severe the bias in the estimated dropout rate.

Common Core of Data (CCD)

The Common Core of Data (CCD) program is a coordinated effort administered by the Center for Education Statistics, U.S. Department of Education, to acquire and maintain data on states and local public school districts. The CCD program includes a universe survey of state education agencies and education agencies of the District of Columbia and outlying areas. The survey collects data on enrollments by grade and numbers of high school graduates in regular day programs each year for each of the state education agencies. The CCD collects data only on public schools, and does not provide separate information on GED or other non-regular day school credentials.

The U.S. Department of Education has reported both national and state-level statistics derived from the CCD data collections. Typically the calculation involves the ratio of the number of high school graduates in a given year to the number of students enrolled in ninth grade three school years earlier. This ratio is frequently described as a "graduation rate," and the difference between the ratio and unity has been called a "dropout rate." The rate is adjusted for the fact that there are ungraded and special education students who do not appear in the denominator, yet may appear in the numerator. There are, though, no means available for adjusting the state-level data for interstate migration, which could affect either the numerator or the denominator of the ratio. A state with high outmigration of high school-aged children over the period in question would have students counted in the denominator of the ratio who do not appear in the numerator, even if they complete high school. Thus, net outmigration would probably attenuate the estimated graduation rate. Conversely, net inmigration leads to students being counted in the numerator of the graduation rate but not the denominator, thereby inflating the estimated graduation rate.

The most serious problem with calling this ratio a graduation rate is the assumption that ninth graders who will eventually graduate do so "on time," in four years of high school. As we have seen, however, some students progress continuously toward graduation more slowly, by failing to accumulate enough credits to graduate, or by failing specific required courses, or by not achieving a passing score on a required state competency test. Other students do drop out of school, but then return to earn a degree at a later time. Since the CCD data collections count only regular day school graduates, many of these students returning to GED or other adult equivalency programs are never counted as graduates in the ratio based on CCD statistics. At best, then, we can think of the ratio derived from the CCD data as an "on-time graduation rate" (Pallas and Verdugo 1986), although it is a fuzzy approximation even of this.

High School and Beyond

Perhaps the best-known contemporary dataset addressing dropout issues is the High School and Beyond (HSB) study. The HSB study was begun in 1980 by the National Center for Education Statistics in the U.S. Department of Education. The study design called for a two-stage, stratified probability sample with schools as the first stage units and students within schools as the second stage units. Up to 36 seniors and 36 sophomores were randomly selected from each school, defining a 1980 Sophomore Cohort and a 1980 Senior Cohort. As the Senior Cohort is comprised of students enrolled as high school seniors in the spring of their senior year, it is of little use for the study of dropouts. The Sophomore Cohort, however, has considerable potential for this purpose.

The 1980 Sophomore Cohort is a representative sample of U.S. students enrolled in the tenth grade in the spring of 1980. The population of students who were not enrolled at that time are excluded from the study by design. Thus, students who had already dropped out and not returned to school by the spring of tenth grade are not part of the HSB study.[6]

The First Follow-Up of the 1980 Sophomore Cohort was conducted from February to June in 1982. The follow-up involved administering surveys and tests similar to those used in the Base Year. In each school, a coordinator identified four groups of students: dropouts, transfers from Base Year schools, early graduates, and students who were still enrolled in their Base Year schools. The eligibility of students for follow-up was determined by their status on the scheduled survey day. If a student had dropped out of school but then returned to full-time school enrollment by the time of the scheduled follow-up survey, that student was eligible for the still-in-school sample. In contrast, the dropout sample consisted of students who the school coordinators indicated were not enrolled in the school on the survey day.

The First Follow-Up dropout questionnaire provides evidence of the ambiguity involved in comparing student reports and administrative records. One of the questions on the dropout questionnaire was, "When did you leave the last high school that you attended?" Among the responding dropouts, 6.5 percent reported that they had left school in 1979. But all of these students were reported by the school as enrolled on the Base Year survey day (ranging from February to June, 1980). In fact, many of these dropouts were present in school to fill out a Base Year questionnaire.

The First Follow-Up dropout questionnaire also asked students, "Do you plan to go back to school eventually to get a diploma or to take a high school equivalency test or GED?" Very few students responded "No" unconditionally. In fact, approxiamtely 14 percent of the students responding to the dropout questionnaire claimed to have already received a GED or equivalent by the time of the First Follow-Up.

The HSB project includes several other sources of data which bear upon dropout-graduate issues. In the fall of 1982, the study obtained high school transcripts from the HSB schools for a large fraction of the original sophomore Base Year cohort. These transcripts indicated whether students were enrolled continuously during their high school years, or whether they had been absent for a semester. The transcripts also provided evidence on whether the student had graduated by 1982.

In addition, the HSB project conducted in 1984 a Second Follow-Up of a subsample of the original Base Year Sophomore Cohort. The Second Follow-Up questionnaire asked respondents, "Did you complete high school?" Approximately 85 percent answered "yes," while an additional 4 percent responded "No, but since earned a high school diploma or equivalency certificate by completing classes in an adult or night school program." About 2 percent indicated that they were still in an adult or high school program working toward a high school diploma or equivalency certificate.

The Second Follow-Up questionnaire, then, suggests that many of the students initially identified as dropouts had returned to school by the spring of 1984, and that most of these had in fact acquired a high school diploma or equivalency certificate. Unfortunately, the questionnaire did not distinguish between obtaining a traditional high school diploma and obtaining a GED or other equivalency certificate.

A very similar pattern is evident from the Third Follow-Up of the Base Year Sophomore Cohort, which was fielded in the spring of 1986. At that time, 82.5 percent of the Base Year sophomores reported that they had graduated with their class or earlier. An additional 2.2 percent indicated they left high school but returned to earn a regular diploma, while 5.6 percent reported having left high school but subsequently earning an equivalent certificate (such as a GED). Less than one percent claimed to be working toward a regular high school diploma at the time of the Follow-Up, and about two percent more of the cohort claimed to be working toward an equivalent high school diploma (such as a GED) at that time. Only about 7 percent of the sample reported that they did not graduate or earn an equivalent certificate, and were not working toward one at the time of the Follow-Up.

The three follow-ups of the HSB 1980 Sophomore Cohort enable us to track the experiences of this group over time. At the time of the First Follow-Up in 1982, when the modal pattern for these students was to be enrolled late in the senior year of high school, 13.6 percent of the sampled students were not enrolled in school and were not high school graduates. By the Second Follow-Up in 1984, about 11 percent reported that they had not received a high school diploma or equivalent. By 1986, 9.7 percent of the original 1980 Sophomore Cohort reported that they had not graduated from high school or earned an equivalent certificate. Over time, then, the proportion of persons in this cohort who reported completing high school has risen, with almost one-third of the students initially identified as dropouts completing high school within four years of the "on-time" educational timetable.

Since the High School and Beyond study pertains to but a single cohort of high school students at risk of dropping out of school, the study is of limited use for developing school dropout and completion indicators for temporal comparisons.[7] This study does hold great potential, though, for studying the causes and consequences of dropping out of school, although to date, research has focused on the former (Pallas 1986; Ekstrom et al. 1986; Wehlage and Rutter 1986). I turn next to some of the measurement issues in studying the causes and consequences of school dropout and completion.

STUDYING THE CAUSES AND CONSEQUENCES OF DROPPING OUT OF SCHOOL

The literature is filled with studies of the causes and consequences of dropping out of high school. These studies stem from several different research traditions. Two of the most important perspectives informing research on school dropouts are the life course perspective and the status attainment perspective.

The Life Course Perspective

Life course analysis focuses on the timing and sequencing of events. Clusters of events comprise stages in the life course. Adulthood, for instance, is characterized by the taking on of adult roles, which represent independence from the family of origin. One of the key elements in the transition to adulthood is the completion of full-time schooling, which marks a transition from the role of student to the role of non-student. Other events in the transition to adulthood include moving out of the house, establishing financial independence by getting a regular job, and forming a family by getting married and/or having children.

There is both individual and group heterogeneity in the social timetables which govern life course transitions, and much of life course research is devoted to understanding the causes and consequences of this heterogeneity (Hogan 1978; 1981; Marini 1985; Modell et al. 1976). This genre of research is highly dependent on information about the timing and sequencing of events in the life course. To study school dropouts from a life course perspective thus requires detailed data on the timing of dropping out of school, as well as the timing of other events in the life course—especially those comprising the transition to adulthood.

The best source of such data is respondents themselves, but even their memories are apt to be unreliable if the events in question occurred in the distant past. One strategy to cope with this is to survey respondents repeatedly at fairly short fixed intervals during the period in which these events are likely to occur. This has been the approach which has directed the High School and Beyond study. High School and Beyond has conducted three follow-ups of the 1980 sophomore and senior cohorts, at two-year intervals. In each follow-up, the respondents report mainly on activities since the most recent follow-up. Thus, in the third follow-up conducted in the spring of 1986, respondents reported on their experiences between February 1984 and spring 1986.

The High School and Beyond questionnaires, while complex, provide detailed information on the timing of various events. Respondents are asked to report on the month and year of start and completion of up to five jobs during the two year period, and the beginning and end points of up to five school enrollments.[8] Respondents also are asked about the timing of marriage, marital dissolution, and parenting. By comparing the reported dates, it is possible to construct a sequence of events.

The Status Attainment Perspective

The status attainment perspective, while also organized around the socioeconomic life cycle (Duncan 1967; Duncan et al. 1972), is largely concerned with achieved educational, occupational, and economic statuses. Status attainment research takes as problematic the relationship between social origins and adult achievements, and attempts to specify the causal mechanisms by which socioeconomic origins are transformed into achieved statuses. With few exceptions (most notably Featherman and Carter 1976), status attainment research traditionally has construed educational attainment as a static characteristic of individuals, rather than a phenomenon that can vary over time. The convention has been to measure educational attainment in terms of the number of years of schooling completed, without regard to the timing or sequencing of school enrollments.

The distinction between life course research and status attainment research has become increasingly blurred. Sociologists of the life course are exploring the socioeconomic consequences of variations in the timing and sequencing of life course transitions (Marini et al. 1987). At the same time, status attainment researchers have taken stock of career contingencies and discontinuities in the socioeconomic life cycle, and their consequences for the customary education, income, and occupation outcomes (Duncan et al. 1972; Featherman and Carter 1976). While it is unwise to generalize about the socioeconomic consequences of variations in the timing and sequencing of role transitions, specific transitions which have been omitted from traditional status attainment models do have demonstrable effects (Marini et al. 1987).

At this point, it is difficult to argue against the collection of event-history data on school enrollments and other events. Tuma and Hannan (1984) compare event-history analyses with other data collection and analysis strategies, and show that event-history data provide the most flexible means for estimating models with differing assumptions about change processes. While there are relatively few studies to date which use event-history methods to analyze school enrollment patterns and other events, we can expect to see them with increasing frequency as the methods become more diffused throughout the discipline.

CONCLUSIONS

A high rate of high school dropouts threatens the image of equality of educational opportunity associated with schooling in the United States. Large urban school districts report that fewer than one-half of their public school students are graduating from high school. Virtually all such districts have dropout prevention programs, even if such programs represent a repackaging of the effective schools movement's recipe for success: strong administrative leadership, high expectations, a safe, orderly climate, and the like. These programs cost money, and there is a great deal of money at stake in the dropout game. New York City, for instance, has been spending an average of thirty-eight million dollars a year on dropout prevention programs in recent years.

Public policy decisions are frequently clothed in the logic of cost-benefit analysis, in which the costs of various programmatic alternatives are compared to their economic benefits. In order for such decisions to be rational and efficient, there must be sound information on the likely costs and benefits of various policy options. Program evaluation is the tool social scientists use to assess these costs and benefits. The evaluation process involves setting goals for a program, converting those goals into measurable program objectives, and assessing the extent to which the program is meeting its objectives. The effectiveness of the program can then be transformed into dollar terms, and compared to the program costs.

For this process to function smoothly, a program must have goals; sometimes these are set by the evaluator, but more frequently they are determined by the policymaker. With respect to the high school dropout problem, it is not clear what the appropriate goal should be. There are many possible goals: that all (or some fixed percentage of) young people graduate from high school by age 18; that all youth graduate from high school by some later age, perhaps age 30; that students earn only regular day school diplomas; that students have continuous enrollment histories; that all students master certain basic literacy and numeracy skills, regardless of whether or not they complete high school.

It is hard to place values on these various goals. We may not know enough about the social, economic, and educational correlates of these goals to judge their relative merits. Lacking a firm knowledge base precludes a social science basis for distinguishing among alternative goals for the high school dropout phenomenon. More research on the consequences of various educational trajectories is needed to inform judgments about the relative desirability of different school enrollment and completion patterns.

The lack of a consensus on what the goals regarding school completion and dropout are greatly complicates the issue of measuring the high school dropout phenomenon. Such goals should drive the measurement strategies and data collection methods used for generating information on school dropouts. Multiple goals imply multiple measures of school dropout and completion activity. The fact that there are a variety of dropout and completion measures in use reflects the diversity of goals, and ought not be taken as a wholesale indictment of educational statistics. What is most important is that the goals and measures be discussed openly, so that their similarities and differences can be taken account of in appropriate ways.

ACKNOWLEDGMENTS

I am grateful to Lawrence Cremin, Phil Kaufman, and the editors for their helpful comments on an earlier draft of this manuscript.

NOTES

1. Not all students enroll in secondary school; some drop out of school in elementary or junior high school. The logic of what follows holds for these early dropouts as well.

2. This varies from state to state. Some states require that a student be out of school to obtain a GED certificate or other alternative credential. Florida's early exit GED program, however, allows students to take the GED test battery and obtain a GED credential while still enrolled in regular day schools.

3. Some have their own internally inconsistent ways, too.

4. The CPS is not designed to produce state-level estimates of educational enrollments or attainments, but can be used to derive regional estimates.

5. Census enumerators are instructed to tell GED recipients to respond "H4," or high school graduate, if the respondent asks what the appropriate response should be for an equivalency degree, but the enumerators do not volunteer this information.

6. These early dropouts are frequently thought of as the "hardcore" dropouts: those worst off academically and socially, and most likely to end up in trouble with the law. If it is true that early dropouts differ appreciably from later dropouts, then the design of the HSB study may produce biased estimates of the relationship of dropout status with other variables.

7. High School and Beyond was, however, designed to parallel the National Center for Education Statistics' National Longitudinal Study of the High School Class of 1972 (NLS-72), which surveyed students late in the senior year of high school. While this precludes cohort comparisons of dropout data, HSB and NLS-72 have been used to test hypotheses about cohort differences in postsecondary access (Alexander et al. 1987).

In addition, the National Center for Education Statistics fielded a new national longitudinal study in 1988 called NELS:88. The design of this study calls for surveying a national sample of eighth graders in the spring of 1988, and following this cohort at two-year intervals. The study is designed to facilitate comparisons with the HSB cohorts. The NELS:88 design is generally regarded to be superior to HSB for studying dropouts, because far fewer students are presumed to have dropped out by the eighth grade than by the tenth grade. Thus, the study should include a greater number of and more representative sample of the population of high school dropouts.

8.   The precise number varies according to the particular questionnaire.

REFERENCES

Alexander, K. L., A. M. Pallas, and S. Holupka. 1987. "Consistency and Change in Educational Stratification: Recent Trends Regarding Social Background and College Access." Pp. 161–185 edited by Robinson, Robert V. *Research in Social Stratification and Mobility*, Vol. 6. Greenwich, CT: JAI Press.

Barber, L. 1984. *Dropouts, Transfers, Withdrawn and Removed Students*. Bloomington, IN: Phi Delta Kappa Center for Evaluation, Development, and Research.

Beltzer, S. 1985. Persistence of GED and Traditional Students at a Public Community College: A Test of a Conceptual Model. *GED Testing Service Research Brief No. 7*. Washington, DC: American Council on Education.

Berg, I. 1970. *Education and Jobs: The Great Training Robbery*. Boston: Beacon Press.

Bowles, S. and H. Gintis. 1976. *Schooling in Capitalist America*. New York: Basic Books.

California Legislature Assembly Office of Research. 1985. *Dropping Out, Losing Out: The High Cost for California*. Sacramento, CA: Author.

Clogg, C. C., M. P. Massagli, and S. R. Eliason. 1988. "Population Undercount and Social Science Research." Unpublished manuscript, Pennsylvania State University.

Cooke, C., A. Ginsburg, and M. S. Smith. 1985. "The Sorry State of Education Statistics." *Basic Education* 29:3–8.

Dougherty, K. 1987. "The Effects of Community Colleges: Aid or Hindrance to Socioeconomic Attainment?" *Sociology of Education* 60:86–103.

Duncan, O. D. 1967. "Discrimination against Negroes." *Annals of the American Academy of Political and Social Science* 371:85–103.

Duncan, O. D., D. L. Featherman, and B. Duncan. 1972. *Socioeconomic Background and Achievement*. New York: Seminar Press.

Ekstrom, R. B., M. E. Goertz, J. M. Pollack, and D. A. Rock. 1986. "Who Drops Out of High School and Why? Findings from a National Study." *Teachers College Record* 87:356–373.

Elder, G. H., Jr. 1975. "Age Differentiation and the Life Course." Pp. 165–190 edited by Inkeles, Alex, James Coleman, and Neil Smelser. *Annual Review of Sociology* Vol. 1. Palo Alto, CA: Annual Reviews, Inc.

Elder, G. H., Jr. 1985. "Perspectives on the Life Course." Pp. 23–49 edited by Elder, Glen H., Jr. *Life Course Dynamics*. Ithaca, NY: Cornell University Press.

Featherman, D. L., and T. M. Carter. 1976. "Discontinuities in Schooling and the Socioeconomic Life Cycle." Pp. 133–160 edited by Sewell, William H., Robert M. Hauser, and David L. Featherman. *Schooling and Achievement in American Society*. New York: Academic Press.

Finn, C. E., Jr. 1987. "The High School Dropout Puzzle." *The Public Interest*. Summer:3–22.

General Educational Development Testing Service. 1986. *The 1985 GED Statistical Report*. Washington, DC: American Council on Education.

Hammack, F. M. 1986. "Large School Systems' Dropout Reports: An Analysis of Definitions, Procedures, and Findings." *Teachers College Record* 87:324–341.

Hogan, D. P. 1978. "The Variable Order of Events in the Life Course." *American Sociological Review* 43:573–586.

Hogan, D. P. 1981. *Transitions and Social Change: The Early Lives of American Men.* New York: Academic Press.

Kaagan, S., and M. S. Smith. 1985. "Indicators of Education Quality." *Educational Leadership* 43(October):21–25.

Karabel, J. 1972. "Community Colleges and Social Stratification." *Harvard Educational Review* 42:521–562.

Kominski, R. 1987. "School Enrollment—Social and Economic Characteristics of Students: October 1983." *U.S. Department of Commerce, Bureau of the Census, Current Population Reports, Series P-20, No. 413.* Washington, DC: U.S. Government Printing Office.

Ladner, R. A. 1986. Educational and Occupational Activities of GED and Conventional High School Graduates in Florida. *GED Testing Service Research Brief No. 8.* Washington, DC: American Council on Education.

Marini, M. M. 1985. "Determinants of the Timing of Adult Role Entry." *Social Science Research* 14:309–350.

Marini, M. M., W. Chan, and J. Raymond. 1987. "Consequences of the Process of Transition to Adulthood for Adult Economic Well-Being." Pp. 87–127 edited by Corwin, Ronald G. *Research in the Sociology of Education and Socialization,* Vol. 7. Greenwich, CT: JAI Press.

McDill, E. L., G. Natriello, and A. M. Pallas. 1986. "A Population at Risk: Potential Consequences of Tougher School Standards for Student Dropouts." *American Journal of Education* 94:135–181.

Modell, J.; F. F. Furstenburg, Jr., and T. Hershberg. 1976. "Social Charge and Transitions to Adulthood in Historical Perspective." *Journal of Family History* 1:7–32.

Morrow, G. 1986. "Standardizing Practice in the Analysis of School Dropouts." *Teachers College Record* 87:342–355.

National Commision on Excellence in Education. 1983. *A Nation At Risk.* Washington, DC: U.S. Government Printing Office.

Neugarten, B. L., and N. L. Datan. 1973. "Sociological Perspectives on the Life Cycle." Pp. 55–69 edited by Baltes, Paul B., and K. W. Schaie. *Life-Span Developmental Psychology: Personality and Socialization.* New York: Academic Press.

Neugarten, B. L., J. W. Moore, and J. C. Lowe. 1965. "Age Norms, Age Constraints, and Adult Socialization." *American Journal of Sociology* 70:710–717.

New York City Board of Education. 1987. *Cohort Dropout Study: The Class of 1986.* New York: Author.

Pallas, A. M. 1986. *The Determinants of High School Dropout.* Center for the Social Organization of Schools Report No. 364. Baltimore, MD: Johns Hopkins University.

Pallas, A. M. 1987. "School Dropouts in the United States." Pp. 158–174 edited by Stern, Joyce D., and Mary Frase Williams. *The Condition of Education, 1986 Edition.* Washington, DC: U.S. Government Printing Office.

Pallas, A. M., G. Natriello, and E. L. McDill. 1987. "The High Cost of High Standards: School Reform and Dropouts." *Urban Education* 22:103–114.

Pallas, A. M., and R. R. Verdugo 1986. "Measuring the High School Dropout Problem." Paper presented at the annual meeting of the American Educational Research Association, San Francisco, CA: April.

Patience, W. M., and D. R. Whitney. 1982. *What Do the GED Tests Measure?* Washington, DC: American Council on Education.

Pincus, F. L. 1980. "The False Promises of Community Colleges: Class Conflict and Vocational Education." *Harvard Educational Review* 50:332–361.

Quinn, L. M., and M. Haberman. 1986. "Are GED Certificate Holders Ready for Postsecondary Education?" *Metropolitan Education* 2:72–82.

Rosenbaum, J. E. 1976. *Making Inequality*. New York: Wiley.

Rubinson, R. 1986. "Class Formation, Politics, and Institutions: Schooling in the United States." *American Journal of Sociology* 92:519–548.

Rumberger, R. W. 1987. "High School Dropouts: A Review of Issues and Evidence." *Review of Educational Research* 57:101–121.

Shryock, H. S., J. S. Siegel, and Associates. 1976. *The Methods and Materials of Demography*. New York: Academic Press.

Spilerman, S. 1977. "Careers, Labor Market Structure, and Socioeconomic Achievement." *American Journal of Sociology* 83:551–593.

Tuma, N. B., and M. T. Hannan. 1984. *Social Dynamics: Models and Methods*. New York: Academic Press.

Wagenaar, T. C. 1987. "What Do We Know about Dropping Out of High School?" Pp. 161–190 edited by Corwin, Ronald G. *Research in the Sociology of Education and Socialization*, Volume 7. Greenwich, CT: JAI Press.

Wehlage, G. G., and R. A. Rutter. 1986. "Dropping Out: How Much Do Schools Contribute to the Problem?" *Teachers College Record* 87:374–392.

Wilson, R. C., P. D. Davis, and J. C. Davis, Sr. 1981. The Success of High School Diploma and GED Equivalency Students in Vocational Programs at Lake City Community College, Florida. *GED Testing Service Research Brief No. 4*. Washington, DC: American Council on Education.

Wolf, J. C. 1980. Predictive Validity of the GED Tests for Two-Year College Study: South Plains College, Texas. *GED Testing Service Research Brief No. 1*. Washington, DC: American Council on Education.

Zelditch, M., Jr. 1971. "Intelligible Comparisons." Pp. 267–307 edited by Vallier, Ivan. *Comparative Methods in Sociology: Essays on Trends and Applications*. Berkeley, CA: University of California Press.

THE MEANING OF EDUCATIONAL ATTAINMENT

Charles E. Bidwell

Educational attainment is a major subject of sociological research. It gained its prime position in the early 1950s. Then, strongly influenced by the liberal-democratic thrust toward social equity, sociologists framed the study of social stratification and mobility as the study of status attainment. From the status-attainment standpoint, individuals' life chances are defined as a function of their own individual attributes and efforts, so that social mobility is to be explained as a consequence of what individuals do to gain attributes, change them, and use them in a quest for economic and social advancement. More specifically, it is occupational advancement that is primarily to be explained because in economically developed societies, wealth, prestige, and power depend on occupation.

Among the findings of status attainment research, one of the most con-

Research in the Sociology of Education and Socialization,
Volume 8, pages 117–138.
Copyright © 1989 by JAI Press Inc.
All rights of reproduction in any form reserved.
ISBN: 0-89232-929-7

sistent and robust is the power of educational attainment to predict how well
people fare in the labor market—the prestige of the jobs that they hold and
their income from work. Despite exhaustive efforts to take into account effects of social origins, personal traits, and social experience, educational
attainment remains the one most powerful predictor of job prestige and income (Jencks 1979:230).

These relationships are strong, and they tend to increase over a lifetime
(Blau and Duncan 1967; Featherman and Hauser 1978; Kelley 1973; Mincer
1974). They obtain irrespective of ethnicity and gender (Blau and Duncan
1967; Featherman and Hauser 1978; Smith and Welch 1986), and they appear
to be as true of Third World and socialist societies as they are of the capitalist
West (Benavot 1985; Treiman and Terrell 1975; Heyneman and Loxley 1983;
Slomczynski, Miller, and Kohn 1981).

In principle, there are many kinds of educational attainment—for example,
increase of knowledge, change of values or other moral commitments, gains
in reasoning powers, and diplomas earned. Nevertheless, in status attainment
research, the dominant measure of educational attainment is the number of
years of education that a respondent has completed. It is not clear which of the
varieties of educational attainment in fact is indexed by years of completed
schooling, nor, in consequence, what mechanisms mediate the relationship
between years of schooling and gains of occupational prestige or income.

Largely in response to the status-attainment findings, sociologists of education have attempted to specify the constituent mechanisms of educational
attainment itself. (For a summary of this literature, see Bidwell and Friedkin
1988.) The results, obtained for the most part from the American public high
school, have generated a protracted debate over the significance and relative
magnitude of educational attainment outcomes attributable to instruction and
other school-specific variables, student body composition, student subcultures, and students' social origins and related out-of-school experiences.

Whether the dependent variable is educational persistence, educational aspiration, or some cognitive or normative outcome, the prime predictors are
students' personal traits, rather than aspects of the school. Students' status
origins are especially important predictors, but by the time of high school
enrollment these effects are mediated in large part by academic ability and
performance, academic and occupational goals, interpersonal supports (originating both in and out of school), and (modestly) academic versus non-
academic curricular track placement. (See Alexander, Eckland, and Griffin
1975; Alexander and Cook 1982; Alexander and Eckland 1975; Alexander
and McDill 1976; Alexander, Cook, and McDill 1978; Alwin 1976; Bain and
Anderson 1974; Hauser 1971; Hauser and Featherman 1976; Hauser, Sewell,
and Alwin 1976; Jencks, Crouse, and Mueser 1983; Rehberg and Rosenthal
1978; Sewell and Hauser 1976; Spenner and Featherman 1978.)

In sum, although in contemporary societies years of completed education is an important, independent predictor of individuals' occupational life chances, there is little about the experience of school, as it has been measured for the U.S. case, that can be specified unequivocally as a mechanism that fosters either persistence in school or the cumulative acquisition of various individual capacities (cognitive or normative) that might reasonably be thought to affect status attainment.

Perhaps the measures of schooling have been insensitive to key instructional variables or other means of socialization, but the findings strongly imply that American high schools serve largely as gatekeepers (Sorokin 1927:Part 2), screening students according to motivation and cognitive capacity in a hierarchically-ordered series of transitions. Wherever these transitions occur in the educational system, students either leave school or continue in a curriculum progressively more specialized in its content and more specific in its bearing on occupational attainment.

One might expect that in our comparatively universalistic, professionalized society, schools screen students without regard to their status origins. Nevertheless, the U.S. studies of educational attainment (as do those in the smaller literature on other Western educational systems) consistently obtain significant coefficients from regressions of attainment on social origins (Bidwell and Friedkin 1988). These coefficients indicate that the social strata, on average, differ significantly with respect to the educational life chances of youth (e.g., Sewell and Hauser 1946:13).

More and more in present-day societies, jobs are allocated in labor markets dominated by bureaucratic organizations that use relatively universalistic standards to hire and later to evaluate and promote employees. In these societies, formal educational programs (in schools primarily, but also in the workplace) are designed to train people to perform on the job and to screen them according to how well they have responded to the training.

Trained capacity—the cognitive skills, motives, and habits of work acquired in these programs—should have its own distinctive effects on occupational life chances, independently of social origins. These effects should occur in initial labor market allocation and in later gains of occupational income and prestige. Consequently, schooling should have a substantive effect on occupational attainment, independently of any contribution by the school to the validation of ascriptive social standing. Even in segmented labor markets, this effect should be observed in the primary, bureaucratized segment.

In short, the powerful, pervasive effects of years of completed education on occupational life chances undoubtedly indicate independent, palpable effects of students' experiences of schooling (and, thus, of the social and curricular organization of schools) on their cognitive and normative capacities. The screening criteria used in schools should be sensitive to the acquisition of trained capacity, as well as to other occupation-related personal traits. Moreover, this screening should show some degree of independence of students' social origins, reflecting the institutional autonomy of the school curriculum and of teachers' professional standards (Sorokin 1927:187–193).

However, because there is no compelling evidence of such effects, what educational attainment means as a variable in the occupational attainment process is unclear. It may indeed denote the substance of trained capacity— the outcome of the instruction and screening that schools conduct. It may also denote the labor market value of an amount of education in itself, reflecting the use of years of completed education by employers as a criterion when they screen job candidates. Possibly the meaning of educational attainment is to be sought more in such institutional connections between education and labor force participation than in substantive linkages provided by what is learned in school. Of course, the symbolic value of educational attainment in labor market allocation may derive in good measure from what schools teach and screen for.

These issues have been posed in the current debate between proponents of educational attainment as indicating the formation of human capital (i.e., instruction and screening) and those who argue that it is a social signal sent by job seekers to employers. I shall consider the meaning of educational attainment by examining the human capital-screening debate. Its terms imply that despite the apparent universality of the educational attainment-occupational attainment relationship, the meaning of this relationship depends upon societal context. Therefore, I shall discuss four principal elements of the process whereby educational attainment may affect occupational attainment: the societal context in which the relationship occurs, the organization of the process into a structure of status-allocation thresholds, the action of educational attainment as a labor market signal, and the substance of what is learned and screened for in school.

THE SOCIAL ORGANIZATION OF EDUCATIONAL ATTAINMENT: SOCIAL CONTEXT

Levine and White (1986) have argued that human identity is by no means universally anchored in achievement. Indeed, they have suggested that in societies less dominated by rationalization and large scale formal organization than are the economically-developed societies (where these social forms engender powerful pressures toward individualism in thought and conduct), identity may be much more firmly grounded in interpersonal bonds and collective loyalties than in individual accomplishment.

Consequently, in traditional societies, such as those with agrarian econo-mies, the school curriculum may place primary stress on cooperative, collec-tivity-oriented modes of conduct and on inculcating group loyalty. Of special interest is Levine and White's postulate that in these societies, cognition is identified with morality rather than with instrumental performance because intelligence and competence are signified by normatively compliant conduct. In achievement-oriented societies, they argue, primary curricular stress is likely to be laid on interpersonal competition, directed toward the demonstra-tion of an individual intelligence that is separable from normative patterns of conduct.

Therefore, in the more traditional society, education may serve primarily to shape conduct into patterns appropriate to ascribed social destinations—for example membership in a status group or local community. In the more individuated society, it may work primarily by endowing persons with skills, information, and certificates that have labor market currency.

In a rather minimal sense, educational attainment means the same thing in both instances. It is an early step in a socially-patterned life history. In three other more significant ways, the meanings are quite different. First, the two types of society differ in the specific content of the education attained. Sec-ond, they differ in the problematics of the link between educational attainment and subsequent life progress—that is, the degree to which the linkage is ascriptive and therefore determinate or achievement-based and therefore prob-abilistic. Third, they differ in the degree to which educational attainment serves cohort by cohort to differentiate (and, thus, to select) individuals on the basis of cognitive or motivational attributes—for example, as Levine and White would have it, on the basis of normatively or instrumentally defined intelligence.

Applied to the relationship between educational and occupational attain-ment, this argument has an honorable sociological lineage. Recall Weber's (1947:242–243,426; Gerth and Mills 1946:426–434) distinction between tra-ditional education ("education for the conduct of a life") and vocational education (formal preparation for the conduct of a technically specialized occupation). With the advance of bureaucracy, he argued, vocational educa-tion would inevitably overtake traditional education as the dominant educa-tional form.

Weber derived this prediction from propositions about markets and status allocation and about formal training and bureaucracy. He assumed that the rise of technically specialized occupations would create an ever more intense demand for correspondingly specialized curricula in the secondary schools and universities, as the basis of social standing shifted from status groups to labor markets and to the universalistic job allocation that bureaucracy entails.

Ascriptive biases in job allocation would be reduced, along with the presence of such particularistic mechanisms as employers' intuition or insight and such social forms as the occupational guild.

At the same time, the rise of mass democracy, which Weber depicted as a concomitant of bureaucratization, would result in bourgeois political ascendancy and would reinforce popular pressures for an equitable distribution of occupational opportunity. So, too, would the spread of the bourgeois individualistic outlook that leads toward strong efforts to pursue family social standing through personal attainment in the market. As a result of these converging, strongly reinforcing social trends, such traditional curricula as generalist liberal studies, which until the late nineteenth century in Europe and England had been a preparation for and emblem of aristocratic and gentry standing, would lose utility for status maintenance and mobility and thus would decline in both enrollment and legitimacy.

In sum, Weber asserted that with the rise of industrial-bureaucratic societies, education becomes less and less a traditionally-defined emblem of elite social standing. It evolves instead into an instrument of work and mobility for an ever-expanding proportion of the labor force.

From the Weberian analysis, one can infer two principal, correlated dimensions along which the relationship between educational and occupational attainment should vary. The first is an incidence dimension—the degree to which educational access is restricted to particular social groups. The second is a content dimension—the degree to which a curriculum is defined (whether popularly or formally) as vocationally useful. The two dimensions are correlated because, to the extent that bureaucracy dominates the arenas of productive social activity, it entails both universalistic status allocation and formal specialist training.

The incidence dimension can be specified with respect to the timing of restricted access. For example, this restriction may occur at the transition from common to secondary education, as in the classic British or European streamed educational system or from baccalaureate to postbaccalaureate programs, as in the more open system of the United States. The incidence dimension also can be specified with respect to the severity of the restriction at any such point—that is, the amount of social heterogeneity in entering and leaving student cohorts.

The content dimension can be specified with respect to the intensity of curricular specialization that occurs with movement toward the vocational pole. The traditional pole is assumed to be characterized by generalist studies, such as the liberal arts curriculum.

Sorokin, like Weber, stressed the context-specific nature of the relationship between educational attainment and social mobility. In *Social and Cultural*

Mobility (1927:164–214), he discussed the "channels of vertical circulation" through which social mobility occurs in various historical periods and societies. He argued that in the present-day West, the possibility of status inheritance has diminished, to be replaced by schools that operate more or less independently of family influence, selecting individuals into positions of greater or lesser social (especially economic) standing. As in Weber's formulation, the principal mechanisms are the spread of labor markets and the differentiation of occupations. As these mechanisms come into play, life chances become less dependent on social ascription and more dependent on academic ability, curriculum content, and the standards that teachers use to evaluate students and move them toward advanced training, certificates, and diplomas.

THE SOCIAL ORGANIZATION OF EDUCATIONAL ATTAINMENT: ALLOCATION THRESHOLDS

The principal elements of Weber's and Sorokin's arguments are (1) the general advance of bureaucracy; (2) universalistic, achievement-oriented role allocation that extends to institutionally autonomous screening of students by schools; and (3) the ascendancy of individualism, embodied in an orientation of individual action toward labor market opportunities. These elements provide a frame for specifying the meaning of educational attainment. To exploit it fully, one would compare societies that contrasted in their degrees of bureaucratization, universalism, achievement orientation, and individualism. However, in this limited essay, I shall focus on those economically-developed societies that are well down the Weberian path.

Consider first how a bureaucratic, achievement-focused social structure orders the relationship between education and occupational life chances. As occupational allocation moves to the center of status allocation and becomes increasingly formalized with respect to evidence of trained capacity, the allocation system takes on a threshold structure in which occupations are stratified according to minimum educational requirements.[1] These thresholds, presumably, mirror a step-wise gradation of occupations that is formed according to complexity, responsibility, income, and, hence, prestige.

As one moves up these gradations, the allocation system differentiates horizontally. That is, the more educationally advanced occupations also are the more technically specialized, so that they require substantively distinctive training—a tendency for the modern labor force to specialize with respect to the content and stratify with respect to the amount of trained capacity that they entail.

The sources of this fan-shaped threshold structure are to be found in the way modern educational systems have institutionalized and differentiated (Durkheim 1977; Clark, Archer 1984; Rubinson 1986). As schools have gained their own institutional standing in society, with a concomitant professionalization of the teaching force, what is taught has evolved into a curriculum composed of blocks—courses of study of varying length and content specificity that are defined in response more to educators' judgment than the predilections of individual students or families.[2]

At the same time, the faculties of the more advanced programs have gained the ability to externalize responsibility for introductory training to teachers in less advanced programs. In this way, the curricular blocks tend to be ordered hierarchically, with completion of more basic programs prerequisite to more advanced courses of study.

The result is a curricular arrangement that is legitimized by educators' professional authority, public policy, and popular belief. This arrangement defines the fan-shaped structure of status allocation thresholds. For all the participants—students, parents, teachers, and employers—this structure defines the acquisition of trained capacity primarily according to the completion of curricular blocks (e.g., graduation from high school or college or from a particular high school track or college major). This definition makes the number of years of school that students complete heavily dependent on the length of the curricular blocks that they enter.

Three implications follow. First, the likelihood of completing any given program should be a strong function of having entered it. Second, the timing of labor force entry (and reentry, for those who interrupt work for education) should be constrained by the timing of program completion and the award of diplomas and degrees. Third, the distribution of educational attainment in the population should tend toward a discontinuous, stair-step shape that reflects the threshold structure.

Contemporary societies vary in the degree to which movement from one level to the next in the threshold structure is selective. They also differ in how tightly the strata are coupled. That is, once a student has finished a curricular block, he or she may face few or many entry criteria for movement to a subsequent block. These criteria may be more or less rigorous, and the number of differentiated curricular pathways that are available at the next threshold may be more or less numerous.

In general, selectivity and coupling are a function of the timing of curricular differentiation. As one moves toward more specialized curricular blocks, the specification of prerequisites tends to become the prime selection device. On average, the more specialized the curricular block that a student completes, the smaller the number of subsequent blocks that are available, but the easier they are to enter. Less specialized blocks may lead to numerous curricular pathways, but only after the student pool has been carefully screened.

In other words, wherever the point of transition from generalist to specialized curricula occurs, selectivity tends to be high and coupling low, with the earlier block leading to many subsequent blocks. Later, selectivity (now within curricular pathways) should be more relaxed, having in effect been accomplished earlier, but coupling should be relatively tight.

For example, in a traditional streamed European structure, when a student moves from common school to secondary school, the intensity of selection is high and the number of potential educational destinations relatively numerous. By contrast, in the transition from grammar school, gymnasium, or lycee to university, the intensity of selection is low and the educational destinations relatively few. In effect, variation in the timing of selective transitions and in the incidence of tighter or looser interstratum coupling provides the structural complement to sponsored as opposed to contest mobility in educational systems (Turner 1960; Kerckhoff 1974).

The concept of threshold structure has obvious implications for the measurement of educational attainment. First, although years of completed school is a continuous variable, educational attainment is discontinuous. Therefore, occupational attainment models that use years of school completed to measure educational attainment will not accurately represent the social organization of educational and occupational attainment. When such models are evaluated, each year of school is given equal weight, even though some correspond to the completion of curricular blocks, others only to progress within blocks.

Second, persistence in school tends to be accompanied by increasingly specialized courses of study. Therefore, years of completed education is not an entirely suitable measure in studies of the mechanisms that affect entry to careers in the technical-specialist sector of the labor market. Although for this purpose a highly content-specific educational attainment measure may not be necessary, it may be desirable to develop measures of the intensity of curricular specialization (e.g., the number of occupations for which the training prepares) or measures that weight the amount of education by the intensity of curricular specialization.

Third, because the number and timing of attainment thresholds and the intensity of curricular differentiation within attainment strata are functions of social context, cross-national or within-society historical comparisons of educational attainment must take these differences into account. For example, although many societies display strong relationships between educational and occupational attainment, the mechanisms that produce this relationship in less economically-developed societies may differ from those at work in more

economically-developed settings. Early selectivity and subsequent tight curricular coupling may produce this relationship in the less developed societies,
while later selectivity and a longer period of loose curricular coupling may do
so in the more developed ones. If so, in the less developed societies, the
tendency toward prolonged education may be mainly a function of status group
origins and ascriptively grounded educational screening, while in the more
developed settings, it may reflect a system of universalistic, merit-centered
educational screening that rewards students for motivation and ability.

Fourth, variation in the threshold structure should create substantive differences in educational attainment. Measuring educational attainment by
years of school completed will not capture these differences. In a differentiated threshold structure, the curricular pathways toward more advanced training undoubtedly provide more opportunities to learn than those that lead more
quickly to the labor market—for example, the academic tracks of American
high schools or the grammar school-university stream of a classic European
system (Fagerlind 1975; Sorensen and Hallinan 1977). If so, the earlier selectivity and tight curricular coupling occur in an educational threshold structure,
the greater should be the average difference in trained capacity (both level and
content) between persons who have completed different curricular pathways.

This difference can be expected in part because of the different amounts of
learning that are possible in programs of different length. But even when the
sheer amount of educational attainment is about the same (e.g., graduates of a
gymnasium or a technical high school), exposure to opportunities to learn
should differ. In part, this difference would arise because, as Sorensen (1987)
has argued, curricular differentiation creates a system of contingent vacancies
in which earlier assignments become crucial for students' educational careers—"a promotion system where more and more students are left without
promotion chances as they progress" (p. 13). In addition to this structural
effect, the earlier the selection of students into tightly coupled curricular
pathways, the greater are the corresponding differences in students' chances
for cognitive change while they are in school (Fagerlind 1975).

In sum, these effects of threshold structures on promotion chances and
opportunities to learn should tend to stratify educational outcomes according
to the length and specialization of curricular pathways. However, this tendency may be partly overcome by the consequences of threshold structures for
motivational changes. The later the timing of curricular selection, the stronger
the effects that one would expect of students' motivation on educational
persistence and other varieties of educational attainment. In other words, if
educational progress has a strong inertial element, then when selection occurs
early and the period of tight curricular coupling is protracted, attainment may
reflect initial placement more than motivation to persist and succeed. At the

least, the consequences of educational persistence for motivational development should be more ambiguous when educational selectivity and tight coupling occur relatively late in the threshold structure. (cf. Kerckhoff 1974).

SYMBOLIC AND SUBSTANTIVE MEANINGS OF EDUCATIONAL ATTAINMENT

In this section, I shall discuss in somewhat more detail the implications of threshold structures for the mechanisms involved in the relationship between educational and occupational attainment. I shall do so with reference to the debate between the social signalling and human capital approaches. I shall suggest that ideas about education as a source of cultural capital may help to resolve certain of the issues posed in this debate.

Signalling

The attainment strata within an educational threshold structure define transitional points in educational and occupational life histories that are likely to be symbolically significant. Their number is comparatively few; they are defined by institutionalized, widely understood and accepted curricular and temporal boundaries; and they are ordered hierarchically according to presumed gradations in the cumulative acquisition, first, of generalized and, then, of specialized knowledge and skill. As a result, crossing or failing to cross each of these thresholds and the formal certification of the corresponding accomplishment are social signals in processes of status attainment.

Sociologists and labor economists have proposed that years of completed education act as a social signal in labor markets (Spence 1973; Arrow 1973; Wolpin 1974; Stiglitz 1975). They have argued that schooling is a process in which individuals are endowed with signals of employability. If the signalling value of education arises primarily from the symbolic aspect of the threshold structure, then the relationship between educational and occupational attainment should approximate a stair-step function in which the more powerful effects correspond to the transition points in the structure (e.g., more powerful effects of certificates held than of simple years of education completed).

This argument ignores the possibility that both amounts and kinds of education produce actual gains in capacity for productive work. It also ignores the possibility that the signalling value of such educational attainments as years of school completed, degrees earned, or track or stream followed to some degree is derived from observed population distributions of skills, work information, and motives that are correlated with the kind of educational attainment in question. Either of these possibilities would produce something like a smooth function in the relationship between school attainment and job prestige and income. Reliance on years of education to measure educational attainment will not permit an evaluation of these competing propositions or of the possible connection between educational productivity and occupational prestige and income attainment.

Human Capital

This limitation is ironic because a principal aim of the signalling theorists has been to criticize the ideas about human capital that for the past quarter century have dominated thinking about the relationship between educational attainment and labor force participation (Rosenbaum 1976; Hope 1984; Schultz 1963; Bowman 1969; Becker 1964; Mincer 1974; Fagerlind 1975). Human capital theory is concerned primarily with the reasons individuals chose to spend more or less time in school, or to spend this time in programs of greater or lesser cognitive and motivational demand. It assumes that schooling has a generally cumulative effect on both the cognitive and motivational aspects of capacity for productive work and, hence, on occupational prestige and income.

In short, human capital denotes trained capacity, and the school is seen as a means for its formation. More specifically, three ways are proposed through which education forms human capital: increasing reasoning powers, imparting knowledge (which interacts with reasoning powers to form cognitive capacity), and developing motives and habits that have to do, on the one hand, with discipline and perseverance and, on the other, with high-order occupational accomplishment. These varieties of human capital formation entail both the instruction and screening of students.

People can use their stocks of human capital as resources in the job search and later as tools for doing the job. In this view, years of completed education can be regarded as a measure of the level of investment in one's own human capital or in the human capital of one's offspring. This investment earns a return in the form of occupational attainment.

Cultural Capital

The cultural capital approach gives special attention to the motivational and informational outcomes of schooling, as they may be created by either instruction or screening (Bourdieu 1977; Bourdieu and Passeron 1979; DiMaggio 1982). The chief thrust of the cultural capital argument is that whatever the status-attainment effects of the more technically instrumental outcomes of schooling (e.g., the certification or the substance of trained capacity), these effects are complemented by the acquisition of the symbols and substance of capacity to conduct oneself within the subculture of an occupational specialty and to follow a style of life appropriate to particular occupational levels, workplaces, or jobs. More specifically, this approach asks how schools may engender in students those secondary status characteristics (e.g., such language forms as standard English or Parisian French) that increase or reduce life chances.

This line of argument has come from a search for the sources of ascriptive bias in status attainment. Specifically, it derives from an effort to determine how ascriptive biases in instruction (especially, the allocation of students to schools and curricula and hence to differing opportunities for learning) or the screening of students in schools affects the distribution of habits, motives, and status-relevant traits within student cohorts.

The cultural capital argument spans and partly integrates the signalling and human capital points of view. From the signalling standpoint, forms of speech, degrees of knowledge about more common or more arcane (and less prestigious or more prestigious) worlds of work, degrees of cultural sophistication, familiarity and ease in one or another style of life, and manifestations of motivation and habituation for work may each be a signal of fitness for patterns of conduct that generate greater or lesser success in a work world. From the human capital standpoint, these varieties of cultural capital may be tools that are in themselves useful in doing work (e.g., fluency in an occupational argot). They may interact with more immediately work-related capacities to increase or decrease the likelihood of one or another degree of occupational attainment (e.g., habituation to regular hours of work, or the drive to earn a high income).

The cultural capital approach implies a weaker stair-step pattern in the relationship of educational to occupational attainment than is to be expected on the basis of signalling theory. The substantive side of cultural capital acquisition should be cumulative, so that years of completed education should be related incrementally to command of the cultural capital required for more advanced, prestigious, and remunerative work. At the same time, the signalling effects of cultural capital may be not much more discontinuous. For example, employers may very well expect each year of a prospective employee's exposure to college to stand for a palpable gain of civility and sophistication.

Comparing the Approaches

The microeconomic analysis of human capital formation does not extend to questions of social mobility. It assumes an allocation process that is sensitive to prospective or actual productivity on the job—resulting in a distribution of persons by job prestige or income that reflects a reasonable fit between individuals' trained capacity and their opportunities to use it.

Signalling theory attends more directly to social allocation, but not because of an interest in social mobility. The primary interest is to make explicit the allocative mechanisms that affect the productive use of labor (e.g., the efficiency of the signals that diplomas, degrees, and the like provide) and to correct what is seen as the over-readiness of human capital theory to assume that correlations between years of schooling and labor force participation necessarily denote mediating effects of work productivity.

Therefore, these arguments stress the symbolic or substantive ways in which educational attainment affects how individuals move into the labor force and through an employment history. As a result, their attention to the meaning of educational attainment has been limited to the question of socialization to economic productivity or of the symbolization of productive capacity. The cultural capital argument broadens this formulation. Increments of cultural capital denote increases in life chances, specifically, chances of occupational prestige and income attainment. These differences of life chances are expected to show a substantial degree of status inheritance by virtue of ascriptive biases in students' access to school.

In sum, human capital theory is a theory of the educational sources of labor productivity from which status allocation derives. Signalling theory is a theory of the allocation of productive labor. Cultural capital theory is a theory of the educational sources social mobility.

Cultural capital theory argues that the bearing of educational attainment on social mobility is not peculiar to labor force participation, however central the economy may be to the formation of life chances. This economic dimension of social stratification may be cross-cut by other status-defining dimensions—such secondary status characteristics as race, ethnicity, gender, lineage, and place of residence. In universalistic status allocation, these cross-cutting dimensions may be bases for discrimination or other allocational bias.

As these dimensions combine with the prime dimension of occupational status, they make the allocation of status more selective in a way that requires the mobile individual to master not only the technical elements of occupational performance, but also to acquire the motives, habits, and elements of a style of life that indicate suitability for one or another position in the occupational structure.

It seems reasonable to suppose that even in a relatively merit-centered system of occupational allocation, getting jobs, raises, and promotions is to some degree affected by the presence or absence of traits that either substantively or symbolically reinforce or substitute for technical qualifications. Such things as having come from the Ivy League, styles of dress and manners, and command of a class or occupational argot may ease social relations at work and affect job productivity more directly.

The multi-dimensional structure that the cultural capital analysts posit may also distribute access to information that is useful in acquiring jobs, doing so in ways that are not perfectly symmetrical with the more technical aspects of job training. For example, schooling may not only produce trained capacity to perform certain jobs, but it may also actively teach students about the work world, about ways to search for jobs (e.g., how to prepare a resume, how to obtain job interviews and conduct oneself in them, or how to use want ads). In addition, school may less directly influence access to information about the work world or about specific job opportunities through the formation of networks of face-to-face ties among students and between students and information sources outside the school, such as the parents of school friends (Granovetter, 1974).

From the standpoint of social equity, these effects pose questions of discrimination and the grounding of differing access to cultural capital. From the standpoint of defining educational attainment, they raise the related questions of the way in which the cumulative experience of education adds to stocks of cultural capital and of the ways in which the several curricular pathways in an educational threshold structure (the curricular blocks and their hierarchical arrangement) introduce ascriptive bias into the distribution of such experience.

EDUCATION AND CAPACITY

Presumably there is some degree of isomorphism between varieties of trained capacity and varieties of social participation, so that certain specific skills, motives, and habits influence productivity or effectiveness in particular occupations or pursuits. An obvious example is the fit between the specialized skills and work activities of such occupations as neurosurgery or nuclear engineering. One also might posit broader relationships, such as a larger contribution of individual initiative or success orientation to productivity in less routine or closely-supervised occupations than in others and a disproportionately greater contribution of such habits as regularity in occupations that are more routine or more closely supervised. Still other elements of capacity may have very generalized consequences for productivity or effectiveness—for example, basic reasoning skills or literacy.

The size of the contribution of schooling to the formation of trained capacity, relative to the contribution of extra-school or post-school experience, remains in dispute. Moreover, the symbolic value of educational attainment—at least years of school completed—may arise as easily from the contributions of out-of-school experience as from in-school experience. Therefore, the duration, substance, and effects of the two forms of socialization would covary.

For example, students who complete high school are more likely than high school dropouts to have had part-time jobs during school and to have participated in youth organizations of various kinds (Michael and Tuma 1984). The high school diploma may be a signal of the acquisition of what is learned from such experiences, just as it is of what is learned in school.

However, I have posited a palpable contribution of education to trained capacity, by virtue of instruction and screening. If this proposition is right, whatever the independent or interactive contributions of out-of-school experience, the effects of educational attainment on occupational productivity, income, and lifetime mobility patterns should be a function of the allocative mechanisms that are embedded in the threshold structures of educational systems.

In other words, to the extent that occupational allocation becomes more selective as one moves up the hierarchy of thresholds or becomes more content-specific because of more intensive curricular differentiation, then educational attainment should affect not only entry level occupational participation, but also longer-term productivity. In this way it should affect longer-term social mobility, displaying the strengthening relationship between educational and occupational attainment that has been found so consistently.

To evaluate these propositions, one must be able to account for the decay of capacity in jobs that provide few capacity-enhancing experiences. One must also be able to account for learning in jobs that provide more of these experiences. These cumulative effects, whether positive or negative, may occur in part by virtue of effects of earlier states of capacity on further learning (e.g., learning to learn) and in part indirectly, as a result of the threshold structure itself. These indirect effects may be expected because, when job allocation is based on educational attainment, the higher the attainment, the higher the probability of capacity-enhancing work.

Evidence about these effects would allow an interesting specification of the social structural and social psychological mechanisms that presumably mediate the relationship between educational and occupational attainment and of the elements of schooling (i.e., socialization, screening, credentialing) involved in the relationship. Comparative estimates of the effects of what students learn, how they are screened, and what educational credentials they earn on on-the-job learning (or unlearning) may reveal a more complex web of relationships than the simple dichotomous opposition of human capital formation and social signalling. However, the difficulty of identifying unambiguous school outcomes suggests that the debate will be joined for some time to come. I shall consider next how this debate might be treated empirically.

SYMBOL AND SUBSTANCE

Completing curricular blocks along any of the progressively branching paths of an educational threshold structure should produce a bundle of reasoning skills, items of information about jobs and the work world, and secondary status traits that affect both job search and job performance.[3] Moreover, aggregate variation in these learning and screening outcomes of curricular blocks should produce widespread labor market expectations that a given amount or kind of education stands for a corresponding kind of trained capacity and related elements of cultural capital. Indeed, the institutionalization of the curricular pathways that form threshold structures should produce a readiness (at least during initial hiring decisions) to accept the symbols of educational attainment as tantamount to the substance of what schools teach and screen for.

It follows that the meaning of educational attainment has inextricably linked substantive and symbolic elements. However, the content of these elements should vary according to the societal context in which a system of education is formed. I have suggested that in present-day bureaucratic societies educational attainment has several meanings. It may denote components of trained capacity for job performance, ancillary bodies of information about the work world, or secondary status characteristics. Each of these denotations, in turn, may be substantive or symbolic, and the symbolic aspect may be either formal (certificates earned) or informal.

Occupational attainment has its own array of meanings, and it is quite likely that different elements of educational attainment contribute in distinctive ways to different aspects of occupational attainment. For example, trained capacity may contribute primarily to work productivity, secondary status characteristics primarily to social acceptability in an occupational or organizational circle.

The issues raised by juxtaposing the signalling, human capital, and social capital approaches have a familiar ring. There is a close fit between the human capital approach and Weber's ideas about the substantive varieties of education and their relation to economic and cultural bases of social stratification. Both assume that with economic development and the rationalization of economic life comes the rise of specialized, instrumentally-valued education that engenders occupationally-useful knowledge and skill. However, Weber did not make a rigid separation between the symbolic or substantive aspects of education (i.e., signalling versus human capital formation). In this vein, I have suggested that to regard the two as parts of a complex of mechanisms in the occupational attainment process is sensible.

This complex is postulated by the cultural capital theorists, and their argument restates and elaborates Weberian ideas about how life chances are formed. His conception of education for the conduct of a life, with its preparation in the values, beliefs, and conventions of a status group is echoed in the notion of cultural capital. However, Weber's formulation was broader. He was concerned to classify forms of education across the sweep of historical societies and specified the primacy of education for life conduct to those earlier ages in which traditional authority relations held sway. For Weber, the master trend in the curriculum and in the bearing of education on individual life chances was vocational because of the centrality of occupations, and occupational specialization, in modern societies.

Weber did not think that life conduct education would disappear entirely. For example, persisting elements of the old liberal curriculum in the secondary schools and universities of Wilhelmian Germany could be understood as an effort by bourgeois families to secure preparation in secondary status traits that would reinforce status claims more centrally grounded in occupational competence and performance. Vocational competence, however close its correspondence to labor market demand, could not be relied on by itself to secure status advantage.

A well-designed empirical effort to clarify the issues posed between advocates of human capital and signalling theory would entail independent measures of (1) work productivity; (2) years of completed education, weighted by curricular content; (3) certification; (4) trained capacity; and (5) various elements of cultural capital. Such research would pose formidable problems. The individual measurement tasks themselves are often difficult—for example, identifying and testing for the cognitive skills or knowledge that are job-specific or more generally useful in occupations. In addition, it would be necessary to obtain evidence of the effect of schooling on various substantive outcomes of occupational productivity and mobility (either learning or screening effects) and, as well, to trace consequences of education for further occupationally useful learning (whether on-the-job or other) that would be estimated independently of the continuing effects of what was learned in school.

I have noted that the relationship of educational and occupational attainment appears to strengthen during a job history, irrespective of societal context. If we are to understand this phenomenon, we must discover the ways in which what is learned in school is mobilized in work—for example, cumulative effects of having learned to learn, in contrast to increasingly productive use of trained capacity. Kohn and his colleagues (1983:53–189) have taken important steps in this direction. Their research suggests a chain of effect in which gains in capacity for complex cognitive activity, acquired in school and on the job, result in recruitment to more complex work. This work, in turn, results in further cognitive gains. Research of this kind must be complemented by equally sophisticated research on other of the mechanisms in the educational-occupational attainment relationship. Such work must use crossnational comparative designs, to reveal differences in the mechanisms in play in different societies.

CONCLUSION

In sum, the relationship between educational and occupational attainment is socially organized. I have described its social organization as a structure of status allocation thresholds that arise because of the evolution of curricular organization in educational systems and believed-in connections between some consequence of being educated and some human capacity (e.g., to work productively or to conduct a life properly). These connections may be established in a variety of ways—for example, through traditional consensus (e.g., the archetypical Weberian connection with status group maintenance and recruitment), efforts to gain monopolistic control of access to such social goods as prestige or income (perhaps through state policy or group organization to control the labor market), or employers' use of tehnical criteria when hiring workers.

Threshold structures order opportunities to learn and criteria that are mobilized in status allocation. They order opportunities to learn—to acquire cultural capital in the dual Weberian sense—in a hierarchy of curricular blocks of varying length, content complexity and specificity, and inter-block coupling. They order status-entry criteria—the criteria employed whenever schools screen students (including the award of certificates and diplomas)—into a hierarchy of selectivity and content specificity. Within this structure, what students learn in school and the credentials that they earn order them, cohort by cohort, with respect to trained capacity, both substantively and symbolically. Thus, individuals are distributed in the division of labor and occupational status structure because of the bearing of the substance and symbolic value of education on occupational life chances and the content of occupational participation (e.g., law or medicine, skilled trades of different kinds).

No doubt the distribution of trained capacity in a population, both its substance and its symbols, affects the institutionalization of thresholds. These effects may at times be mediated by markets—ample supplies of trained capacity driving up status-entry requirements or allowing them to differentiate horizontally, while scarce capacity drives requirements down and tends to make status entry criteria more homogeneous or more general. These institutionalizing effects may also occur because of self-interested action by groups of the capable—for example, the strategic behavior of the organized occupations to restrict recruitment to their ranks.

I have suggested certain theoretical possibilities and difficulties likely to be encountered in research on educational and occupational attainment. I have stressed the promise of a Weberian reading of the cultural capital approach, and I have advanced some specific propositions derived from a juxtaposition of the different lines of argument about educational and occupational attainment. In brief, I have argued for a research program that would include the analysis of:

1. the mechanisms through which threshold structures are established,
2. the effects of education on trained capacity, and
3. the relationship between the substance and symbolization of trained capacity.

I have argued that each of these lines of analysis will make distinctive demands on the measurement of educational attainment. At the least, simple years of education completed is not likely to be theoretically appropriate, whatever the research agenda. Better measures of educational attainment and a resulting body of more useful evidence might now advance the field.

NOTES

1. I shall ignore here the degree to which this requirement is based upon accurate assessments of the effects of training on job productivity.

2. In the aggregate, of course, these predilections, whether aggregated in educational markets or in public policy, can have substantial long-term effects on what educators propose and what they can effect curricularly.

3. Whether this bundle of trained capacities and accompanying information and status characteristics is produced in school by virtue of instruction or screening does not affect what educational attainment means in status attainment—even though it is a central question for the analysis of schooling and its effects.

REFERENCES

Alexander, K. L. and M. Cook. 1982. "Curricula and Coursework." *American Sociological Review* 47:626–640.

Alexander, K. L., M. Cook, and E. L. McDill. 1978. "Curriculum Tracking and Educational Stratification: Some Further Evidence." *American Sociological Review* 43:47–66.

Alexander, K. L. and B. K. Eckland. 1975. "Contextual Effects in the High School Attainment Process." *American Sociological Review* 40:402–416.

Alexander, K. L., B. K. Eckland, and L. J. Griffin. 1975. "The Wisconsin Model of Socioeconomic Achievement: A Replication." *American Journal of Sociology* 81:324–363.

Alexander, K. L. and E. L. McDill. 1976. "Selection and Allocation within Schools." *American Sociological Review* 41:963–980.

Alwin, D. F. 1976. "Socioeconomic Background, Colleges, and Postsecondary Achievement." Edited by W. H. Sewell, R. M. Hauser, and D. L. Featherman. *Schooling and Achievement in American Society.* New York: Academic.

Archer, M. S. 1984. *Social Origins of Educational Systems.* Beverly Hills, CA: Sage.

Arrow, K. 1973. "Higher Education as a Filter." *Journal of Public Economics* 2:193–216.

Bain, R. K. and J. G. Anderson. 1974. "School Context and Peer Influences on Educational Plans of Adolescents." *Review of Educational Research* 44:429–445.

Becker, G. S. 1964. *Human Capital.* New York: Columbia.

Benavot, A. 1985. *Education and Economic Development in the Modern World.* Ph.D. dissertation, Department of Sociology, Stanford University.

Bidwell, C. E. and N. E. Friedkin. 1988. "The Sociology of Education" edited by Neil Smelser. *The Handbook of Sociology.* Beverly Hills, CA: Sage.

Blau, P. M. and O. D. Duncan. 1967. *The American Occupational Structure.* New York: Wiley.

Bourdieu, P. 1977. "Cultural Reproduction and Social Reproduction" edited by J. Karabel and A. H. Halsey. *Power and Ideology in Education.* New York: Oxford.

Bourdieu, P. and Jean-Claude Passeron. 1979. *The Inheritors.* Chicago: University of Chicago Press.

Bowman, M. J. 1969. "Economics of Education." *Review of Educational Research* 39:641–670.

Clark, B. R. 1983. *The Higher Education System.* Berkeley: University of California Press.

Collins, R. 1979. *The Credential Society.* New York: Academic.

DiMaggio, P. 1982. "Cultural Capital and School Success: The Impact of Status Culture Participation on the Grades of U.S. High School Students." *American Sociological Review* 47:189–201.

Durkheim, E. 1977. *The Evolution of Educational Thought.* London: Routledge and Kegan Paul.

Fagerlind, I. 1975. *Formal Education and Adult Earnings.* Stockholm: Almqvist and Wiksell.

Featherman, D. L. and R. M. Hauser. 1978. *Opportunity and Change.* New York: Academic.

Gerth, H. and C. W. Mills. eds. 1946. *From Max Weber: Essays in Sociology.* New York: Oxford.

Granovetter, M. 1974. *Getting a Job: A Study of Contacts and Careers.* Cambridge, MA: Harvard.

Hauser, R. M. 1971. *Socioeconomic Background and Educational Performance.* Washington, D.C.: Rose Monograph Series, American Sociological Association.

Hauser, R. M. and D. L. Featherman. 1976. "Equality of Schooling." *Sociology of Education* 49:99–120.

Hauser, R. M., W. H. Sewell, and D. L. Alwin. 1976. "High School Effects on Achievement," edited by W. H. Sewell, R. M. Hauser, and D. L. Featherman. *Schooling and Achievement in American Society.* New York: Academic.

Heyneman, S. P. and W. A. Loxley. 1983. "The Effect of Primary School Quality on Academic Achievement across Twenty-nine High- low-income Countries." *American Journal of Sociology* 88:1162–1194.

Hope, K. 1984. *As Others See Us: Schooling and Social Mobility in Scotland and the United States.* Cambridge: Cambridge University Press.

Jencks, C., J. Crouse, and P. Mueser. 1983. "The Wisconsin Model of Status Attainment: A

National Replication with Improved Measures of Ability and Aspiration." *Sociology of Education* 56:3–19.

Kelley, J. 1973. "Causal Chain Models for the Socioeconomic Career." *American Sociological Review* 38:481–493.

Kerckhoff, A. C. 1974. "Stratification Processes and Outcomes in England and the U.S." *American Sociological Review* 39:789–801.

Kohn, M. L., C. Schooler, et al. 1983. *Work and Personality: An Inquiry into the Impact of Social Stratification.* Norwood, N.J.: Ablex.

Lazear, E. 1977. "Education: Consumption or Production?" *Journal of Political Economy* 85:569–597.

Levine, R. A. and M. I. White. 1986. *Human Conditions: The Cultural Basis of Educational Development.* New York: Routledge and Kegan Paul.

Michael, R. and N. B. Tuma. 1984. "Youth Employment: Does Life Begin at 16?" *Journal of Labor Economics* 2:464–476.

Mincer, J. 1974. *Schooling, Experience, and Earnings.* New York: National Bureau of Economic Research.

Rehberg, R. A. and E. R. Rosenthal. 1978. *Class and Merit in the American High School.* New York: Longman.

Rosenbaum, J. E. 1976. *Making Inequality.* New York: Wiley.

Rubinson, R. 1986. "Class Formation, Politics, and Institutions: Schooling in the United States." *American Journal of Sociology* 92:519–548.

Schultz, T. W. 1963. *The Economic Value of Education.* New York: Columbia University Press.

Sewell, W. H. and R. M. Hauser. 1976. "Causes and Consequences of Higher Education: Models of the Status Attainment Process," edited by W. H. Sewell, R. M. Hauser, and D. L. Featherman. *Schooling and Achievement in American Society.* New York: Academic.

Slomczynski, K. M., J. Miller, and M. L. Kohn. 1981. "Stratification, Work, and Values: A Polish-United States Comparison." *American Sociological Review* 46:720–744.

Smith, J. P. and F. R. Welch. 1986. Closing the Gap: Forty Years of Economic Progress for Blacks. *Technical Report R-3330-DOL.* Santa Monica, CA: Rand Corporation.

Sorensen, A. B. 1987. "The Organizational Differentiation of Students in Schools as an Opportunity Structure," edited by M. T. Hallinan. *Conceptualizations of School Organization and Schooling Processes.* New York: Plenum.

Sorensen, A. B. and M. T. Hallinan. 1977. "A Reconceptualization of School Effects." *Sociology of Education* 50:273–289.

Sorokin, P. A. 1927. *Social and Cultural Mobility.* New York: Harper.

Spence, M. 1973. "Job Market Signalling." *Quarterly Journal of Economics* 87:355–374.

Spenner, K. I. and D. L. Featherman. 1978. "Achievement Ambitions." *Annual Review of Sociology* 4:373–420.

Stiglitz, J. 1975. "The Theory of 'Screening,' Education, and the Distribution of Income." *American Economic Review* 65:283–300.

Treiman, D. J. and K. Terrell. 1975. "Sex and the Process of Status Attainment: A Comparison of Working Women and Men." *American Sociological Review* 40:174–200.

Turner, R. H. 1960. "Sponsored and Contest Mobility and the School System." *American Sociological Review* 25:855–867.

Weber, M. 1946. *The Theory of Social and Economic Organization.* Glencoe, IL: Free Press.

Wolpin, K. 1974. "Education and Screening." Department of Economics, University of Chicago.

PART II

MEASUREMENT AND DESIGN ISSUES

HAVE INDIVIDUALS BEEN OVEREMPHASIZED IN SCHOOL-EFFECTS RESEARCH?

Ronald G. Corwin and Krishnan Namboodiri

Many years have passed since W. Lloyd Warner, Robert J. Havighurst, and Martin B. Loeb published their perceptive account of the role schooling plays in the social mobility process. *Who Shall Be Educated?* (1944) is seldom mentioned anymore, but status attainment research might have taken a different direction had this work been consulted when the data bases being used to explain social mobility were designed. With penetrating insight the book laid out the parameters and the issues that still plague research estimating how formal education intervenes in the status attainment process. Asserting that education is one of the most important elevators, the authors likened schooling to an "enormous, complicated machine for sorting and ticketing and

Research in the Sociology of Education and Socialization,
Volume 8, pages 141–176.
Copyright © 1989 by JAI Press Inc.
All rights of reproduction in any form reserved.
ISBN: 0-89232-929-7

routing children through life'' (p. 49). Yet, through case narratives, they demonstrated there is no simple connection between mobility within the restricted school hierarchy and mobility within the larger social order (e.g., p. 35). Success in school, they concluded depends on more than intellectual ability. It depends as well upon economic status, position and social personality.

Since then, a voluminous body of statistically sophisticated research on the status attainment process has accumulated based on surveys and census data. The findings have refined the insights, but the basic conclusions of *Who Shall Be Educated?* have not been refuted. While not as rigorous as work being done today, the range of dynamic variables included in the study proved sensitive to differences among groups and social contexts. It is therefore unfortunate that the book has provided so little guidance for surveys that have come to dominate this genre of research. Many of its sound observations seem to have been forgotten until recently. Now, however, isolated critics are echoing similar observations.

Twenty-three years after the publication of *Who Shall Be Educated?*, Peter Blau and Dudley Duncan's (1967) watershed study demonstrated the power of a parsimonious model that would re-direct social mobility research towards the variables and measures that are commonly employed today. As in the Warner, Havighurst and Loeb study, they found a distinct relationship between the educational attainment of individuals and their occupational achievement, concluding that education is the most important determinant of occupational status among the variables considered, with a zero order correlation of .60 and a path coefficient of .39 (pp. 402–403). (See also, Featherman and Hauser 1978). However, unmeasured factors, in addition to SES and education, accounted for most of the variance in occupational achievement. While acknowledging that socioeconomic background is not trivial, Blau and Duncan concluded that most of the major determinants of occupational attainment remain unknown.

Eight years later, William Sewell and Robert Hauser (1975) published another landmark study based on surveys of Wisconsin high school graduates. Their analysis supported the conclusion that socio-economic background explained no more than 15 percent of the variance in years of education. Academic ability was nearly of equal importance. The relationship between SES background and education, while persistent, was especially negligible when a person's academic achievement, occupational aspiration level and ability are taken into account. A variety of factors contributed to the occupational attainment of this sample, but reminiscent of Warner *et al.* (1944) and of Blau and Duncan's conclusions, they observed that the path to higher occupational status is through education, and that education is the single most important variable (p. 107). However, their analysis also indicated educational attainment strongly depends upon intellectual ability; see also Alexander, Eckland, and Griffin (1975).

Note that, first, educational attainment enters these models either as an intervening or an independent variable. Second, the typical measure of educational attainment is either years of schooling completed or the person's performance on standardized tests. Third, information about individuals is often aggregated and treated as a system level attribute. There are some troublesome issues with these conventions, some of which were raised in *Who Shall Be Educated?*.

THE EDUCATION-OCCUPATION CONNECTION: RIVAL VIEWS

One issue concerns exactly what it is about years of education that gives one an advantage in the labor market. Or, put another way, what do years of formal education completed actually measure? The relationship between education and occupation has been accounted for in a variety of ways. Some explanations rely on socialization; others use an institutional perspective. Almost no attention has been given to macro-level cohort explanations.

Socialization-type Explanations

Socialization explanations emphasize the acquisition of intellectual ability, and/or social and cultural capital, interpersonal skills, and values learned indirectly through experiences and opportunities encountered in school.

The Ability Dimension

Many writers assert or assume that educational achievement has much to do with intellectual *ability*. Measures of ability and high school grades figure prominently in Sewell and Hauser's attainment models, for example. They observe that intelligence becomes more important than socioeconomic status as the person advances through the educational system, concluding that both SES origins and ability are important determinants of higher educational attainment. The priority these authors attach to ability is reflected in this comment:

> It is apparent from our analysis that the path to high occupational status is through higher education. Higher status families appear to make greatest use of this route, in part by providing the genes and the stimulating environment that result in superior cognitive abilities and school performance (p. 107).

The Social Capital Dimension

However, the link between ability and educational attainment is at best modest. Surveys indicate that measured intelligence explains no more than 15–30 percent of the variance in high school grades (cf. DiMaggio 1982; Sewell and Hauser 1975). What else is involved? Sewell and Hauser state that, in addition to nurturing ability, some families encourage high educational and occupational aspirations. Well educated parents transfer their advantage to their children by coaching them in linguistic and academic skills and by encouragement. Kelley and Kline (1981) refer to the type of advantage that can be inherited from one generation by the next as *human capital.* Coleman (1987) calls it *social capital,* which includes not only support provided by families, but also the opportunities, demands and rewards provided by communities and organizations such as schools. Teachman (1987) reports a relevant analysis based on Project Talent data. His measure of a family's educational resources is simple—whether there is a place in the home to study, available reference books, a dictionary or encyclopedia and a daily newspaper. Yet, the composite measure had a positive impact on educational aspirations and (for men) on grades, net of family background.

The Cultural Capital Dimension

Social capital, as construed by Coleman, is not exclusively controlled by families. For example, it includes opportunity structures within schools. DiMaggio (1982) believes that schools provide the opportunity, in particular, to acquire forms of *cultural* capital. Employing Weber's (1968) concept of *status groups* based on principles of consumption and lifestyle, he explains differences in educational attainment through the advantage some individuals gain in school by identifying with prestige status cultures centered around art, music and literature. Other individuals reject such lifestyles and thus lose status (Willis 1973). The notion of cultural capital, though not the term, was also suggested by Warner et al. (1944, p. 141), who observed that technical competence must be complemented by civic and social skills as a prerequisite to success in the modern complex world. While those authors believed schools should teach technical skills and provide competent instruction, they observed that personal habits also play an important role in status attainment (p. 37). "Growing up," they said, "consists in learning how to behave, and learning how to behave means acquiring the proper responses to the batteries of social stimuli which compose our social order." (p. 18). Recently, others have made similar observations (Etzioni 1982; Hern 1978).

DiMaggio's thesis is that teachers favor students who have acquired cultural capital, and in fact educational attainment is a very imperfect proxy for cultural capital. Whereas Bourdieu (to be discussed) had maintained that elites use status cultures to reinforce their positions, Dimaggio argues that participation in status cultures is often used by upwardly mobile students to overcome their family handicap. Cultural capital was measured using data from Project Talent on students' attitudes, activities and information. Among women and among males from lower and middle-status households, the measure was positively correlated with grades. A low correlation with parents' education supports the thesis that cultural capital is not merely a reflection of what is learned in the home, and therefore can be used as a social elevator for young men and women from low income families.

The Interpersonal Skills and Values Dimensions

Interpersonal skills represent another non-cognitive dimension transmitted by schools (Collins 1979; Kerckoff 1976; Sewell, Haller and Ohlendorf 1970). Also, many writers emphasize the importance of the values teachers endorse through overt and subtle cues. Dreeben (1968) observed that schools teach children how to adjust to tensions between particularistic family settings and universalistic norms used in the market place, including beliefs about winning and losing, how to cope with failure, and differences between cooperation and cheating. Other writers have described causal paths from education to status attainment that include intervening variables variously described as "passive obedience and loyalty" learned in school (Bowles and Gintis 1976) and "coping strategies" that individuals use to confront problems routinely encountered in organizations, such as retreatism, ritualistic conformity, innovation and rebellion (Corwin 1986; Merton 1957). For example, Claus (1986) reports students who were reluctant to complete a project could get another student or the teacher to do it for them.

Institutional Explanations

There is another way of looking at the education-occupation relationship which Kerckoff calls the *allocation perspective*. Individual attainment is still the focus, but more emphasis is given to (a) the agencies responsible for assigning individuals to social positions and (b) the existing structural constraints.

Legitimacy and Discrimination in the Allocation Process

Work organizations sometimes employ educated workers because it makes them look good. Correspondingly, educational qualifications are used symbolically by elites for purposes of legitimation as well as for instrumental purposes. Blau and Duncan pointed out that superior status no longer can be directly inherited but must be legitimized "by actual achievements that are socially acknowledged" (p. 430). Thus, education assumes increasing significance for social status in general and for the transmission of social standing from fathers to sons in particular. According to Blau and Duncan, superior family origins increase a son's chances of attaining superior occupational status in the United States in large part because they help him to obtain a better education. The implication is that family status is more important than social connections individuals establish on their own.

Bourdieu (1977) maintains that the real function of educational credentials is to certify the cultural capital that has already been acquired in the home (Bourdieu 1977:493,502; see also Collins 1975, 1979). This has little to do with forces that operate within the education system. Curriculum, pedagogical methods, the relationship between teacher and students, and methods of selection give economically privileged children an advantage over children of the less privileged and less educated. Teachers put much more emphasis on such things as speech patterns, tastes, and interpersonal skills—all of which are products of family background—rather than social and technical skills and values acquired in the school. His position suggests the following hypotheses. (a) students from upper-status homes receive higher grades even if they do not do well in tests or assignments, and they are given good recommendations by their teachers, no matter how poorly they perform in school work. This helps them to get good jobs (even if they are not qualified). (b) children from lower-status homes, no matter how well they do in school work, receive lower grades and less enthusiastic recommendations from teachers, denying them good placements. (c) students from lower-status homes, no matter how smart they are, get fewer opportunities to show their academic ability as they are sidetracked into courses and curricula that are relevant for a career in sports and the like. In these ways the education system militates against upward social mobility. This position has some holes, however. For example, it does not explain the gains blacks have made during the past 20 years.

In contrast to Bourdieu, Blau and Duncan seem to view legitimation as a by-product resulting from a person's actual accomplishments. They found no basis for the myth that poverty is inherited, concluding that there is little discrimination against white ethnic groups in occupational life. There is no guarantee that a son of a highly placed father will be highly placed. True, superior family origin increases a son's chance of obtaining better education, which in turn increases his chance of superior occupational attainment. But, actual occupational attainment is something that one accomplishes through education, not something that one just inherits from parents. Thus, Blau and Duncan concluded that, notwithstanding the legitimizing function of education, universalism discourages discrimination against ethnic minorities. However, their position also seems extreme. Many writers have concurred with Warner et al., who observed that while "outwardly, school is that institution which sorts out people by achievement, the young people are inspected not only for brains and learning ability, but also for skin color, pronunciation, cut of clothes, table manners, parental bank account" (p. 50, 73; see for example, Cicourel and Kitsuse 1963; Rist 1973).

A generation after *Who Shall be Educated* Kerckoff (1976) was calling for more sensitive measures of discrimination in the allocation process within and between schools, measures to assess the influence of school personnel in the tracking process, assignment of grades, choice of courses, participation in extra-curricular activities, and disciplinary practices. Current models, he observed, explain less than a third of the variance in grades, and most of this reflects the association of grades with intelligence. In short, finding employment is not solely a function of either the number of vacancies, or the individual's talents and educational attainments. There is a complex allocation process which includes dominant social values, social networks, and employment practices. Moreover, it should be added, social mobility may hinge on more than jobs.

Structural Constraints

The amount of mobility possible through education is a function of the supply and demand for an educated population. Dismissing the myth that "there is plenty of room at the top" as a fiction in a society that is no longer expanding, Warner et al. were acutely sensitive to the supply-demand ratio. If too many people are pushed up through the educational system, they warned, competition for good jobs will become fierce and "some people will have to take positions below the level for which they have been trained," causing feelings of dissatisfaction (p. 150). However, they did not mention the corollary to this "overeducation" problem, namely that jobs requiring a lot of education do not necessarily require more skill.

Given inadequate information and measurement problems, it is not yet possible to assess with accuracy the extent to which levels of education are out-stripping demand (Spenner 1985; Rubinson 1977). Clogg and Shockey's (1984) approach to measuring overeducation illustrates some of the problems. They measure overeducation within an occupation by computing the percentage of its members with education levels over one standard deviation above the mean level of years completed for the occupation as a whole. This approach supposes that (a) there is ceiling on the education needed for particular jobs, (b) occupations are stable, and (c) necessary skills can be clearly delineated. However, suppose that some occupations have been "undereducated" and are now in the process of upgrading. For example, not long ago the typical classroom teacher did not possess a B.A. degree. Now, almost all do. Many have M.A.s, and a number of states have regulations requiring teachers to complete at least five years of education or a master's degree. Moreover, within teaching, some existing and evolving positions require additional education. Is teaching becoming an overeducated occupation, or is it catching up to the weight of its responsibilities? What is the education ceiling for such an occupation? And, how does one draw the skill boundaries? Skill demands are more elastic for some occupations than for others. What seems to be over-education may also be seen as a strategic margin of safety available to an occupation for coping with atypical critical situations. For example, it may be the case that most accountants do not need C.P.A. certificates for most of the work they do, but conceivably the extra training proves useful in rare, extreme situations.

The concept, overeducation, seems to imply that the sole purpose of formal education is to train workers for jobs. But beyond imparting training that may have direct bearing on one's chances in the job market, schooling affects a person's appreciation of art, literature, music, history, sports and many other activities. Thus, it ultimately shapes one's preferred lifestyle, including uses of leisure time and participation in civic, cultural and other non-economic activities. Lifestyle, in turn, affects an individual's prestige, social status, and chances of upward social mobility. Moreover, for many people school activities have a consumption side, just as a job "well done" carries with it an intrinsic satisfaction in addition to any tangible output.

Macro-Level Explanations

Institutional level approaches have the advantage of embedding individuals within larger social contexts. However, the individual's mobility continues to be the central concern, and thus researchers remain steadfastly preoccupied with micro-level interpretations of the educational process. The research questions still characteristically concern finding out *who* gets ahead and how the *individual's* background, formal schooling and ability may contribute to that persons's status.

Structural Approaches

Other approaches ignore differences among individuals, their family backgrounds and educational attainment, and seek the causes of mobility in labor market structures, legal constraints, and demographic conditions (e.g., Parcel 1987). For example, dual economy theory calls attention to how characteristics of firms located in the core and the periphery of the economy influence the fates of those who are channeled into one or the other type of firm. Cohort analysis is concerned with whether entire cohorts differ in levels of status attainment, and if so, whether the differences are associated with formal education within the cohort. What matters, in other words, is whether the *aggregate* levels of education and occupational status achievement are associated. Identifying the particular individuals who gain or lose status is of no concern here.

For example, if cognitive ability is a prerequisite for social mobility, then it is first necessary to determine whether cohorts differ in ability composition, and then whether they also have different rates of mobility. We are not here interested in why one individual within a cohort may have more or less ability makeup than others, but whether the distributions of two cohorts differ in an understandable way. Suppose two cohorts with the same innate ability makeup have been exposed to two different systems of education. The question then is, do they also have different mobility patterns?

An Illustration

To make the picture a little more complicated, we can recognize that pupils who enter formal educational institutions leave at different times (e.g., after completing years 8, 9, 10, 11, 12, 13, etc.) A certain proportion leaves after duration a, a + 1, etc. These proportions can be denoted by q_a, $q_{a + 1} \cdots$ For a cohort, the age pattern of leaving corresponds to the educational makeup of the cohort. The question is whether two subcohorts that differ in this age pattern also differ in their occupational makeup at age 30. Put differently, is the path to high occupational status through education? The same question has often been asked at the micro level, but the answer will be different. However, the macro and micro level answers differ. To see the difference between the two answers, consider the following table.

Occupational Prestige/Income

Education	Cohort 1				Cohort 2		
	Occ 1	Occ 2	Total		Occ 1	Occ 2	Total
Education 1	75	75	150	Education 1	90	60	150
Education 2	25	25	50	Education 2	10	40	50
Total	100	100		Total	100	100	

The two cohorts are identical in educational and occupational make-up. But while there is no association between the two variables for cohort 1, for cohort

2 the chance of attaining occupation 2 is much higher for those with education level 2 than for those with education level 1.

If the two cohorts are pooled, the association becomes:

$$165 \quad 135$$
$$35 \quad 65$$

This pooled table shows that better educated individuals have a greater chance of attaining a better job, but it obscures the macro-level patterns described above. One could easily imagine a situation in which there is no cohort-by-cohort variation in ability, family background, educational attainment, or occupational composition, and yet there is a persistent micro-level association between educational and occupational attainment.

HAS PERFORMANCE ON TESTS BEEN OVEREMPHASIZED?

Among the rival views, the ability hypothesis has often been favored in the research on status attainment. Correspondingly, sociologists with an interest in schooling have focused much of their attention on explaining the variance in the test scores of individuals. Project Talent, and subsequently the Equal Education Opportunity Survey (EEOS), dramatically shifted attention away from an exclusive focus on inputs (such as facilities and teacher characteristics) to a particular outcome, namely standardized achievement test scores (SATs). In one influential analysis after another, sociologists have more or less taken for granted that achievement as measured by standardized tests is the schooling outcome most worth explaining. SATs have been used in many major studies in recent years including the eight year study in the 1930s (which used many other criteria as well), Project Talent and the EEOS in the 1960s, the National Longitudinal Survey (NLS) in the 1970s, and more recently the analysis of high school and beyond data (Coleman-Hoffer and Kilgore 1982). Perhaps the prevailing sentiment among some prominent sociologists in this field is succinctly expressed by Coleman, Hoffer, and Kilgore (1982) when they assert "although these cognitive skills constitute only one type of educational outcome, it is one on which there is little disagreement and one which is relevant to both elementary and secondary education."

The Search for Ability

The truth is that the validity of SATs has never been fully accepted, even as they were becoming firmly entrenched in the fabric of American education.

Teachers rarely consult standardized test results (Herman and Dorr-Bremme 1983), and few administrators consider them to be terribly useful (Sproull and Zubrow 1981). Testing was plagued by major public criticisms during the 1920s and again in the late 1950s and mid-seventies. From Hoffmann's book, *The Tyranny of Testing* and Vance Packard's *The Naked Society,* to a series of articles in the *National Elementary Principal* in 1975, critics have leveled devastating attacks on standardized testing. Yet, achievement tests are being constructed today in the same manner they were 50 years ago and being used in social research without much thought given to their meaning.

The Impetus for Testing

The waves of public criticism noted above did not deter the march of testing technology. Haney (1984, p. 615) writes that by mid-century mental testing clearly had become well established in education in the United States. There was already a precedent by 1889 when Joseph Mayer Rice was commissioned by *Forum* magazine to prepare an appraisal of public education. Determined to render an objective assessment, he placed no reliance on reports by school officials (Cremin 1964:4). Some regard his survey as probably the very first to use a standardized test of ability (Cronbach et al. 1982; Haney 1984). Tests were used in the early part of this century to demonstrate that large numbers of children were overage for their placement in school. This type of criticism sparked a school efficiency movement. By 1925, school superintendents were routinely using standardized tests to create homogenous grouping and curricular tracks (Haney 1984). Again during World War II tests were used extensively to screen draftees for work assignments.

The use of tests received further impetus with the National Defense Education Act of 1958 which provided federal funds to establish and maintain a program for testing aptitudes and abilities of students in public secondary schools for the purpose of identifying outstanding students. However, it was the Elementary Secondary Education Act of 1965, which mandated evaluations of all Title I programs for children from low income families, that researchers must thank for the wide availability of student achievement test scores today. SATs received still another boost in the education amendments of 1974 requiring the U.S. Office of Education to develop models embodying uniform methods of evaluation to yield comparable results across the Title I programs of different local education agencies. It has been estimated that up to 90 percent of local Title I evaluations used norm-reference tests for estimating program effectiveness (Reisner et al. 1982). However, in recognition of the shortcomings of such tests, the National Assessment of Education program was created. That body uses other approaches to assessment which potentially might be more effectively utilized by social scientists. At the present time some influential members of congress are supporting proposed legislation for a national education examination that would entrench testing even more deeply in the process of education.

What is Wrong with SATs?

Ironically, even as the use of SATs was becoming so widespread, many educational researchers were becoming highly critical of the use of such tests for program evaluation. In the words of Hanson and Schutz, (1986, p. 101) "standardized achievement tests continue to be used as the primary criterion measures in the evaluation of basic skills programs despite explicit recommendations against this practice by many testing and evaluation experts." Among the half dozen sources cited by Hanson and Schutz there are two legendary figures in testing and evaluation, Ralph Tyler and Oatis Burrows. All of the critics argue that SATs are designed and constructed for selection purposes and hence are poor indicators of instructional program accomplishment. Several objections have been raised about the validity of SATs in general which have direct implications for their utility as measures of schooling outcomes.

First, the way such tests are constructed make them poorly suited for making comparisons among schools or organizational units within schools. Testing in schools began with the purpose of ranking students to select those most likely to benefit from special instruction (Haertel 1985). Many of the early testers, including Binet viewed intelligence tests as a device to help solve a practical problem, namely the identification of children in need of special instruction. Accordingly, the key to constructing SATs is the power of each test item to discriminate among test takers. This quality is referred to as a norm-reference test (NRT). Such criterion can be justified when the purpose is to select and categorize test takers. However, using them to assess differences among organizations is another matter. Since SATs are designed to maximize variance among individuals *within* classrooms, they are poorly adapted to the purpose of identifying sources of variance *between* classrooms, schools and other organizational units. Aggregating test scores tends to mask rather than accentuate the variances (see also Alexander and Griffin 1976; and Hubert Blalock's discussion in this volume).

Secondly, because of the way they are measured, NRTs can result in unrecognized mismatches between what is being tested and what is taught in schools. Thus, Hansen and Schutz (1986) conclude that SATs provide a generally poor fit with instruction as usually covered in a given basic skills program. Despite the label "standardized *achievement* tests" it is more appropriate to see them as measures of general competence, having a heavy middle class bias, rather than achievement within schools. As Herbert Blalock stresses (see pages 60–61), it is essential to distinguish school outputs from their products, and general competency tests are ill-suited for that purpose precisely because they do not necessarily reflect what schools are attempting to achieve. A better way to distinguish outputs from products is to construct tests more closely tied to specific schools and curricula and synchronized with instruction.

On this point Hansen and Schutz compared the results of three types of tests that corresponded more or less to the instructional programs being evaluated. They concluded that the SAT provided results "that are of little use and are often actually misleading for program evaluation purposes" (p. 110). They observe that when the instructional scope was definite, the proficiency attained was uniformly high. When the instructional scope was indefinite, proficiency was only moderately high. Moreover, the program evaluation interpretation was in sharp contrast to the interpretation based on grade equivalent score analysis, which showed student attainment below the norm.

Third, because the objective of SATs is to maximize variance among examinees, items covering important topics or skills are eliminated when all the examinees get the items right or wrong. Many writers advocate another form of test, the criterion referenced tests (CRTs), as an antidote to NRTs (see Popham 1978a, 1978b, 1980). When tests are used only to rank examinees, the validity can be established by simple correlations of test scores with total score. However, criterion referenced interpretations do not depend on comparisons to the performance of other examinees. The purpose is to determine what each individual can or cannot do in terms of specific behaviors. Testing for functional literacy is an example. Functionally literate high school graduates should be able to summarize orally a newspaper article, fill out a credit card, job or license application, learn to operate appliances by reading the instructions, make informed choices among products in the supermarket, and read popular literature.

Fourth, a closely related criticism is that neither norm referenced nor criterion referenced tests assess complex reasoning skills. They put a premium on speed and efficiency rather than on thoughtful reflection. A machine-scored multiple-choice test cannot pretend to provide anything more than an *indirect* measure of what children know or how they think. Recognizing a correct answer on a test is a quite different skill, relying on a different form of reasoning, than actually creating the answer to a test. Achievement tests usually use a fixed format from which the test taker must choose, and situations where school learning will be applied rarely present problems in this neat, closed form. The relationship between test performance and out-of-school performance is weak indeed. Except for their ability to predict future socio-economic status (SES) and further schooling, the predictive power of academic achievement tests has been disappointing (Collins 1979; McClelland 1973).

Finally, because they are being used to compare and assess the performance of teachers, schools, school districts and states, SATs have become very vulnerable to political influences. For several years virtually every state education department has released information showing that children in their particular state are reading, writing, and calculating above the national average. Since this is impossible, the figures may more closely reflect a lag or manipulation than performance. For example, some schools adapt their courses to the tests, and teachers may alter their teaching to anticipate what their students will need to know. Some districts routinely release samples of tests and tutor students. Still other districts excuse students with learning problems from the tests. An added complication is that curriculum the norms themselves may not be changed rapidly enough to reflect actual changes in test performance.

Implications

Testing is ingrained throughout the society. SATs are generally used in the interstices of the social institution as a signal that socialization experiences have been completed—entry into elementary school, placement in special classes, transition from high school to college and from college to jobs. Tests are used by state and federal level civil service agencies, and by schools and colleges to screen applicants. However, these uses of tests have different implications than using them to assess the effects of instruction over a given time interval.

There is a place for SATs in social research. They may sometimes be suitable for measuring the cumulative effects of years of schooling, provided that the appropriate time span can be identified. What we are asking is, how long can social scientists continue to ignore the criticisms? How long can we rely on such a narrow measure of outcomes? Research based exclusively on SATs as output measures for schools may have caused damage to the enterprise of schooling by narrowing curricular choices and focusing teaching-learning on specific test items to the neglect of the character formation functions of schools (Etzioni 1982; Hansen and Schutz 1984; Steadman 1987). More to the point, the extensive use of SATs seems to have deflected the attention of sociologists from the fundamental sociological issues which only this discipline is capable of addressing.

WHAT OUTCOMES SHOULD BE MEASURED?

For over two decades then, eminent sociologists have employed routine economic models to explain perplexing psychological processes associated with learning. But cognitive achievement, however measured, is not the most important outcome of American public schools. Formal education has made other, more salient, contributions. Some of them, including some of the outcomes mentioned earlier in this chapter, will be considered further in this section.

Schooling Outcomes in Historical Perspective

Over two decades ago one of the authors (Corwin 1965, pp. 70–88) reviewed the evolution of goals in education and came to some conclusions that are relevant to this discussion:

> The initial settlement of America must be understood in terms of the Protestant revolt . . . the Puritans aimed at nothing less than the complete domination of the society . . . and not surprisingly, the school, which in Europe traditionally had been the handmaiden of the church, was completely dominated by religion in the colonial period . . . the original primary function of schools was neither political nor vocational, but religious . . . traces of religion's early influence (remain); it can be detected in stress on deportment and character training . . . narrowly moral criteria often have tended to take precedence over intellectual ones in hiring and evaluating teachers. . .
>
> As the influence of religion declined, educational practices eventually became tailored to the needs of business . . . (however) it was only after labor unrest had developed in the middle of the nineteenth century that business leaders seriously turned their attention to the support of public education . . . it occurred to them that public schools could indoctrinate children with the business ideology as easily as they had formed religious character . . . indeed, compulsory education itself came in the wake of mass unemployment and after labor leaders had begun to give active support to public education . . . laws requiring children to remain in school until the age of 16 followed closely upon laws establishing the same minimum age requirements for child labor in industry. . .
>
> It is certain that any group whose primary concern is to influence the younger generation will be carefully watched by political leaders. . . . As levels of government have achieved more control, the goals of education have become more narrowly prescribed in terms of the interests of the state. In many circles, education is believed to be equivalent to citizenship training . . . patriotism to a local legion or to a specific country. . .

Also, play has been institutionalized within schools as leisure time, extra-curricular activities in the public schools evolved through periods of abstinence, tolerance, and eventually institutionalization (Frederick 1959). Today, teachers supervise extra-curricular activities as part of their normal duties, and academic credit is assigned to some activities for which a teacher assumes full responsibility. As some leisure activities became institutionalized, however, others were omitted and ignored. Struggles for favorite status developed among the teachers responsible for various activities.

Recent Developments

During some periods within recent years, there has been intensive concern about the ineffectiveness of schools as measured by cognitive outcomes. After the 1958 National Defense Education Act the federal government encouraged schools to give more attention to the cognitive achievement levels of categories of students and subjects. But again, the purpose was directly related to international competition, particularly the search for scientific talent, not to the general intellectual commitment of schools. During the past decade the school effectiveness and back-to-basics movements, spearheaded by coalitions of leaders from business, politics, and education, have re-emphasized the cognitive outcomes. During 1983 alone a wave of more than 20 reports and studies of schools in the United States promoted an environment of dissatisfaction with public education of seemingly crisis proportions. One panel of distinguished Americans warns that the "educational foundations of our society are presently being eroded by a rising tide of mediocrity that threatens our very future as a nation and as a people" (National Commission on Excellence in Education 1983). The subsequent debates have produced a lengthy list of recommendations for the reform of school curriculum and teaching practices, the time students spend in school, and ways to attract and retain competent teachers. Although the evidence for the charges is frail and uneven (cf. Peterson 1983), not since the Conant report (1959) has the American high school been under so much pressure to raise academic standards.

Yet, the clamor probably will not change the priorities within local schools and classrooms. Similar movements have been deflected many times before. The triumph of the comprehensive classroom structure in elementary schools (and in modified form in high schools) is testimony to the continuing priority of cultural over intellectual goals. As Conant (1967) emphasized in his historical account, the comprehensive school is ideally suited to the task of assimilating minorities in multi-ethnic, stratified communities. Specialized classrooms, programs, and schools may be better equipped for the purpose of tailoring teaching resources to different ability levels, intellectual talents, and learning difficulties. But the public historically has rejected specialization as a solution other than in its most primitive forms, such as grouping and tracking. The forms of specialization that have evolved have been used for custodial purposes and job training rather than to help students learn intellectual skills.

Comprehensive schools are believed to be superior settings for forming moral character and for sustaining democracy.

Implications

Clearly then, schools were founded for conflicting purposes. They have always emphasized moral, normative, and political forms of socialization as well as experience with co-curricular leisure activities. Indeed, their primary purpose may very well be to form character (e.g., Etzioni 1982). Cognitive outcomes are only one of many competing priorities, and they seldom have been the most important. Privileged groups expect public educators to help them secure their property and keep other people from asserting their power. Low income, disfranchised groups look to them for help in improving their position in society. In recent years many other writers have reiterated the theme that schools were set up to socialize compliant workers and to Americanize children from alien, offensive backgrounds (Bowles and Gintis 1976; Rubinson 1986). Collins (1979:110) echoed the familiar idea that the arguments for public high schools and for compulsory attendance were based on rationalizations about good citizenship, political stability, and moral qualities, and only infrequently about learning skills and benefits to industry. "Compulsory attendance laws," he wrote, "grew out of two related issues: truancy and control over recalcitrant youths." Secondary education was conceived primarily as socialization, and the curriculum was initially established to emphasize classical studies quite remote from commercial life.

It is curious that from all of this, Collins concludes that the primary function of schools is certification rather than socialization. True, they do not merely teach intellectual and technical skills. True, they do certify. But they also socialize. True, diplomas and degrees are used by employers to gain power advantages and favorable public images. But we think the argument that employers look only at superficial credentials has been carried too far. The position probably has been aided by surveys which pay more attention to measuring the formal qualifications of individuals than to changes in their character make up. But realistically, certification is primarily a mechanism for controlling socialization, not a substitute for it. Credentials certify that someone has been subjected to certain types of socialization experiences in addition to the acquisition of specific skills. The history of education is a struggle over who will control the certification process precisely *because* of the presumed power of schools to socialize youth. In any case, research strategies that focus exclusively on the cognitive outcomes of schooling cannot be easily justified unless one is willing to overlook the historical character formation functions of schools.

But of course the issue is more complex than simply determining whether educational organizations do socialize the individuals who are certified. Much of the learning takes place outside schools and colleges—in the family, the community, the church, and the workplace. Therefore formal educational institutions must start with the foundation laid by the training system outside schools and colleges. The research challenge lies in determining the relative contributions of school and these extra-school training systems, both for intellectual and skill development and for indoctrinated values such as masculinity, femininity, leadership, courage, compassion, caring, inventiveness, entrepreneurship, neighborliness, citizenship, justice, etc.

The following table (Table 1) was prepared as a means of summarizing some of the diverse outcomes others have attributed directly or indirectly to systems of formal education. In preparing this taxonomy it has been assumed that no one expects all students who finish a given grade (e.g., the tenth) to have learned equally well everything they were exposed to in their courses. It has been assumed further that everyone may not necessarily be exposed to the same content areas. Thus, students in various tracks may differ in the kinds of knowledge to which they have had access. Also, it has been assumed that among learning outcomes one expects from students are attitudes and behaviors that are not specifically related to content areas of courses. As noted, schools have been expected to transform the young into contributing members of society, imbue them with a strong commitment to certain cultural ideals, increase their skills in interpersonal relationships, contribute to their physical and mental well-being, and so on (Goodlad 1979). It is not taken for granted that teachers try to imbue students from different backgrounds with the same set of non-subject-related behaviors. It may very well be, for example, that teachers emphasize patterns such as independent and critical thinking, creativity, and questioning more among students from upper classes than among those from lower classes. A point worth emphasizing is that subject-related outcomes and non-subject related outcomes are likely to be interrelated. Furthermore, all outcomes are likely to be influenced by what goes on in the school and what takes place elsewhere (e.g., the family, community, etc.) If this is so, it has important design and analytical implications concerning investigations aimed at estimating school effects.

Diverse Functions of Schools

A generation ago Warner et al. lamented that many parents are interested only in whether schooling helps their children get well paying jobs, to the neglect of other social functions schools perform. The other functions they mentioned were: providing a basis of communication and common core of

Table 1. A Taxonomy of Developments or Outcomes That Can be Traced
Directly or Indirectly to the Operation of the Education System

---

MACRO-LEVEL

New entrants to the labor force and to other types of functional membership in society:
number and composition (by educational attainment) of leavers from the education
system.

Demand for higher education and new admissions to institutions of higher learning.

"Wastage" at school resulting from dropping out, repetition of courses, grade levels, and
so on.

Impact on various industries such as teacher training, textbook publishing industry,
construction industry, and transportation industry attributable directly or indirectly to
schools' need for inputs from them.

Impact on research pertaining, for example, to educational testing services, to the creation
of instructional materials, to the development of methods of evaluation of intervention
programs (e.g., in assessing whether schools perpetuate or moderate socioeconomic
inequalities across generations), to the construction of process models (e.g., those
focusing on flows of pupils from grade to grade or on resource requirements, or
scheduling with reference to individual schools; those viewing education system as an
integral part of the wider socioeconomic system) and so on.

School-related issues fueling political action (e.g., the mobilization of political forces in the
United States during the period since the 1950s in frequent efforts to alter or protect
school-finance-related arrangements) or serving as testing grounds for lobbyists, citizen
groups, future leaders, etc.

School system serving as a push or pull factor with respect to population migration between
territorial communities.

Impact in local and state economies, including other service industries (such as hospitals,
fire and police services) that compete for limited tax dollars.

MICRO-LEVEL

Information absorbed and assimilated with respect to matters that fall under the sciences
and humanities.

Personal reputation of students and teachers.

Skills acquired with respect to communication, comprehension, computation, athletic and
physical prowess, manual dexterity, management of crises in interpersonal relations
and/or organizational contexts.

Attitudes, orientation, and values pertaining to patriotism, respect for others' rights,
industriousness, self-discipline, commitment, critical thinking, self-direction, creativity,
cooperation, conforming to rules and expectations.

---

traditions and values, teaching children to work and live together, and preparing people to challenge and improve the social order; most of this is not
measured by standardized testing.

The ability to write clearly and creatively, to speak before groups, and
familiarity with the arts and the theater are usually considered basic skills, but
they are not well represented in standardized achievement tests. Kerckoff

(1976) further suggests that learning interpersonal skills, manual dexterity and the ability to use autonomy effectively are equally important outcomes. Understanding how organizations work and a person's ability to cope with organizational problems are skills that often are learned informally in the process of attending school. Such skills are at least as critical as technical competence for occupational success (Corwin 1986; Schein 1968). More generally, it is often understood that students will become politically astute and interested in political events.

Other products of schools include the quality of life they provide, and the opportunity for students to participate in decisions that affect them. In view of the high incidence of teenage suicide, alienation is another important dimension, a kind of inadvertent product that may be associated with certain schooling practices. For example, student alienation may be related to rules, specialization, teacher's education and other bureaucratic aspects of schools (Anderson 1966). On a more positive note, Etzioni (1982) stresses the importance of self discipline, or commitment, as a prerequisite to learning, and presumably to occupational success as well. Commitment, he believes, is fostered when authority relationships between adults and students are based on respect for students and reinforced by praise and other positive sanctions.

Typically, individual data are collected and aggregated to the level of organizations, and therefore the usual evaluation produces data on *individuals* to answer questions about the *organization* (Light 1979:551; Baron and Bielby 1980:738). Instead, organizational data are needed to evaluate that which is distinctively organizational about schools. One example of this kind of output from schools concerns what they do to and for communities. They are sources of community identity, cheap labor and college recruitment. Furthermore, concentrations of teenagers in and around schools sometimes terrorize neighborhoods, while in other cases schools are centers of civic activity. The reputation of schools attracts or repels parents, and firms often decide where to locate based on the reputations of the schools. School districts also act as political arenas and testing grounds for political candidates, and they often become political targets. In view of the recurrent controversies among the public over course content, textbooks, academic standards and disciplinary policies, it also would be relevant to know the extent to which lobbyists, citizen groups, and students participate in the important decisions reflecting priorities, policies and practices. These variables affect the ability of schools to accommodate diversity and flexibility in the changing heterogeneous society, and to be responsive to emerging public issues (see also, Lotto 1983). Given value conflicts among the general public, opportunities for citizens to participate in education programs provide a substitute for the absence of a clear mandate.

Implications

We have thus far been considering outcomes one at a time. This makes sense only for outcomes that are independent of one another, or that are negatively correlated, such that emphasis on one is detrimental to others. But in practice they often occur simultaneously and are present or absent in varying degrees. They may be positively correlated and reinforce one another; for example, a good performance on tests may also contribute positively to character development. Or, they may have a compensatory relationship such that if one is achieved, some others can be ignored; if learning a foreign language sharpens grammatical skills, it is not necessary to teach grammar as a separate subject. Or, an outcome may be a perquisite to others, and some will be incidental *by-products* of other outcomes. For example, as a by-product of learning mathematics, a person develops skills in logic, more effective study habits, and a generalized ability to discipline oneself. Field trips to museums, or to observe a legislative body, can enhance a student's awareness and interest in art and politics. This might occur even though test scores in these subjects do not improve, and conversely, high test scores in these subjects do not necessarily signal changes in values and behavior to the extent they are by-products of something other than cognitive performance.

It seems certain that outcomes form complex and often highly interdependent patterns. Yet, the approach that customarily has been taken is to select one dependent variable—usually test scores, sometimes literary skills, and only rarely more complex outcomes such as political awareness—and focus exclusively on it. While perhaps this tack can be defended on pragmatic grounds, we are uneasy with the over-simplification that results. Instead, we urge that models should be used which respect the multi-dimensional property of outcomes that, realistically, can be expected of schools. Rather than a single dependent variable, research designs for schooling outcomes should use clusters of dependent variables.

Methods of Analysis Commonly Employed: Is There a Better Option?

As is well known, even when the focus is on a single dependent variable, inappropriate methodology may lead to misleading inferences. Failure to take into account relevant variables (e.g., the conditions that affect test performance) is a case in point (Haney 1984). It is indeed surprising that test builders were not sensitive to the pitfalls of omission of relevant factors, given the developments in statistical methodology prior to World War I. History of statistics shows that by the 1920s regression analysis, permitting in social research the sifting, evaluating, and comparing the effects of independent variables on a dependent variable, had started to predominate applications in social research (see, e.g., Stigler 1986). Even many of the basic notions of experimental designs (Fechner 1860) had been developed several decades before World War I. So if test builders were not guided by regression models, the basic notions of analysis of variance, or the fundamental premise that experimental outcomes are affected by an endless variety of factors, it is not because the ideas were unavailable. They had been expounded in detail in extant publications (see, however, Stanley 1971).

A number of scholars have recently addressed the issue of appropriate methodology when attempting to measure the so-called school effects. For example Alexander, McPartland, and Cook (1981: 4, 23) refer to the advantages of focusing on "outlier" (exceptional) schools, and using covariance models. Steadman (1987) refers to a technique focusing on extreme-differences based on outliers, and reports that when this technique is used the estimate of the impact of schools on test scores is two to three times the corresponding estimate obtained by other techniques.

Although the notion of hierarchical layers of contexts (e.g., classroom within school within school district within state within region in the United States) has been often mentioned in the literature (see, e.g., Herriott and Hodgkins 1973), formal models reflecting the structure have not been frequently used in the analysis of educational outcomes. To give a flavor of multi-layer models, let us consider schools, classrooms within schools, and pupils within classrooms. A multi-layer model for the measurements on a response variable (e.g., a test score) is

$$Z_{kij} = \omega_{kij} + \vartheta_{ki} + \varphi_k \tag{1}$$

where Z_{kij} is the measurement for the jth pupil in the ith classroom within the kth school, ω_{kij} is a "pupil effect," ϑ_{ki} a "classroom effect," and φ_k is a "school effect." At each layer we set up a model relating the corresponding "effect" to a set of appropriate explanatory variables. Thus we may set

$$\omega_{kij} = \alpha_0 + \alpha_{1(ki)}W_{1(kij)} + \ldots + \alpha_{p(ki)}W_{p(kij)} + e_{kij} \tag{2}$$

$$\vartheta_{ki} = \beta_0 + \beta_{1(k)}X_{1(ki)} + \ldots + \beta_{q(k)}X_{q(ki)} + u_{ki} \tag{3}$$

$$\varphi_k = \gamma_0 + \gamma_1 Y_{1(k)} + \ldots + \gamma_r Y_{r(k)} + v_k \tag{4}$$

where e_{kij}, u_{ki}, and v_k are residuals, assumed to be random, with expectations zero and standard deviations $\sigma_e(ki)$, $\sigma_u(k)$, and σ_v respectively; the W's are explanatory variables at the pupil level, X's those at the classroom level, and Y's at the school level. The "effect" coefficients (the α's, β's, and γ's) may also be assumed to be random variables. For example we may assume that

$$\alpha_{l(ki)} = \delta_0 + \delta_1 X^*_{ki} + \epsilon_{ki} \tag{5}$$

which says the pupil-level "effect" of the lth explanatory variable is a linear function of a property of the classroom involved plus a random residual.

Computer programs are now available to estimate such models (see, e.g., Goldstein, 1987; also see Mason and Wong, 1985). If all covariances of residuals are zero, the variance of Z can be partitioned into components for school, class, and pupil. The model can be extended to cover longitudinal data on individuals, with covariates (measured explanatory variables) or a multilevel, nested structure. It can be further extended to cover two or more response variables, giving rise to, for example, multivariate, multilevel mixed (random and fixed) effects models. This last class of models is of interest for analyzing the time patterns of a multiplicity of schooling outcomes, i.e., time (e.g., age) patterns of changes brought about by schooling in a specific multi-trait complex (cognitive skills, problem-solving abilities, value orientations, and so on).

HAS THE ESSENCE OF THE EDUCATIONAL PROCESS BEEN CAPTURED?

Starting with the Equal Education Opportunity Survey (Coleman et al. 1966), a number of surveys have suggested or implied that the quality of schooling has little discernible relationship to intellectual achievement, esepcially in comparison to the overwhelming effects of home background. The following remark is typical:

> . . . factors in the student's family background are probably of considerably greater importance in determining aspiration levels than are the characteristics of the school he attends or the neighboi,o˷d in which he resides. This finding has been confirmed by other writers . . . (Sewell and Hauser 1975, p. 7).

Crudeness of the Measures

Conclusions such as these, which seem to challenge the efficacy of schools as places of learning, are necessarily based on superficial measures of school properties, because critical features of schools have not been faithfully trans-lated into survey questions. For example, most of the school-level measures included in the EEOS pertained to resources or school facilities such as per pupil expenditures; volumes-per-student in the school library; the presence or absence of science laboratories; and teachers' college majors verbal scores, experience, and years of education (see Corwin 1975, pp. 146–149). The U.S. Civil Rights Commission team included measures of the comprehensiveness of the curriculum and extra-curricular activities.

Needed Measures

With their intuitive grasp of how schools work, Warner et al. clearly saw the impact of course offerings and how students are assigned to them (p. 75), peer cultures (p. 64), and the priority given to class distinctions over ability as teachers "reshuffle" students into curricular programs. Similar views were expressed more forcefully later (Alexander and McDill 1976; Cicourel and Kitsuse 1963; Oakes 1985; Rosenbaum 1975; 1976). In 1976, Kerckoff called for systematic data regarding the way teachers and counselors make decisions to assign grades, divide a class into reading groups or other functional units, advise on course choices or encourage participation in extra-curricular activities. Perhaps more important than ability grouping and tracking practices is the fluidity with which students move through tracks. A host of ethnographies published since the 1970s have documented numerous instances of overt and subtle discrimination practices, many related to the inflexibility of ability grouping which typically have not been tapped in survey designs. If grouping were used in earnest as a learning mechanism, the results could be very different from the numerous recorded instances when it has served primarily as an instrument of social control.

One must include high on the list of candidates for affecting outcomes the decision-making process, rules, professional norms and educational standards, evaluation practices and incentive and systems, teaching styles, formalization, specialization among the faculty, classroom control structure, peer cultures, and work-study opportunities. For example, are students encouraged to ask questions, to help design their own learning experiences, to speak in public, to write analytically or creatively, or to participate in community civic, social and political programs? Mortimore and Yamoor (1987) further suggest that the way the curriculum is structured may teach youths how to use autonomy and to cope with the complexities of jobs, and that norms regarding tardiness and absenteeism, for example, may affect later job performance. *Configurations* of such properties, which may be thought of as the organization's learning "climate," generate the experiences that in turn shape what is really learned in school.

From his reading of the effective schools literature, Steadman (1987) found still other properties associated with schools that have high test scores: (1)

they emphasize cultural pluralism and bilingual education and are responsive to students' ethnic and racial identities; (2) serve small neighborhoods and cultivate parental support by bringing parents into the educational program through parent/teacher councils, conferences and workshops to help them supervise learning at home; (3) provide special programs in areas beyond the basics, such as art, drama, history, ecology, and anthropology; (4) use a relaxed, humane approach to discipline. The unanswered question is whether these patterns are causally linked.

Finally, it has been frequently noted that the fundamental unit of analysis should be the classroom, rather than the school, because that is the action setting, the place where authority relationships, assignments, and evaluations are negotiated (Alexander, McPartland, and Cook 1981:7,21; Barr and Dreeben 1983; Metz 1978; McNeil 1981). Both classroom and school-wide measures are needed.

The following taxonomy summarizes critical dimensions of the schooling process that should be considered. In preparing this taxonomy, it has been assumed that the student produces "education" by combining his or her own time with the goods and services he or she receives. It is recognized that the focus should be the classroom, which is nested within the school, which, in turn, is nested in the school district within a territorial community that forms part of a higher-order entity such as a state, which in turn is nested in a still higher order unit such as a country. It is recognized further that each student in a classroom has a history of schooling (e.g., a low-track history, generated by a tracking system that does not necessarily give due attention to the student's potential,) and that this history partly determines the goods and services that reach the student and the fraction thereof that he or she uses in creating "education." The classroom activity is viewed as one involving teacher-curriculum, teacher-student, student-curriculum, and student-peer interactions. These interactions take place in an environment which extends beyond the classroom to the school, the community, the state, and so on, each with a history. There are varying techniques to present instructional stimuli, to translate the stimuli to learning, to store and retrieve what has been learned. Instruction as understood herein extends beyond reading, writing, and arithmetic, to the sciences and humanities, to proper citizenship, and to self-direction, independence, creativity, and so on.

As emphasized just now schooling takes place in classrooms within schools nested in school districts which are in turn nested in territorial communities within political and administrative divisions within nations. Furthermore, since what we usually mean by education is much more than schooling, we should consider in addition to schools (their environment, structure, and functioning) other units that impart education (the family, the church, etc.).

An additional complication we should emphasize is that the educational

Table 2.   A Taxonomy of Critical Dimensions of Schooling Process

1. Teachers

    Academic and social backgrounds
      Values and beliefs
      Early socialization and socialization during professional training programs
      Norms and ideologies about teaching endorsed by peers
    Supply and demand
      Number of qualified teachers
      Competitive position of district/school
        with respect to other districts
        with respect to other industries (activities)
      Output of graduates from teacher training colleges
    School's recruitment process
      Applicable teacher certification standards and procedures
      Accreditation status and resources of schools/districts

2. Students

    Composition of student body
      Ability, values, and dispositions
      Ethnicity, social class and other ascribed characteristics
      Characteristics of parents and neighborhood
    School's policies and practices
      With respect to admission, testing, promotion and tracking
      Number and clarity of rules governing the above
      Enforcement practices

3. Relationships between Teachers and Students

    Personal Relationships
      Particularism and universalism between teachers and students
      Mutual trust, alienation and social distance
      Priority teachers give to subject matter and to personal development of students
    Authority Relationships
      Time spent by teacher on pupil control
      Punitiveness, consistency and fairness of teachers in disciplining students
      Emphasis on student conformity to teacher authority and established classroom
        routine
      Emphasis on student autonomy and independence (self-direction, creativity, critical
        thinking)
      Student involvement in classroom decision making

4. Curriculum and Teaching Technologies

    Content and coverage
      Specificity
      Time allocated to content areas
    Effectiveness of techniques used
      For the presentation of stimuli (textbooks and other publications, visual aids,
        lectures)

Table 2. *(Continued)*

For the absorption and assimilation of information (reading, writing, doing exercises, discussing, taking tests, disciplining oneself)
For storage and retrieval (memorizing, using pocket calculators, computers, notes, etc.)
Effectiveness of beliefs about learning and learning theories used
Clarity of goals
Variety and types of activities organized
Materials such as textbooks and visual aids used
Tests given
Time set aside for learning activity
Time required to do homework

5. Relationships between Students and Curriculum

Student participation in shaping the curriculum
Formal procedures within the school
Informal influences within classrooms, such as negotiation
Translation of instructional stimuli into learning
Time spent on learning activity, i.e., combining with own time the goods and services offered to produce "education"
Off-task activities, e.g., day-dreaming

6. Relationships among Students

Number and makeup of student subcultures
Peer pressure to conform to or to deviate from patterns of behavior expected in classroom and school
Cliquishness
Trust, cooperation, and goodwill among students
Competition among students for grades and recognition
Basis of prestige—grades, athletics, social and cultural skills, socio-economic status
Basis of peer esteem—the degree to which students like and help one another classroom discord—arguing, fighting with each other in the class

7. Administrative Structure

Power and Authority structure
Respective roles of school administration, school district boards, state agencies, federal agencies
Composition and constituency of school boards
Professionalization of teachers and teacher organizations
Division of labor
Specialization among units and teachers within schools/districts
Services of supporting staff such as counselors

8. External Environment

Legal-political system
Laws and regulations which determine opportunities, options and constraints
Priorities supported by government agencies

Table 2.   (Continued)

Pressures exerted by organized and unorganized citizen groups
Role of parents, law-enforcement officers, courts, citizen groups, etc., as disci-
    plinarians, adjudicators, reformers, etc.
Resources
Wealth of school district and of the state
Distribution of resources among/within regions, states, districts, and schools
"Out-of-school" resources, such as public libraries, reading materials in the home,
    and the like available to students
Competing demands for resources and priorities attached to them (in the family,
    community, state, and national budgets)
Demography and ecology of the community and school
Mobility and heterogeneity of the school population, rates of economic and political
    change
Socio-political composition of school district and state
Physical (classroom facilities—crowdedness, noise and other disturbance coming
    from outside; school building facilities)
Relationships among components of the education system
Social classroom nested within school
School nested within school district
School district nested within territorial community
Territorial community nested within state
State nested within nation

---

process is something that is spread over a long time interval. This sensitizes us
to the time pattern of learning. We expect that by the time a student graduates
from one cycle (primary, junior high, senior high, etc.) he or she should have
absorbed a certain amount of information, acquired a certain set of skills,
become indoctrinated with certain values, outlooks, and so on. The time
pattern of progress toward these end results may be nonlinear. Thus, the
progress during the second year in high school may not be the same as that in
the first year in high school, and so on. It is possible that the progress made
during a given interval (e.g., the senior year in high school) may be a function
of the level reached by the beginning of the interval.

Sørenson refers to a negative feedback model. (See the Sørensen-Hallinan
1977, paper in *Sociology of Education*) Also see the Entwisle-Alexander
paper, for the present volume. According to the Sørensen-Hallinan model, the
rate of change in the information level is a linear function with negative slope
of the information level attained. In symbols $dy(t)/dt = s + by(t)$, where $y(t)$
is the information level as of time t, $dy(t)/dt$ is the rate of change in it, and s
and b are constants, the latter being negative. However, the negative feedback
model may not always reflect reality. It may very well be that the more one

learns the greater (rather than less) will be one's appetite for learning more. Thus exposure received in the classroom may *at times* stimulate exploration in the school library, in the community library, at home, and so on, in a rather explosive fashion. Therefore the amount of information a student absorbs on a subject matter during a given interval is not necessarily constrained by the exposure given in the classroom, contrary to the Sørensen-Hallinan postulate. Also if there is a test, the chances are that more information is absorbed and assimilated as the time of the test nears than before. Some students, on the other hand, may be in the habit of absorbing the information supplied when or soon after it is supplied. For them the pace of learning is likely to be more even, since information supply tends to be spread somewhat evenly over the duration of the course. [This seems to be true of mathematics, biology, etc.] If, however, a fixed amount of information is presented all at once (as in the case of computer assisted independent study), then the rate of change in the information absorbed and assimilated may show different time patterns for different students, depending upon such things as study habits.

The time dimension of the education process thus seems to elude simple theorizing. Be that as it may, one has to address it. How the time dimension is handled has implications for data collection and analysis (see the remarks in the chapter on education as a component of a larger social system; also see the Entwisle-Alexander chapter).

Some of the factors that affect learning (e.g., absorption and assimilation of information) may be time dependent (see Blalock's chapter). Thus over the span of three years covering the high school cycle, many changes may occur in the school, in the community, in the nation, and in the world. Some of the changes may significantly affect the outcomes of the education process. Obviously, the data and analytical problems created by time-dependence of covariates may be less serious for short "observation" periods (e.g., one semester or even one year) over which one examines the change (e.g., in the information absorbed and assimilated.)

Some Progress

It is perhaps unfortunate that the surveys which have been most influential—such as the EEOS and Sewell and Hauser's study that used the vacuous measure, "years of education"—often have not been informed either by organizational theory or by the accumulating body of sociological research on schools. We have just lived through an era of research on schools which has been on a tangent preoccupied with a few socioeconomic variables and test scores, but grossly disconnected with the sociology of complex formal organization.

However, there has been progress. For example, Alexander and Cook (1982) have developed a sophisticated model of the curriculum process to estimate the actual effects of tracking in comparison to prior course work and grades; see also, Hotchkiss and Dorsten (1987). A significant stride was made in 1982 when Coleman and his colleagues published *High School Achievement*. Their measures tapped many aspects of the educational process including the specialized and advanced math and English course work taken, hours spent on homework, student absences, disciplinary climate, student-professional staff ratios, student misconduct, including fighting and threats to teachers. In addition, they demonstrated important differences between public and private Catholic schools; the social climate of Catholic schools interacted with the effects of students' background in determining both achievement and dropout. Kerckoff, Campbell, and Trott (1982) also found that differences among types of schools and the qualifications that are certified affected educational outcomes in Great Britain. Hopefully, these are signs of a new appreciation for the potential significance of properties of schools.

HOW GOOD ARE THE DATA?

Probably no one would seriously oppose the kinds of variables we have mentioned. The real problem is that the availability of these kinds of data is at best uneven. The difficulty is reflected in this comment by Sewell and Hauser (1975, p. 111):

> We also are cognizant of the interests of social scientists in dependent variables other than years of schooling, occupational status, and earnings, such as critical thinking, tolerance, humanitarianism, citizenship, responsibility, and other valued traits. Perhaps we can develop models to explain these outcomes, but at present we do not have the necessary data to study them.

There is a clear need for better, more widely available information despite a substantial increase in the number of data archives in the past decade (Durstein 1984). Referring to some of these data bases, Coleman et al. (1982) lament that "their principal deficiency is superficiality of measurement, leading either to measurement errors or to failure to measure the right characteristic of schools." Yet they are willing to overlook the difficulties, satisfied that "large scale surveys constitute one of the most important means for discovering what it is about schools that makes them more or less effective in accomplishing their goals." If the quality of our research is to rest solely on the data currently available the future seems bleak indeed.

Data Vacuums

Responsibility for government-sponsored surveys is divided among various federal agencies. This division of labor has created large voids in what can be learned about schooling. In their ambitious assessment of available data bases in education, Plisko, Ginsburg, and Chaikind (1986) observe that no national data base provides good information on home activities of children and no national survey has looked at the home environment and the preschool environment together. While a few data bases contain some information on schooling processes, they usually apply to specific areas, such as provisions for special education for the handicapped. Moreover, many national data bases do not allow for district and school level comparisons.

The NLS provides information on cognitive achievement and student background, but nothing on resources and only incomplete information on school characteristics such as curriculum and standards. High School and Beyond (HSB) is the only existing data base with extensive information on family background and school guidance, but it says little about critical inputs. While it provides some information on curriculum resources, this information is very incomplete and relegated to supplemental surveys (e.g., in school climate, teaching practices, and working conditions). Moreover, the HSB is an entirely new enterprise. It does not build directly on the National Longitudinal Survey (NLS) even though most of the questions are comparable. The lack of coordination reflects the deep-seated discontinuities among totally independent data bases in existence today.

However, shortcomings in the available data bases can not be used forever as an excuse for uneven, primitive measures and models. At some point social scientists must assume responsibility for the data they use.

CONCLUSIONS

The issues raised here suggest the following conclusions.

- The statistical models that for a generation have dominated research on status attainment have been responsible for significant strides in our ability to explain the role education plays in the social mobility process.
- However, the existing models are too simple and need to be expanded in at least two ways.
    - First, to remain faithful to the multi-dimensional character of schooling outcomes, models should be elaborated to include more than one dependent variable at a time. An applicable equation was

described which can be used to deal with more than one dependent variable at a time.

- Second, analyses based on the individual level should be supplemented with macro-level structural and demographic approaches. A mutli-level model was presented that can be used to nest classrooms within schools and schools within school districts.

- More and better measures are needed for non-cognitive types of schooling outcomes. Correspondingly, social scientists should acknowledge the limitations of standardized test scores and stop relying so heavily on such measures.
- More and better measures of school structures and processes should be added as independent and intervening variables.
- Statistical explanations should be supplemented with other forms of understanding. Complex truths that are summarized in formulae and statistical patterns can be illustrated through case materials capable of including complex, dynamic processes involved in different contexts.

ACKNOWLEDGMENTS

We wish to thank Roy Edelfelt and Linda Dorsten for their comments on an earlier draft of this chapter.

REFERENCES

Alexander, K. L., and M. Cook. 1982. "Curricula and Coursework: A Surprise Ending to a Familiar Story." *American Sociological Review* 47:626–640.

Alexander, K. L., and L. J. Griffin. 1976. "School District Effects on Academic Achievement: A Reconsideration." *American Sociological Review* 41:144–52.

Alexander, K. L., and E. L. McDill. 1976. "Selection and Allocation Within Schools: Some Causes and Consequences of Curriculum Placement." *American Sociological Review* 41:963–80.

Alexander, K. L., J. McPartland and M. A. Cook. 1981. "Using Standardized Test Performance in School Effects Research," edited by Alan C. Kerckhoff and Ronald G. Corwin. *Research in Sociology of Education and Socialization.* Greenwich, CT: JAI Press.

Alexander, K. L., B. K. Eckland, and L. J. Griffin. 1975. "The Wisconsin Model of Socioeconomic Achievement: A Replication." *American Journal of Sociology* 81:324–42.

Anderson, J. G. 1968. *Patterns of Control and Their Consequences in Formal Organizations.* In W. G. Monahan, 1973. (ed). *Theoretical Dimensions of Educational Administration.* New York: Macmillian.

Barr, R., and R. Dreeben. 1983. *How Schools Work*. Chicago, IL: University of Chicago Press.

Baron, J. N. and W. T. Bielby. 1980. "Bringing the Firms Back In: Stratification, Segmentation, and the Organization of Work," *American Sociological Review* 45:737–765.

Blau, P. M. and O. D. Duncan. 1967. *The American Occupational Structure*. New York: John Wiley & Sons.

Borman, K. 1981. "Review of Recent Case Studies on Equity and Schooling," edited by Alan C. Kerckhoff and Ronald G. Corwin. *Research in Sociology of Education and Socialization*. Greenwich, CT: JAI Press.

Boudon, R. 1977. "Education and Social Mobility: A Structural Model." Pp. 173–86, edited by Jerome Karabel and A. H. Halsey. *Power and Ideology in Education*. New York: Oxford University Press.

Bourdieu, P. 1977. *Reproduction in Education, Society, Culture*. Beverly Hills, CA: Sage.

Bowles, S. and H. Gintis. 1977. "I.Q. in the U.S. Class Structure." Pp 215–331, edited by Jerome Karabel and A. H. Halsey. *Power and Ideology in Education*. New York: Oxford University.

Burstein, L. 1984. "The Use of Existing Data Bases in Program Evaluation and School Improvement." *Educational Evaluation and Policy Analysis* (Fall) 6:307–318.

Cicourel, A. V. and J. I. Kitsuse. 1963. *The Educational Decision Makers*. Indianapolis, IN: Bobbs-Merrill.

Claus. 1986. *Opportunity or Inequality in Vocational Education? An Ethnographic Investigation*. Ph.D. Dissertation, Cornell University, 1986.

Clogg, C. C. and J. W. Shockey. 1984. "Mismatch Between Occupation and Schooling: A Prevalence Measure, Recent Trends and Demographic Analysis." *Demography* 21.

Coleman, J. S. 1987. "Families and Schools." *Educational Researcher* 16 (August/September):32–38.

Coleman, J. S. 1961. *The Adolescent Society*. New York: Free Press.

Coleman, J. S., et al. 1966. *Equality of Educational Opportunity*. U.S. Office of Education. Washington, D.C.: Government Printing Office.

Coleman, J. S., T. Hoffer, and S. Kilgore. 1982. *High School Achievement: Public, Catholic, and Private Schools Compared*. New York: Basic Books.

Collins, R. 1975. *Conflict Sociology: Toward an Explanatory Science*. New York: Academic Press.

Collins, R. 1979. *The Credential Society: An Historical Sociology of Education and Stratification*. New York: Academic Press.

Collins, R. 1971. "Functional and Conflict Theories of Educational Stratification." *American Sociological Review* 36:1002–10.

Conant, J. B. 1967. *The Comprehensive High School: A Second Report to Interested Citizens*. New York: McGraw-Hill.

Conant, J. B. 1948. *Education in a Divided World: The Future of the Public Schools*. Cambridge MA: Harvard University Press.

Conant, J. B. 1959. *The American High School Today: A First Report to Interested Citizens*. New York: McGraw-Hill.

Corwin, R. G. 1986. "Organizational Skills and the "Deskilling" Hypothesis." Pp. 221–43, edited by Kathryn M. Borman and Jane Reisman. *Becoming A Worker*. Norwood, NJ: Ablex Publishing Corp.

Corwin, R. G. 1975. *Education in Crisis: A Sociological Analysis of Schools and Universities in Transition*. NY: Wiley.

Corwin, R. G. 1965. *A Sociology of Education: Emerging Patterns of Class, Status, and Power in the Public Schools*. New York: Appleton-Century-Crofts.

Cremin, L. 1964. *The Transformation of the School.* Vintage.

Cusick, P. A. 1973. *Inside High School.* New York: Holt.

Dreeben, R. 1968. *On What is Learned in School.* Reading MA: Addison-Wesley.

DiMaggio, P. 1982. "Cultural Capital and School Success: The Impact of Status Culture Participation on the Grades of U.S. High School Students." *American Sociological Review* 47:189–201.

Etzioni, A. 1982. "Schools: Educational Experiences First—Parts I and II." *American Education* 18:(November)6–10; and (December)2–7.

Featherman, D. L. and R. M. Hauser. 1978. *Opportunity and Change.* New York: Academic Press.

Fechner, G. T. 1860. *Elemente der Psychophysik, Vol. 1.* Trans. 1966 by H. E. Adler as *Elements of Phsychophysics,* edited by Davis H. Howes and Edwin G. Boring. New York, NY: Holt, Reinhart, & Winston.

Frederick, R. W. 1959. *The Third Curriculum: Student Activities in American Education.* New York: Appleton-Century-Crofts.

Goldstein, H. 1987. *Multilevel Models in Educational and Social Research.* London: Charles Griffin & Co., Ltd.

Goodlad, J. I. 1979. *What Schools Are For.* Bloomington, IN: Phi Delta Kappa.

Haertel, E. 1985. "Construct Validity and Criterion-Referenced Testing." *Review of Educational Research* 55:23–46.

Haertel, E. 1986. "The Valid Use of Student Performance Measures for Teacher Evaluation." *Educational Evaluation and Policy Analysis* 8:45–60.

Haney, W. 1984. "Testing Reasoning and Reasoning About Testing." *Review of Educational Research* 54:597–654.

Hanson, R. A. and R. E. Schutz. 1986. *"A Comparison of Methods for Measuring Achievement in Basic Skills Program Evaluation."* *Educational Evaluation and Policy Analysis* 8:101–113.

Herriott, R. E. and B. J. Hodgkins. 1973. *The Environment of Schooling: Formal Education as an Open System.* Englewood Cliffs, NJ: Prentice-Hall.

Hotchkiss, L. and L. E. Dorsten. 1987. "Curriculum Effects on Early Post High School Outcomes." Pp. 191–219, edited by Ronald G. Corwin. *Sociology of Education and Socialization.* Volume 7. Greenwich CT: JAI Press.

Hurn, C. J. 1978. *The Limits and Possibilities of Schooling: An Introduction to the Sociology of Education.* Boston: Allyn and Bacon.

Karabel, J. and A. H. Halsey. 1977. *Power and Ideology in Education.* New York: Oxford University Press.

Ketznelson, I. and M. Weir. 1985. *Schooling for All: Class, Race, and the Decline of the Democratic Ideal.* New York: Basic Books.

Kelley, J. and H. S. Klein. 1981. *Revolution and the Rebirth of Inequality: A Theory Applied to the National Revolution in Bolivia.* Berkeley, CA: University of California Press.

Kerckhoff, A. C., R. T. Campbell and J. M. Trott. 1982. "Dimensions of Educational and Occupational Attainment in Great Britain." *American Sociological Review* 47:347–364.

Kerckhoff, A. 1976. "The Status Attainment Process: Socialization or Allocation?" *Social Forces* 55:368–81.

Light, D. 1979. "Surface Data and Deep Structures: Observing the Organization of Professional Training." *Administrative Science Quarterly* (December) 24:551–559.

Lotto, L. S. 1983. "Revisiting the Role of Organizational Effectiveness in Educational Evaluation." *Educational Evaluation and Policy Analysis* 5:367–378.

Mason, W. M. and G. Y. Wong. 1985. "The Hierarhical Logistic Regression Model for Multi-level Analysis. *Journal of the American Statistical Association* 80:513–524.

McClelland, D. C. 1973. "Testing for Competence Rather Than Intelligence." *American Psychologist* 28:1–14.

McNeil, L. M. 1981. "Negotiating Classroom Knowledge: Beyond Achievement and Socialization." *Journal of Curriculum Studies* 3.

Merton, R. K. 1957. "Social Structure and Anomie," edited by R. K. Merton. *Social Theory and Social Structure,* pp 131–160. Glencoe IL: The Free Press.

Metz, M. H. 1978. *Classrooms and Corridors: The Crisis of Authority in Desegregated Secondary Schools.* Berkeley CA: University of California Press.

Mortimore, J. T., and C. Yamoor. 1987. "Interrelations and Parallels of School and Work as Sources of Psychological Development," edited by Ronald G. Corwin. *Research in Sociology of Education and Socialization,* Volume 7. Greenwich CT: JAI Press.

National Commission on Excellence in Education. 1983. *A Nation at Risk.* U.S. Washington D.C.: Department of Education.

Oakes, J. 1985. *Keeping Track: How Schools Structure Inequality.* New Haven, CT: Yale University Press.

Parcel, T. L. 1987. "Theories of the Labor Market and the Employment of Youth," edited by Ronald G. Corwin. *Research in Sociology of Education and Socialization,* Volume 7. Greenwich CT: JAI Press.

Peterson, P. E. 1983. "Did the Education Commission Say Anything?" *The Brookings Review* (Winter): 3–11.

Plisko, V., A. Ginsburg and S. Chaikind. 1986. "Assessing National Data on Education." *Educational Evaluation and Policy Analysis* 8:1–16.

Popham, W. J. 1980. "Domain Specification Strategies," edited by R. A. Berk. *Criterion-Referenced Measurement: The State of the Art.* Baltimore MD: John Hopkins University Press.

Popham, W. J. 1978. *Criterion-Referenced Measurement.* Englewood Cliffs NJ: Prentice Hall.

Rist, Ray C. 1973. *Urban School: Factory for Failure.* Cambridge MA: MIT Press.

Robinson, R. V. and M. A. Garnier. 1985. "Class Reproduction among Men and Women in France: Reproduction Theory on Its Home Ground." *American Journal of Sociology* 91:250–280.

Rosenbaum, J. E. 1975. "The Stratification of Socialization Processes." *American Sociological Review* 40:48–54.

Rosenbaum, J. E. 1976. *Making Inequality: The Hidden Curriculum of High School Tracking.* New York: Wiley Interscience.

Rubinson, R. 1986. "Class Formation, Politics, and Institutions: Schooling in the United States." *American Journal of Sociology* 92:519–48.

Schein, E. H. 1968. "Organizational socialization." *Industrial Management Review* 2:37–45.

Sewell, W. H. and R. M. Hauser. 1975. *Education, Occupation, and Earnings: Achievement in the Early Career.* New York: Academic Press.

Sewell, W. H., A. O. Haller, and G. W. Ohlendorf. 1970. "The Educational and Early Occupational Status Attainment Process: Replication and Revision." *American Sociological Review* 34:82–92.

Spenner, K. I. 1979. "Temporal Changes in Work Context." *American Sociological Review* 44:968–75.

Spenner, K. I. 1985. "The Upgrading and Downgrading of Occupations: Issues, Evidence, and Implications for Education." *Review of Educational Research* 55:125–154.

Sproull, L., and D. Zubrow. 1981. "Standardizing Testing from the Administrative Perspective." *Phi Delta Kappan* 62:628–31.

Stanley, J. C. 1971. "Reliability," edited by R. L. Thorndike. *Educational Measurement* (2nd ed). Washington D.C.: Council on Education.

Stigler, S. M. 1986. *The History of Statistics: The Measurement of Uncertainty Before 1900.* Cambridge MA: The Belknap Press of Harvard University Press.

Teachman, Jay D. 1987. "Family Background, Educational Resources, and Educational Attainment." *American Sociological Review* 52:548–557.

Walters, P. B., and R. Rubinson. 1983. "Educational Expansion and Economic Output in the United States, 1890–1967: A Production Function Analysis." *American Sociological Review,* 48:480–93.

Warner, W. L., R. J. Havighurst and M. B. Loeb. 1944. *Who Shall Be Educated?: The Challenge of Unequal Opportunities.* New York: Harper & Brothers.

Weber, M. 1968. *Economy and Society.* New York: Bedminister Press.

Willis, P. 1977. *Learning to Labour.* Westmead, England: Saxon House.

THE ADVANTAGES AND DISADVANTAGES OF LONGITUDINAL SURVEYS

Robert W. Pearson

INTRODUCTION

Longitudinal surveys, in which repeated observations are made of the same individual subjects, have existed for some time in the social sciences. A quick scan of research would find them employed at least as early as 1928, when Stuart Rice studied the changing presidential preferences of Dartmouth college students (Rice 1928). Perhaps more readily recalled are Theodore Newcomb's classic studies of the effects of a liberal environment at Bennington College on young women from conservative families (Newcomb 1943). Panel designs were further extended when Paul Lazarsfeld and colleagues studied

Research in the Sociology of Education and Socialization,
Volume 8, pages 177–199.
Copyright © 1989 by JAI Press Inc.
All rights of reproduction in any form reserved.
ISBN: 0-89232-929-7

the 1940 U.S. presidential campaign through a stratified random sample of about 2,400 Erie County, Ohio, citizens (Lazarsfeld, Berelson, and Gaudet 1944).

Longitudinal studies became especially prominent in the 1960s and 1970s in the United States as the federal government turned its attention and resources to a domestic public agenda in which research and evaluation played an increasing part. As the technology of data collection, storage, and analysis developed, so too did the call for and subsequent investment in longitudinal surveys. In the United States, for example, some 13 national longitudinal surveys were conducted in the 1950s while 64 surveys of this kind were carried out in the following two decades (Taeuber and Rockwell 1982). Panel studies quite simply permitted the study of change that other study designs (principally, cross sectional surveys) could not. These surveys were asked to evaluate the effects of social programs and to unravel the processes by which individuals change. The surveys facilitated the development of several fields of inquiry, including—but not limited to—labor economics, developmental psychology, voting behavior, and evaluation research. Conversely, theoretical and conceptual developments within these fields called for the use of longitudinal surveys.

The love affair with longitudinal data appears to have been short lived, however. This earlier affection has been replaced with an increasingly if not as yet widely shared appreciation of the limits of longitudinal surveys. Kerckoff (1980), for example, raised the question of the value of longitudinal studies (relative to cross-sectional ones) in the first volume of the series of JAI publications on the sociology of education, and such questioning has continued. More recently, the editors of a volume on longitudinal analysis of labor market data would begin the volume provocatively by saying,

> Longitudinal data are widely and uncritically regarded as a panacea. Given the substantial cost of collecting such data, it is surprising that so little attention has been devoted to justifying the expense. The conventional wisdom in social science equates "longitudinal" with "good," and discussion of the issue rarely rises above this level (Heckman and Singer 1985, p. xi).

Similar questioning can be found in other fields of research. For example, Hirschi and Gottfredson assert in their review of research on the relationship between age and crime that "Funding agencies seem convinced by researchers that the longitudinal study is necessary for the proper study of crime" (Hirschi and Gottfredson 1983, p 582). They argue instead that the causes of crime are similar across age cohorts and that cross-sectional designs are likely to produce more knowledge per dollar of research than are longitudinal designs, which Hirschi and Gottfredson believe to be relatively more costly to conduct (Greenberg 1985; Hirschi and Gottfredson 1985; Murray and Erickson 1987).

The recent concern with longitudinal or panel surveys stems in part from the substantial investment in such data made during the past 20 years. There is also a suspicion that several important panel studies have reached or have gone beyond their maximum usefulness. Members of the policy and research communities now discuss these limitations as well as their comparative advantages in the reflective mood that was catalyzed by reductions in the data collection and social science budgets of the early part of the Reagan administration (Pearson 1985).

The purpose of this chapter is to review several of the strengths and weaknesses of longitudinal surveys that have emerged from these discussions. The chapter will make special note of the manner in which these research designs have been oversold on one hand and underused on another. I will begin with a brief discussion of the characteristics of longitudinal surveys that distinguish them from and which they share with other survey-based research designs. I then turn to a discussion of the several advantages and disadvantages of these instruments of social observation and draw attention to several claims about these data collection strategies that appear to be not well established, even if widely believed.

The principal point of the chapter is a relatively simple one—which survey design is most appropriate for a particular purpose is a complicated function of a large number of factors. These include, but are not limited to, the use to which the data are put; the cognitive capacities and interests of respondents; legal and ethical restraints on the study of human subjects; the nature and quality of theories or assumptions about social processes and behavior; and the inferential abilities of different research designs. Unfortunately, these simple points are too often ignored. The research literature and the decisions concerning the choice of research designs appear to have become increasingly interested in choosing one rather than another design. Too little attention is paid to their fruitful combination, both within the survey research tradition— the focus of this chapter—and between this tradition and more qualitative research approaches.

WHAT ARE LONGITUDINAL SURVEYS?

Discussions of panel or longitudinal studies usually focus on their principal characteristic: repeated observations of the same persons or units through time. These research designs are often contrasted with aggregate time series data, cross-sectional surveys (perhaps themselves repeated), matched comparison methods, clinical trials, and experiments. Although useful, these contrasts and comparisons are often not precisely correct. Aggregate time series and repeated cross sectional research designs, for example, can be conceptualized as repeated observations of a single entity (e.g., the country) in which the observed characteristics of that unit are an aggregation or composite of the characteristics of its constituent parts (or a sample of those parts). And experimental research designs typically include the repeated measurement of individuals. Experimental assignments are indeed not unknown to panel surveys (or cross-sectional designs for that matter), and recent work has sought to integrate the two sampling strategies in which randomization is a common component in sample selection (Boruch 1975; Fienberg and Tanur 1986, 1987b).

Although the most prominent longitudinal studies in the social sciences and in policy analysis are large probability samples of a national population (e.g., voting age citizens, high school seniors), many such research designs are used among smaller populations. These studies include, for example, the Woodlawn Study, the Baltimore Follow-up of Teenage Mothers and Their Children; and the Cornell Early Intervention Consortium Study (cf. Migdal, Abeles, and Sherrod 1981; Verdonik and Sherrod 1984).

The focus of this chapter, however, is the relatively large, nationally-based longitudinal survey. These include, for example, the Panel Study of Income Dynamics (PSID) and the various cohorts of the National Longitudinal Surveys of Labor Market Experience (NLS). More directly related to education, one finds the National Longitudinal Survey of the Senior Class of 1972 (NLS72), the High School and Beyond Study of sophomores and seniors in 1980 (HS&B), and the National Education Longitudinal Surveys of 1988 (NELS88), all of which constitute the U.S. Department of Education's Center for Education Statistics' ongoing National Education Longitudinal Studies program. The general aim of this program is to study the educational, vocational, and personal development of young people and the personal, familial, social, institutional, and cultural factors that may affect that development (Sebring et al. 1987).

HS&B, for example, is a survey of approximately 58,000 high school sophomores and seniors who were first interviewed in the spring of 1980 and subsequently reinterviewed every other year—the third followup interviews being completed during the spring and summer of 1986. The sample is based on a multi-stage stratified national probability sample of over 1,100 secondary schools, within which 36 senior and 36 sophomores were selected. Special efforts were made to identify twins or triplets of these sample members, who were then invited to participate in the study—producing a separate Twin Data File. Schools were oversampled if they were: schools that included a high percentage of Hispanic students, Catholic schools with high percentages of minority group students, alternative public schools, and private schools with high-achieving students. An additional supplemental sample was drawn of students attending overseas Department of Defense Dependent Schools. In addition to questions asked of the students, questionnaires were completed by an official in each participating school, and by teachers and parents of the students in the sample. A series of cognitive tests for each cohort were conducted. High school transcripts of the sophomore cohort and postsecondary education transcripts and financial aid data for the senior cohort were collected. Waves employed various modes of implementation—principally group administration and mail-back questionnaires, with telephone or personal interviews used with those who had not responded to prior efforts. Response rates to any particular questionnaire or test ranged from 81 to 91 percent (Sebring et al. 1987).

Although longitudinal surveys differ from one another and from other research designs in important respects, their essential characteristics are strikingly similar. Each is a complex social technology. Their parts include the people who design the questionnaires, the interviewers who administer the survey instrument, and the coders who reduce open-ended responses to manageable sets of responses. They are a technology without clearly written blueprints. No patents are issued for the clever techniques that have been invented for converting the nonresponses of recalcitrant sample subjects, for locating sample members who have moved between waves of a panel survey, for determining whether a sample household has "died" through a change in its composition, or for splicing old and new questions together. Much of our knowledge about their operation remains tacit. In the best case, this understanding is codified in such publications as the *Handbook of Survey Research* or is passed between practitioners within survey research organizations as a consequence of the networks of relations that are formed through professional associations and by the working relations that develop in the use, evaluation, and marketing of this technology (cf. Converse 1987). In the worst case, the knowledge is lost and rediscovered as old problems reemerge. Some of the problems that confront the successful creation and maintenance of this technology are relatively mundane or archane to whose who use these instruments. Their understanding of the relative advantages and disadvantages of one design versus another is often based on prevailing opinions, not all of which are well established.

THE ADVANTAGES AND DISADVANTAGES OF LONGITUDINAL SURVEYS

Discussions of the advantages and disadvantages of a particular research design are difficult to conduct in the abstract. This is so for several reasons.

First, the discussion needs to be framed in a comparative perspective. Is the question one of the relative advantages and disadvantages of one longitudinal panel vs. another? Is it the relative merits of longitudinal vs. other designs? The former question faces secondary analysts of existing survey data. The latter question—the principal focus of this chapter—confronts those who sponsor and design research.

These are often two distinct, though overlapping, levels of concern. Users of such data may find several surveys that are ostensibly relevant to a given topic, but have few tools for judging the equivalence of their measures. It is difficult to confirm, validate, and replicate research results across surveys. Paralleling the users' concerns, those who fund or design surveys must consider which studies to initiate, maintain, or terminate, and for what reasons? What combination of ongoing data collection programs will meet the present and future needs of research and public policy? Clearly, legitimate replication may be hard to distinguish from unnecessary redundancy. Although reliance on a single data source invites biased or inconclusive results, investments in similar or equivalent data series are likely to yield diminishing returns. Put briefly, each additional instrument may not lead to an equally valuable increment in knowledge.

Second, discussions of the advantages and disadvantages of longitudinal surveys (and other research designs as well) are difficult because their evaluation depends on a variety of conditions. These conditions include:

- The questions one wishes to answer.
- The skills and analytic competences of the investigator or the "user friendliness" of the data.
- The sample size, target population, substantive content, and design of the survey.
- The timeliness of the survey.
- The quality of the information.
- The documentation and dissemination of the data.

The evaluation of longitudinal surveys as well as other survey research designs also depends on subtler factors. For example, there are substantial costs associated with gaining a working knowledge of the structure (and anomalies) of a large data set, costs that are not entirely transferable to another survey. These impediments to use are frequently confronted by analysts because many data collection programs do not devote resources to the creation of adequate documentation, data-based management structures, or the creation and distribution of users' access utility programs or constructed variables (David 1980, 1985).

Many analysts use several different longitudinal data sets in their research. But when they do, they are often aided by students, research assistants, and computational facilities that minimize the costs of doing so. That is to say, the use (and usefulness) of these and other relatively large data sets or instruments cannot be considered apart from a wider set of instrumentalities which include students, assistants, training programs, computational and analytical technologies, instructional materials, and the availability of research funds for secondary analysis.

Standards or guidelines for the conduct of longitudinal surveys exist (Bailar and Lanphier 1978; Boruch and Pearson 1988). These guidelines include, for example:

- The facility with which the survey may be linked to other data or ancillary studies.
- The ability of multiple users to simultaneously access and analyze the data.
- The ease with which its sample may be augmented or modified.
- The extent to which the anonymity of respondents is protected.
- The frequency with which its data use and resource-sharing programs are evaluated.
- The extent to which efforts to replicate other studies take into account the shifting semantics of language and the importance of the changing sociohistorical context of the questionnaire, as well as the context of particular questions within the questionnaire.
- The extent to which justification and explanation are provided for the following questions: (a) How does any failure to replicate other studies diminish the ability to understand social or individual change? or (b) Is the study's success in replicating other studies an unnecessarily redundant allocation of research resources?
- The devotion of resources to the measurement and reporting of nonsampling error.
- The explicit use of theories to inform what data to collect, as well as the use of data to inform the development of theory.
- The use of mechanisms for minimizing nonresponse and attrition and for subsequently adjusting for the nonresponse and attrition that invariably occurs (e.g., through weighting and/or imputation).

The guidelines cannot be used, however, a priori to compare one longitudinal survey to another because such evaluation relies heavily on the uses to which the results or findings of the studies are to be put. If the findings of a study are known before the data are collected, there would be little need to conduct the study. (For similar conclusions concerning the intractability of judging the relative value of different data, see David and Peskin 1984.)

Comparisons of longitudinal with other research designs are difficult because many of the advantages and disadvantages of panel designs are shared by other designs. Nonresponse, confidentiality, data access are problems or concerns that face each (Boruch and Cecil 1979). Moreover, some disadvantages or difficulties posed by longitudinal surveys are also part of their strength. For example, how one defines and measures such ever-changing phenomena as the "family" is a problem that accompanies the increased ability to conceptualize and measure these dynamic phenomena (Koo 1985; Citro and Watts 1985; Citro, Hernandez, and Moorman 1986).

Equally important, some problems or disadvantages can be avoided or minimized if anticipated and if appropriate quality control mechanisms are built into the technology. For example, sample attrition of panel members can be reduced if sufficient attention and resources are devoted to collecting information from sample respondents about friends or relatives who are likely to know where a respondent may move between waves of an interview. The effects of attrition can be monitored and, through imputational or weighting algorithms, compensated for during the analysis of the data.

The comparison of different survey research designs are often inappropriate because they tend to criticize one research design while more or less explicitly extolling the virtues of an alternative, as if their discussion was part of a debate in which it was important that one type of research design "win," while others "lose." We should instead begin by agreeing that different designs can in principle be combined to take advantage of their relative merits and to overcome their relative disadvantages. One ought to ask what combination is most effective or efficient for answering one's questions rather than which *one* research design is best.

Although comparisons of the relative advantages of longitudinal surveys should be made cautiously, research and experience suggest that longitudinal surveys have several generic advantages and disadvantages that are relatively well established.

The *advantages* of longitudinal designs include, for example:

- The development of reliable measures of individual change. (Retrospectively collected data are subject to telescoping, memory decay, etc.) Similarly, these designs permit the measurement of subjective phenomena as current states rather than as recalled states. (Consider the difficulty of asking a respondent to rate his or her health or happiness four years ago.)
- The development of concepts that are characteristically dynamic rather

than static. (The burgeoning multidisciplinary research on life-course perspectives owes part of its vitality to the creation and distribution of panel studies. See, for example, Baltes 1979; 1983).

• Better descriptions of the dynamics of change. (The typical episode of family poverty or welfare receipt has been shown through panel data to be considerably briefer than was assumed in studies using repeated cross-sectional surveys. See, for example, Duncan et al. 1984; Corcoran et al. 1985; and Duncan, Hill, and Hoffman 1988.) Similarly, longitudinal designs permit the estimation of individual levels and rates of transition between states or conditions for which cross-sectional data may only provide gross or aggregate measures of group change.

• The ability to conduct analyses that control for unmeasured attributes of individuals, thus improving the ability to distinguish between the influence of enduring individual differences (e.g., race and gender) and the influence of having previously experienced the condition that is under investigation (e.g., previous unemployment leading to current unemployment).

The *disadvantages* of panel designs include:

• Nonresponse bias (especially through panel attrition) may be high and analytically troublesome. (Respondents for whom subsequent interviews cannot be completed may differ in analytically important ways from those who remain in the survey.)

• Response and learning effects (i.e., "panel effects") may prejudice responses. (People who are interviewed about their voting behavior tend to vote more frequently thereafter.)

• Errors in the measurement of variables (and the correlation of these errors) and changes in the accuracy, reliability, and validity of such measures may spuriously create the appearance of change.

• Panel data, unless regularly refreshed or augmented, may provide useful or accurate estimates of the population from which the original sample was drawn, but not from the current population, which may be of interest.

• Panels always involve a moving target. Panel surveys of families, for example, must cope with movement into and out of families, the formation of new ones, and the dissolution of old.

Let us consider in more detail the first of the listed advantages and discuss several features often included in such lists that are not well established. (For several discussions of the strengths and weaknesses of longitudinal surveys see, for example, Ashenfelter and Solon 1982; Boruch and Pearson 1988; Duncan, Juster, and Morgan 1984; Duncan and Kalton 1985; Fienberg and Tanur 1987a; and Subcommittee on Federal Longitudinal Surveys 1986.)

The Limits of Retrospection. The repeated observations of longitudinal surveys permit an investigation of change in phenomena that can be measured in the present. They rely less than, say, a single cross-sectional survey design on the memory of respondents' prior conditions. This principal limitation of the ability of cross-sectional research designs to assess individual change is one of the major relative advantages of longitudinally designed studies.

Increasing evidence and recent theoretical developments in cognitive psychology and survey methodology question, in more sophisticated ways than in the past, the trustworthiness of retrospective—or memory-based—responses to survey questions. Some research has found that certain kinds of memory-based data are flawed not only by temporal confusion and forgetting, but are systematically influenced by the respondent's current emotional state and beliefs about life and self.

Memory is basically reconstructive (cf. Bartlett 1932). And this reconstruction often involves the "top down" processing of the past that includes the development or use of scripts and narratives about the self or society, as well as the organization of details about the past. These scripts, schemata, self narratives, or stereotypes define more or less coherent sets of beliefs around which more detailed images are actively (although not necessarily consciously) organized or distorted. If by virtue of sharing a common culture, the respondent's schemata or theories of self or society are the same as those of the questioner (e.g., that adult mental distress follows from childhood problems), then research that relies on retrospective questioning techniques typically found in cross-sectional surveys may be systematically biased in the direction the questioner expects. The resulting "theory validation" of retrospective studies may simply be the result of widely—even if only implicitly—shared cultural stories, narratives, stereotypes, or folklore whose accuracy is unknown and unprovable (Dawes and Pearson 1987).

Several studies substantiate this conclusion. In two separate but similar experiments, for example, Conway and Ross (1984) examined randomly selected participants in a program designed to improve study skills and a control group of nonparticipants who indicated a desire to participate in the program but who were placed on a waiting list. Participants and control group members were questioned both before the beginning of the study skills program and at its conclusion. At both times, they were asked to assess their own study skills (e.g., how much of their study time was well spent, how satisfactory were their note taking skills, etc.) and the amount of time they studied.

At the second interview they were also asked to recall what they reported during the first session concerning skills and study time.

At the initial interview, participants and control group members did not significantly differ on any measure of skill, study time, or on additional information about grades on a psychology examination taken prior to the study skills program. Nor did these two groups differ in their recall of hours spent studying; there was a slight tendency for subjects in both conditions to recall studying less than they initially reported.

Recall of skills produced marked differences, however. Program participants recalled their study skills as being significantly worse than they initially reported. On the average, waiting list subjects recalled their study skills as being approximately the same as those they reported initially (p. 743). Participants in the study skills program appeared to exaggerate their improvement in a direction consistent with their theories of what ought to be—taking a course should improve skills—but they did so by retrospectively derogating their initial status. They did not exaggerate their current skills, but reconstructed their memory of the past to combine: (1) a theory that they *should* have improved because of the instruction and (2) a relatively accurate assessment of their current level of skills. In both studies, the study skills program did not have a significant effect on academic performance, as measured by subsequent psychology examinations or average grades for the semester. The recall of past events and conditions were in error, and these errors were in a direction that was consistent with what the students thought that the past should have been as a result of their current conditions and prior participation in a study skills program.

In another study, Collins, Graham, Hansen, and Johnson (1985) compared the agreement (or lack thereof) between past reported use and recalled use of tobacco, alcohol, and marijuana among a group of high school students over a 30-month period. They also estimated the extent to which biased recall was a function of current use among those whose behavior changed. In every case, recalled use was less than reported use at both one year and 30 months after the first interview. For example, 67 percent of the subjects reported in an initial interview having smoked at least part of a cigarette. One year later, 49 percent recalled having done so. These findings of memory "loss" or "decay" are widely replicated in a number of studies (cf. Wagenaar 1986; Bradburn, Rips, and Shevell 1987).

Importantly—but less fully recognized in the survey research literature—the influence of patterns of current use was most pronounced for those whose use changed. "When all students were considered, the bias [in recalled use] due to current use was significant but relatively small, ranging from about 12 percent to 23 percent of the total R^2 at the one-year interval, and from 25 percent to 29 percent of the total R^2 at the [30-month] interval. However, calculations based only on students whose use changed from wave to wave showed that 28 percent to 51 percent of the total R^2 was attributable to current use for [30-month] recall'' (pp. 307–308). As the authors note, retrospective data appear to be accurate for those subjects who are asked to report about past behavioral patterns from which they have not departed. But for those whose behavior has changed—often that group in whom we are most interested—errors in the recall of past behavior were strongly associated with current behavior. To exaggerate their conclusion, stability makes truth tellers of us all; current behavior makes liars of those of us who change.

Survey research has become increasingly aware of the distortions and misrepresentations of the past that are engendered by retrospective questions (cf., Turner and Martin 1984, p. 296; Sudman and Bradburn 1982, pp. 43–51; Schuman and Kalton 1986, pp. 644–647). In a recent validation study of employment-related information, for example, Mathiowetz (1986) and Duncan and Mathiowetz (1985) found that when a firm's employees were asked (in July 1983) whether they had been unemployed at any time during 1981 and 1982, 15 percent were in error concerning 1981 and seven percent were in error concerning 1982. Validation studies of retrospective reports have also observed substantial error in the recall of hospitalizations (Cannell, Fisher, and Baker 1965) and of victimizations (Turner 1972).

Obviously, longitudinal research designs themselves may rely upon recall, as well as other cognitive processes. Their dependence on retrospective accounts is in part a function of the length of time between waves of a panel study and the need to measure experiences prior to the first interview. Panel designs have the advantage of providing opportunities to employ bounded recall techniques (asking respondents to recall events since the last interview) and to use information provided in a previous interview to reinstate prior context and to provide cues to facilitate their recall. The relative advantage of longitudinal surveys in this regard is often grounds for choosing this design over cross-sectional surveys.

Costs: A Red Herring. The list of strengths and shortcomings of longitudinal research provided above is not exhaustive. But it excludes their cost as a relative disadvantage. One can find numerous references to the expensiveness of longitudinal designs (cf., Murray and Erickson 1987, p 109), a belief that appears to be widespread. Unfortunately, this belief is not well established and the limited attempts to empirically assess the relative costs of longitudinal and cross-sectional surveys have shown under certain assumptions that longitudinal surveys may be *less* expensive than repeated cross-sectional surveys

(Duncan, Juster, and Morgan 1984). No one can argue that surveys such as the PSID, HS&B, and NLS72 are relatively expensive instruments to create and maintain. But these costs are largely a function of the number or special character of sample members required by the study; not necessarily their longitudinal design.

Surely, longitudinal surveys require the added expenses of tracing and tracking respondents as they move between waves of interviews, costs that are unique to a research design that follows subjects through time. Locating and securing the cooperation of sample respondents during an initial interview, however, reduces the costs associated with drawing new sampling frames or screening households for the desired universe of sample members. These features also permit the use of relatively less expensive modes of administering subsequent waves of the survey (e.g., phone, mail back questionnaires) than may be required in cross-sectional national samples.

Evaluating the relative costs of longitudinal surveys depends a great deal on what one chooses to compare them to. In this regard, we are faced with the difficulties posed by the proverbial comparison of apples and oranges. It is only suggestive—but nonetheless in opposition to the belief about their expense—that the average field cost of completed interviews of the 1987 General Social Survey[1] of NORC was $400. The average costs of each completed interview of the 10th wave of the Youth Cohort of the National Longitudinal Survey of Labor Market Experience[2] was $333 (Carter 1987). Similarly, the total cost of the first year of interviews of the National Post Secondary Student Aid Study of 1987 was $7.2 million; its first year follow-up is currently estimated to cost $3.0 million (Carroll 1987).

The comparative costs of different survey designs compound the difficulty of simultaneously weighing their advantages and disadvantages. A relatively ambiguous attitude toward panel surveys in assessing the effects of job training programs, as suggested for example by Heckman and Robb (1985), could be turned on its head by altering assumptions about the comparative costs of these different designs. Indeed, if one assumes relatively equal expenses, or cost advantages to panel designs, it would be prudent to select panel rather than cross-sectional designs (holding a great many other factors constant) because panel designs permit the use of a wider variety of statistical and theoretical assumptions. The application of a wider range of assumptions provides a useful means of testing how sensitive conclusions are to different assumptions. That is to say, one can analyze a panel study as if it was a repeated cross-sectional design, but not vice versa.

The largest costs of such studies lie in the creation and maintenance of the organization that is required to collect the data and in the burden which such surveys impose on their respondents. This commitment of resources is largely fixed and shared with other large survey-based designs; whether panel, experimental, or cross-sectional. Ongoing instruments of data collection—which longitudinal surveys such as High School and Beyond are by design—are more likely to present opportunities for linkage or augmentation with side studies, experiments, topical modules than are "one-shot" data collection programs, which single cross-sectional surveys can often be, an advantage to which we return below.

Causal Inference: An Oversold Advantage. Longitudinal survey designs do not, however, as is often incorrectly claimed, permit unequivicable inferences about causation. Surely, the temporal dimension of longitudinal surveys provides strong priors for assuming that *a* leads to or causes *b* if *a* is observed to occur before *b*. But there are several dangers in making such strong causal inferences from panel designs. One's anticipation of future events can influence current behavior, for example. And selection biases (i.e., people found in a program often differ in unmeasureable or unmeasured ways from nonparticipants) invariably trouble the estimation of program effects.

Heckman and Robb (1985), for example, examined three survey designs and associated econometric techniques to determine whether one was "better" than the others in assessing the consequences of a public policy interventions, e.g., a youth employment training program. They compared (1) single retrospective cross-sectional, (2) repeated cross-sectional, and (3) panel designs and their corresponding analytical techniques. Heckman and Robb showed that each design and corresponding analytical technique requires untestable assumptions in evaluating the earnings effects of participation in training programs. Their research argued that many of the assumptions of cross-sectional analytical techniques were no more or less justifiable than those upon which the panel designs were based, although some assumptions could be—although too infrequently are—the object of independent study.

Although panel studies permit one to trace spells and transitions and to order conditions in sequences that suggest causation, longitudinal surveys cannot do so without the aid of assumptions. This point is forcefully illustrated by Lord's paradox (1967, 1968, 1973) and its discussion by Holland and Rubin (1986).

Lord introduces the paradox as follows:

> A large university is interested in investigating the effects on the students of the diet provided in the university dining halls and any sex differences in these effects. Various types of data are gathered. In particular, the weight of each student at the time of his arrival in September and his weight the following June are recorded.

Lord used two hypothetical statisticians to illustrate the paradox which lead each to draw different conclusions from the same data. The first statistician based his conclusions about the effect of the diet on the difference between the distribution of weights for males and females. The data showed no differences in the mean weight of each group between the beginning and the end of the observation period. This statistician concluded that the diet had no effect. Lord showed, however, that this inference can be made only by making explicit assumptions about what the students' weight would have been (and the corresponding weight gains or losses) in comparison with some alternative (unobserved) diet.

Statistician 2 computed a covariance adjusted difference of weights for males and females, and arrived at different conclusions derived from the differences in weight gains for males and females of equal initial weight. Males gained more in such comparisons. But these descriptive conclusions, correct insofar as they go, do not address the question first posed about the effects of the diet. Statistician 2 could make such inferences, but as Lord persuasively argued, only with certain assumptions about unobserved alternative diets. These alternative assumptions are untestable; there are no statistical procedures for making them correctly.

Other attempts to understand how different models generate the same data, or how similar models can generate or represent different data, have produced a greater sensitivity to the problems of making causal inferences from the research designs of panel studies (and other observational designs such as matched comparison groups and cross-sectional surveys). Fraker and Maynard (1985, 1987), for example, analyzed data from several sources to compare the estimated earnings effects from participating in an employment and training program. They compared estimates of training effects derived from (1) control groups of the National Supported Work Demonstration program that were selected in accordance with experimental research designs and (2) comparison groups constructed from the Current Population Survey. Matched comparison designs involve the creation of samples of respondents (typically drawn from such surveys as the Current Population Survey) who are similar in important respects to the participants in a program that one seeks to evaluate. These research designs are common in program evaluations in part because information about program participants is regularly collected at their enrollment or discharge from the program. Experiments in which a number of eligible individuals are randomly precluded from participating in a program (and later compared to those who are allowed to enroll), on the other hand, are at times difficult to conduct or proscribed by ethical and legal considerations.

Fraker and Maynard's comparisons of experimental versus nonexperimental estimates of training program effects on annual earnings showed that comparison group procedures and analytical models produced estimates of large negative effects on the earnings of youth both during the program's employment period and after. The experimental design revealed estimates of program earnings for youth that were modestly positive during the program, and negligible thereafter. Comparisons of the effects of training on AFDC recipients revealed similar positive effects between the experimental and matched comparison designs. The differences in results between unemployed youth and AFDC recipients suggest that the greater earnings and employment variability of youth may result in more biased selection into the employment program, which in turn makes the task of defining a comparison group and an analytical model more difficult. Corroborative evidence to this work can be found in LaLonde (1986).

The implication of these marked differences in results is that the longitudinal and cross-sectional designs (or other nonexperimental designs) alone do not permit one to unravel the many causes and consequences of social and economic change or of program interventions. Perhaps more disturbing to those who must rely on such data, these research designs may produce the wrong answer when the behavior of the population under study is undergoing considerable change (as are the employment activities of youth). Experimental designs are superior to panel designs in making causal inferences.

Rarely is the use of or investment in data made "on purely statistical grounds" alone, however. In addition to costs, choices are constrained by legal, ethical, and administrative considerations (Riecken et al. 1974). Considerable experience (much from studies of states and municipalities) has produced a greater appreciation of many of the difficulties of importing laboratory-oriented experimental designs into the field. It is often difficult, for example, to sustain the separation of treatment and control groups in the field. Moreover, some of the problems associated with the design and implementation of panel studies, such as attrition, apply equally to experimental designs (Betsey, Hollister, and Papagiorgiou 1985). Experiments are useful for assessing the relative differences among program variations on a common set of outcome variables. But experimental designs have their own scientific and administrative shortcomings. For example, treatments are often limited to a narrow set of variables and to specialized samples, and so their results may be of limited generalizability. Moreover, they are often difficult to administer and require substantial managerial skills to conduct. These limitations, among others, have retarded the use of experimental designs in the social sciences and in the evaluation of government programs. On the other hand, the design, implementation, and analysts of field experiments is possible, and some evidence exists of a renewed interest in them (c.f. Maynard 1987; Bloom, Borus, and Orr 1987; and Cottingham and Rodriguez 1987).

Coupling Experimental and Longitudinal Designs: A Not Fully Realized Potential. Longitudinal surveys are often an appropriate technology for describing the timing, duration, and sequence of individual change. And they are often better in this regard than alternative nonexperimental observational research designs because of the problems these alternatives confront when relying on retrospective measures of past conditions. Under certain conditions, longitudinal surveys appear to be no more expensive to conduct than repeated cross-sectional surveys. But their ability to draw causal inferences has in general been overdrawn. Although temporal order provides prima facie evidence for causation, it is insufficient.

Increasingly, the research community is considering the fusion of longitudinal and experimental survey designs in which randomly assigned treatments or interventions are given to some members of an ongoing longitudinal survey. Coupling experiments and longitudinal surveys capitalizes on the strongest merits of each design. That is, one obtains both the information produced by national probability samples—often conducted over a considerable length of time—and the information produced by smaller comparative experiments in which causal inferences are more appropriately deduced. Insofar as the experiments can be adjoined systematically, their generalizability will be enhanced.

Joining experiments to ongoing longitudinal surveys also permits one to use the experiments to calibrate estimates of program effects that are derived entirely from the longitudinal survey. That is, the biases engendered by using estimates that are based on longitudinal data can be assessed, and periodically corrected, through controlled experiments. Thus, longitudinal studies are likely to be more policy-relevant and less ambiguous with respect to biases in estimating program effects. Experiments are likely to benefit from their greater generalizability, lower costs, and more manageable administration.

Joining experiments to ongoing longitudinal surveys has its origins in the debate among scholars and bureaucrat-scholars about how much one can depend on longitudinal data. The justification for the coupling of longitudinal surveys and randomized experiments appeared in the early 1970s. In particular, the Social Science Research Council's Committee on Experimentation as a Method for Planning and Evaluating Social Interventions devoted considerable attention to the problem of generalizing from experiments. The enterprise capitalized on work carried out by Campbell, Borgotta, Watts, Newhouse, Rivlin, and others (Riecken et al. 1974; and Boruch and Riecken 1975;

Boruch 1975). The interest in joining these two technologies also shares an interest with those who have discussed the more generic issue of combining experimental and sampling structures (Fienberg and Tanur 1986; 1987b).

There is no doubt about the need for social experiments in understanding change (Berk et al. 1985). The National Academy of Sciences' Committee on Youth Employment Programs, for example, examined major studies to understand whether one could draw firm conclusions about program effects from earlier research. The committee concluded, among other things, that longitudinal surveys are no substitute for randomized experiments when the object is to estimate the effectiveness of youth employment programs. Moreover, they urged the use of randomized experiments for this purpose (Betsey, Hollister, and Papagiorgiou 1985).

Coupling randomized designs to longitudinal surveys can also be traced to a technical advisory committee for employment program evaluation appointed by the U.S. Department of Labor. The DOL sought to learn whether analyses of manpower programs based on conventional longitudinal surveys lead to adequate estimates of program effects. Adequacy was assessed, for example, by comparing estimates of effects based on longitudinal surveys against estimates based on randomized trials. The conclusion of this exercise was that the two estimates are *not* always in accord. Indeed, they differ remarkably depending on what population is the subject of inquiry (Fraker and Maynard 1985, 1987).

Proposals for adjoining experiments to longitudinal and some cross-sectional studies have been presented formally to policy boards responsible for enhancing data bases and their utility. The groups include the Policy Advisory Board of the National Center for Educational Statistics, the Policy Advisory Board of the National Assessment of Educational Progress (Boruch and Sebring 1983), the National Science Foundation's Human Resources Division, and others. The idea is implicit in standards developed by Bailar and Lanphier (1978) for evaluating how well a survey is carried out. Surveys such as the National Longitudinal Study of the High School Class of 1972 (NLS72), and High School and Beyond (HS&B) could serve as a host vehicle for randomized field experiments on, say, the effectiveness of certain types of counseling and student loans or the effectiveness of methods of teaching (Mundel 1979). The larger sample and main data collection effort could inform the design of such tests (suggesting, for example, to which students to target the intervention); the HS&B infrastructure could facilitate the conduct of the experiments; and the rich background information that HS&B provides could facilitate the interpretation of the experimental results (Boruch and Pearson 1988).

Obviously, changes in standard practices that are suggested here would introduce costs and difficulties, at least until their implementation permitted organizations to identify and remedy the problems that naturally arise with any new technology. And surely, there are a number of programs that could not be evaluated through such a coupling of designs because of the nature of the intervention or the limited number or location of possible respondents even in relatively large national longitudinal surveys. Randomly varying policy responses to violent domestic disputes could not be comfortably grafted onto HS&B, for example. Unfortunately, the development and application of this general strategy has yet to be adequately tested.

SUMMARY AND CONCLUSION

Longitudinal surveys are an important technology for the measurement of individual change and development. Considerable resources have been devoted during the last two decades to their creation and maintenance. These instruments of social observation have contributed a great deal to the development of several fields of inquiry, and promise to continue to do so.

Recent years have seen a growing restlessness with these research designs, however. Their limitations—especially those related to causal inference—are increasingly recognized, although their relative strengths have continued to argue for their use as important new instruments of data collection. Their support and criticism is the healthy consequence of the continual scrutiny that a principal tool of social analysis should undergo.

Their relative strengths, however, have not yet been systematically and regularly coupled with the strengths of another research design—experiments. The promise of combining these methods and of moving beyond the discussion of the strengths and weaknesses of a particular research design still lays before us.

ACKNOWLEDGMENTS

This chapter was partially supported by a grant from the National Science Foundation's program of Measurement Methods and Data Improvement, Grant # SES-8511609. The chapter benefited from the helpful comments and suggestions of Robert F. Boruch, Calvin C. Jones, and Nancy A. Mathiowetz.

NOTES

1. This survey of approximately 2,000 respondents was a face-to-face stratified probability sample of the adult noninstitutionalized population of the United States, which included a special supplemental sample of minorities for that year.

2. This survey of approximately 10,000 respondents is a cohort of youth (age 14–21 during the first year of the survey in 1979) which included oversamples of females and minority youth and a special military sample.

REFERENCES

Ashenfelter, O. and G. Solon. 1982. *Longitudinal Labor Market Data: Sources, Uses, and Limitations.* A paper presented at a conference sponsored by the National Council on Employment Policy, An Assessment of Labor Force Measurements for Policy Formulation, Washington, D.C. (June).

Bailar, B. A. and C. M. Lanphier. 1978. *Development of Survey Methods to Assist Survey Practices.* Washington, D.C.: American Statistical Association.

Baltes, P. B. 1979. "Life-span Developmental Psychology: Some Converging Observations on History and Theory." In *Life-Span Development and Behavior.* Vol. 2., edited by P. B. Baltes and O. B. Brim, Jr. New York: Academic Press.

Baltes, P. B. 1983. "Life-span Developmental Psychology: Observations on History and Theory Revisited." In *Developmental Psychology: Historical and Philosophical Perspectives,* edited by R. M. Lerner. Hillsdale, N.J.: Lawrence Erlbaum Associates.

Bartlett, F. C. 1932. *Remembering: A Study in Experimental and Social Psychology.* Cambridge: Cambridge University Press.

Berk, R. A. et al. 1985. "Social Policy Experimentation." *Evaluation Review* 9:387–429.

Betsey, C., R. Hollister, and M. Papagiorgiou. 1985. *Report of the Committee on Youth Employment Programs.* Washington, D.C.: National Research Council.

Bloom, H. S., M. E. Borus, and L. L. Orr. 1987. "Using Random Assignment to Evaluate an Ongoing Program: *The National JTPA Evaluation.* A paper presented at the annual meeting of the American Statistical Association, San Francisco (August 17–20).

Boruch, R. F. 1975. "Coupling Randomized Experiments and Approximations to Experiments in Social Program Evaluation." *Sociological Methods and Research.* 4:31–53.

Boruch, R. F. and H. W. Riecken. eds. 1975. *Experimental Testing of Public Policy.* Boulder, Colorado: Westview Press.

Boruch, R. F. and J. S. Cecil. 1979. *Assuring the Confidentiality of Social Research Data.* Philadelphia, PA: University of Pennsylvania Press.

Boruch, R. F. and R. W. Pearson. 1988. "Assessing the Quality of Longitudinal Surveys." *Evaluation Review* 12:3–58.

Bradburn, N. M., L. J. Rips, and S. K. Shevell. 1987. "Answering Autobiographical Questions: The Impact of Memory and Inference on Surveys." *Science* 236:157–161.

Cannell, C. F., G. Fisher, and T. Bakker. 1965. *Reporting of Hospitalization in the Health Interview Survey, Vital and Health Statistics,* Series 2, No. 6. Washington, D.C.: U.S. Government Printing Office.

Carroll, D. 1987. Personal Communication, December 8, 1987.

Carter, W. 1987. Personal Communication, December 7, 1987.

Citro, C. F., and H. W. Watts. 1985. *Patterns of Household Composition and Family Status Change.* Paper presented to the American Economic Association, New York, New York.

Citro, C. F., D. J. Hernandez, and J. E. Moorman. 1986. *Longitudinal Household Concepts in SIPP.* Paper presented to the American Statistical Association, Chicago, Illinois, May 30.

Collins, L. M., J. W. Graham, W. B. Hansen, and C. A. Johnson. 1985. "Agreement between

Retrospective Accounts of Substance Use and Earlier Reported Substance Use." *Applied Psychological Measurement* 9:301–309.

Converse, J. M. 1987. *Survey Research in the United States: Roots and Emergence 1890–1960.* Berkeley, CA: University of California Press.

Conway, M. and M. Ross. 1984. "Getting What You Want by Revising What You Had." *Journal of Personality and Social Psychology* 47:738–748.

Corcoran, M. E., G. J. Duncan, G. Gurin, and P. Gurin. 1985. "Myth and Reality: The Causes of Persistence of Poverty. *Journal of Policy Analysis and Management* 4:516–536.

Cottingham, P. and A. Rodriguez. 1987. "The Experimental Testing of the Minority Female Single Parents Program." A paper presented at the annual meeting of the American Statistical Association, San Francisco (August 17–20).

David E. L. and H. M. Peskin. 1984. "Theory of an Optimal Database." *Review of Public Data Use* 12:45–53.

David, M. 1980. "Access to Data: The Frustration and Utopia of the Researcher." *Review of Public Data Use* 8:327–337.

———. 1985. "The Language of Panel Data and Lacunae in Communication about Panel Data." A paper presented at the annual meeting of the IFO/IASSIST, Amsterdam, Holland, May. (Also reprinted as Center for Demography and Ecology Working Paper 85–20).

Dawes, R. M. and R. W. Pearson. 1987. "The Effect of the Present on Retrospective Data: Measuring the Then, Now." New York: Social Science Research Council, mimeo.

Duncan, G. J., F. T. Juster, and J. N. Morgan. 1984. "The Role of Panel Studies in a World of Scarce Research Resources." In *The Collection and Analysis of Economic and Consumer Behavior Data: In Memory of Robert Ferber,* edited by S. Sudman and M. A. Spaeth. Champagne, Illinois: Bureau of Economic and Business Research.

Duncan, G. J., R. Coe, M. E. Corcoran, M. Hill, M. S. Hoffman, and J. M. Morgan. 1984. *Years of Plenty, Years of Hope.* Ann Arbor: Survey Research Center, University of Michigan.

Duncan, G. J. and G. Kalton. 1985. "Issues of Design and Analysis of Surveys across Time." A paper presented at the centenary session of the International Statistical Institute, Amsterdam.

Duncan, G. J. and N. A. Mathiowetz. 1985. *A Validation Study of Economic Survey Data.* Ann Arbor, MI: Institute for Social Research, mimeo.

Duncan, G. J., M. S. Hill, and S. D. Hoffman. 1988. "Welfare Dependence within and across Generations." *Science.* 239:467–471.

Fienberg, S. B. and J. Tanur. 1986. "From the Inside Out and the Outside In: Combining Experimental and Sampling Structures." *Technical Report No. 373,* Carnegie Mellon University (December).

———. 1987a "The Design and Analysis of Longitudinal Surveys: Controversies and Issues of Costs and Continuity. In *Designing Research With Scarce Resources,* edited by R. W. Pearson and R. F. Boruch. New York: Springer-Verlag.

———. 1987b. "Experimental and Sampling Structures: Parallels Diverging and Meeting." *International Statistical Review* 55:75–96.

Fraker, T. and R. Maynard. 1985. "The Use of Comparison Group Designs in Evaluation of Employment Related Programs." Princeton, N.J.: Mathematica Policy Research, mimeo.

———. 1987. "The Study of Comparison Group Designs for Evaluations of Employment-related Programs. *The Journal of Human Resources* 22:194–227.

Greenberg, D. F. 1985. "Age, Crime and Social Explanation." *American Journal of Sociology* 91, 1–21.

Heckman, J. J. and R. Robb, Jr. 1985. "Alternative Methods for Evaluating the Impact of

Interventions." In *Longitudinal Analysis of Labor Market Data,* edited by J. J. Heckman and B. Singer, 156–246. New York: Cambridge University Press.

Heckman, J. J. and B. Singer. eds. 1985. *Longitudinal Analysis of Labor Market Data.* New York: Cambridge University Press.

Hirschi, T. and M. Gottfredson. 1983. "Age and the Explanation of Crime." *American Journal of Sociology* 91: 359–374.

————. 1985. "Age and Crime, Logic and Scholarship: Comment on Greenberg." *American Journal of Sociology* 91: 22–27.

Holland, P. W. and D. B. Rubin. 1986. "Research Designs and Causal Inferences: On Lord's Paradox." In *Survey Research Designs: Towards a Better Understanding of Their Costs and Benefits.* edited by R. W. Pearson and R. F. Boruch, 7–37. New York: Springer-Verlag.

Kerckhoff, Alan C. 1980. "Looking Back and Looking Ahead." Pp. 257–271, edited by Alan C. Kerckhoff. *Research in Sociology of Education and Socialization,* Vol 1: *Longitudinal Perspectives on Educational Attainment.* Greenwich, CT: JAI Press.

Koo, H. 1985. "Short-term Change in Household and Family Structure." Paper presented to the American Statistical Association, Las Vegas, Nevada.

LaLonde, R. 1986. "Evaluating the Econometric Evaluations of Training Programs with Experimental Data." *American Economic Review* 76 (4):604–20.

Lazarsfeld, P. F., B. Berelson, and H. Gaudet. (1944) 1960. *The People's Choice: How the Voter Makes Up His Mind in a Presidential Campaign.* 2nd ed. New York: Columbia University Press.

Lord, F. M. 1967. "A Paradox in the Interpretation of Group Comparisons." *Psychological Bulletin* 68:304–305.

————. 1968. "Statistical Adjustments When Comparing Preexisting Groups." *Psychological Bulletin* 72:336–337.

————. 1973. "Lord's paradox." In *Encyclopedia of Educational Evaluation.* Anderson, S. B. et al. San Francisco: Jossey-Bass.

Mathiowetz, N. A. 1986. "Episodic Recall and Estimation: Applicability of Cognitive Theories to Survey Data." Paper presented at a Seminar on the Effects of Theory-Based Schemas on Retrospective Data, June 26–28, New York: Social Science Research Council.

Maynard, R. 1987. "The Role of Experiments in Employment and Training Evaluations." A paper presented at the annual meeting of the American Statistical Association (August 17–20).

Migdal, S., R. P. Abeles, and L. R. Sherrod. 1981. "An Inventory of Longitudinal Studies of Middle and Old Age." New York: Social Science Research Council

Mundel, D. Memo to Franklin Zweig. 1979. Congressional Budget Office (November 15).

Murray, G. F. and P. G. Erickson. 1987. "Cross-sectional Versus Longitudinal Research: An Empirical Comparison of Projected and Subsequent Criminality. *Social Science Research* 16, 107–118.

Newcomb, T. M. (1943) 1957. *Personality and Social Change: Attitude Formation in a Student Community.* New York: Dryden.

Pearson, R. W. 1985. "The Changing Fortunes of the U.S. Statistical System, 1980–1985." *Review of Public Data Use* 12:245–269.

Rice, S. A. 1928. *Quantitative Methods in Politics.* New York: Knopf.

Riecken, H. W. et al. 1974. *Social Experimentation.* New York: Academic.

Schuman, H. and G. Kalton. 1986. "Survey methods." Pp. 635–697 in *The Handbook of Social Psychology,* 3rd ed., edited by G. Lindzey and E. Aronson. Reading, MA: Addison-Wesley.

Sebring, P., B. Campbell, M. Glusberg, B. Spencer, M. Singleton, and C. D. Carroll. 1987.

High School and Beyond 1980 Sophomore Cohort Third Follow-Up (1986) Data File User's Manual, Volume 1. Chicago: National Opinion Research Center.

Subcommittee on Federal Longitudinal Surveys, Federal Committee on Statistical Methodology. 1986. *Federal Longitudinal Surveys.* Washington, D.C.: Office of Management and Budget.

Sudman, S. and N. M. Bradburn. 1982. *Asking Questions.* San Francisco: Jossey-Bass.

Taeuber, R. and R. C. Rockwell. 1982. ''National Social Data Series: A Compendium of Brief Descriptions. *Review of Public Data Use* 10:23–111.

Turner, A. G. 1972. ''The San Jose Methods Test of Known Crime Victims.'' Washington, D.C.: National Criminal Justice Information and Statistics Service, Law Enforcement Assistance Administration, U.S. Department of Justice.

Turner, C. F. and E. Martin. eds. 1984. *Surveying Subjective Phenomena,* Volume 1. New York: Russell Sage Foundation.

Verdonik, F. and L. R. Sherrod. 1984. *An Inventory of Longitudinal Research on Childhood and Adolescence.* New York: Social Science Research Council.

Wagenaar, W. A. 1986. ''My Memory: A Study of Autobiographical Memory over Six Years.'' *Cognitive Psychology* 18:225–252.

MEASUREMENT ERROR IN SECONDARY DATA ANALYSIS

Alan C. Acock

Measurement error is omnipresent in secondary data. Four issues are striking. First, many who design and execute the original surveys pay too little attention to measurement error. Second, researchers analyze data disregarding measurement error. Third, when measurement error is estimated its consequences are often ignored. Fourth, corrective action is often misdirected.

There are three sections. First, we discuss measurement models. We compare the strict operationalism of the neo-positivists to a multi-level conceptualization of measurement. Second, the consequences of measurement error are reviewed. This discussion is based on an interval level model assuming random error. The General Social Survey is used to illustrate the effects of measurement error. Some attention is given to a categorical measurement model, systematic error, and full versus limited information solutions. The

Research in the Sociology of Education and Socialization,
Volume 8, pages 201–230.
Copyright © **1989 by JAI Press Inc.**
All rights of reproduction in any form reserved.
ISBN: 0-89232-929-7

third section reviews sources of measurement error in secondary analysis and various solutions. Topics include the number of questions, the type and location of questions, external validity of samples, collapsing data, missing data, problems for multi-group comparisons, correlated errors, and the effects of outliers on error variance estimates. The conclusion presents implications for graduate training, secondary analysis, and theory construction.

MEASUREMENT MODELS AND MEASUREMENT ERROR

Social science research has come a considerable way from the strict operationalism that characterized positivist and neo-positivist research. We recognize that there are latent variables, not directly observed, containing variance that is only partially tapped by operationalizations. This involves a *multi-level conceptualization of measurement* (Acock 1979; Bagozzi 1980; Bailey 1984; Feigl 1970) represented in Figure 1.

On the one hand, we have abstract, theoretical concepts such as class and liberalism. We develop theories causally linking such abstractions. The domain of content of theoretical concepts extends beyond the operational definitions used in any particular study. They have systemic meaning. Examples of such theoretical concepts abound in socialization and education research:

> What Marx meant by 'class' or 'capitalism' is made manifest only in the whole corpus of his writing, as is Freud's meaning of 'libido,' or Durkheim's of 'anomie.' . . . The chances are, indeed, that a key term of this kind is 'defined' several times and in several different ways. This diversity does not necessarily mark a lapse of either logic or of memory, but the occurrence, rather, of systemic meaning (Kaplan 1964:64).

Beneath these theoretical concepts shown in Figure 1 are more specific, but still latent, concepts such as position in social relations of production and attitude toward abortion. These concepts, their linkage to the higher level theoretical concepts, and their causal relationships are the domain of mid-range theory.

The third level, the only one that we observe empirically, consists of indicators of these concepts. For example, family income and respondent's education might be used to measure the position in social relations of production and an hypothetical three-item scale might measure attitude toward abortion. With secondary analysis of survey data the isomorphism between the second (latent concepts) and third (empirical indicators) level is a core problem in measurement. The crucial problem is that we do not always have the best indicators to represent the latent variables as is illustrated by this example. This is the necessary trade-off in order to test relationships.

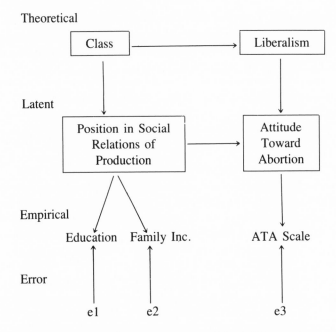

Figure 1.   Mûlti-Level Model of Social Research

A fourth level contains the measurement error associated with each of the indicators. Indeed, this measurement error can be further described as partly random or stochastic error and partly systematic error. We consider both types of error below.

A strict operational or positivist approach looks at the linkage between reported education and family income on the one hand and the attitude toward abortion scale score on the other hand. The implicit assumptions are that there is no measurement error in any of these three variables and that position in social relations of production and attitude toward abortion have no surplus meaning beyond that recorded through the three indicators.

Traditionalists see the conceptualization presented in Figure 1 as introducing vagueness into our models because it allows for surplus meaning of the higher-order concepts. However, there are advantages to concepts having a surplus of meaning. Costner (1969:245) argues that such concepts allow us to integrate ideas from a variety of different empirical studies, many of which have used slightly different indicators of the higher-order concepts. We are, in fact, interested in the relationship between class and liberalism rather than between reported education and computed attitude, or reported family income and computed attitude.

The direction of the causal flow in Figure 1 shows a clear theoritical hierarchy. Higher-order concepts determine lower-order concepts and lower-order concepts determine the measures used to operationalize them. This is the reverse of strict operationalism, which argues that the measures determine the concept (see Blalock 1968; Bailey 1984).

By using such procedures as Latent Structure Analysis and Analysis of Covariance Structures, we can move beyond the restrictions of strict operationalization. It is possible to estimate and incorporate estimates of measurement error into our models. We see below that the results can be dramatic.

CONSEQUENCES OF MEASUREMENT ERROR

What Measurement Error Does. Most research on the effects of measurement error assume interval level data and is based on classical measurement theory (Lord and Novick 1968). Typically, the observed score (X) is the sum of the true score (X_t) on a latent variable plus a random error (u):

$$X = X_t + u.$$

We assume that the random error component is "unbiased"—meaning that $E(u) = 0$, thus, the $E(X) = E(X_t)$. This is not true if any bias in the error leads us to over- or underestimate the true score of certain groups (e.g., women, minorities, the aged).

By algebraic manipulation several consequences of random measurement error can be revealed. This is simplified using a bivariate regression model (see Goldberger 1973:3–4):

$$Y = \beta X_t + v, \tag{2}$$

where β is the *unstandardized* population regression coefficient. For convenience, we assume the means of X_t and v are 0.0 and that they are independently distributed. It follows that: (1) $Var(X) = Var(X_t) + Var(u)$, (2) $Cov(XY) = \beta[Var(X_t)]$, and (3) $Var(Y) = \beta^2[Var(X_t)] + Var(v)$. We may express the predicted value of Y as an effect of X:

$$Y' = \beta^*X, \tag{3}$$

where

$$\beta^* = Cov(XY)/Var(X)$$
$$= \beta\{Var(X_t)/[Var(X_t) + Var(u)]\}. \tag{4}$$

Ordinary least squares gives us an unbiased estimate of β^*. Goldberger (1973) indicates it is a mistake to say we have a biased estimate. However, β^* is a mixture of structural parameters as defined by (4); $\beta^* \neq \beta$ when Var(u) $\neq$ 0. In other words, β^* is the product of the true β and the realiability of X, Var(Xt)/[Var(X_t) + Var(u)]. In effect, *we have an unbiased estimator of the wrong structural parameter!*

By extension (see Kessler and Greenberg (1981:138–139), the *standardized* regression coefficient (equal to r in the bivariate case) is attenuated by the square root of the reliability, $\{\text{Var}(X_t)/[\text{Var}(X_t) + \text{Var}(u)]\}^{1/2}$. When there is error in the dependent variable, there is no attenuation of the unstandardized coefficient, β, but the standardized coefficient will be attenuated by the square root of the reliability of the dependent variable, $\{\text{Var}(Y_t)[\text{Var}(Y_t) + \text{Var}(v)]\}^{1-2}$. When there is error in the dependent *and* independent variables the standardized coefficient is attenuated by $[\text{Var}(X_t)/[\text{Var}(X_t) + \text{Var}(u)]\}^{1/2}$ $\{\text{Var}(Y_t)/[\text{Var}(Y_t) + \text{Var}(v)]\}^{1/2}$. This multiplicative effect makes the attenuation dramatic even when there is a small amount of error in both variables.

Several treatments have outlined the effects of random measurement error on estimators when variables are at the interval-level. Bohrnstedt (1983, see also, Schwartz 1985) reports:

1. $E(X) = E(X_t)$,
2. the $\text{Var}(X) > \text{Var}(X_t)$,
3. the bivariate correlation (XY) < the true correlation (X_tY),
4. errors in the dependent variable do not affect estimates of the true unstandardized regression coefficients, and
5. in the multivariate case the "observed partial correlation coefficients and regression coefficients are usually, but not always, smaller than the true coefficients (1983:76)."
6. When error is present in both the independent and dependent variable the attenuation is multiplicative.

The last two effects are troublesome. What they mean in everyday practice can be seen in results from the 1986 General Social Survey in which we make varying assumptions about measurement error. We use a very simple model to show the effects of measurement error.

Our model is shown in Figure 2; the results are in Table 1. Taking a strict operationalist approach, we assume perfect measurement in all four variables. As is shown in Table 1, this results in the following OLS estimation equation:

$$\text{Abort.Att} = .195(\text{Educ}) + 0.32(\text{Fam.Inc}) - .380(\text{Relig}). \qquad (5)$$

This model explains 19.9 percent of the variance in the attitude toward abortion. What happens if we have measurement error in one or more of the variables? At one extreme, we can assume minimally adequate measurement.[1] With our single-item indicator of attitude toward abortion we assume that $\alpha = .50$. Similarly, we can make the same assumption about religiosity and family income (these assumptions cannot be tested since each uses a single item indicator). Table 1 presents maximum likelihood estimates using LISREL for the model in Figure 2 assuming low reliability for each variable:[2]

$$\text{Abort.Att} = .509(\text{Educ}) - .204(\text{Fam.Inc}) - .745(\text{Relig}). \qquad (6)$$

Table 1. Influence of Measurement Error on Estimates Using Education, Family Income, and Religiosity to Predict Attitude Toward Abortion

Model	Educations β	t	Family Income β	t	Religiosity β	t	R^2
Assume Perfect Measurement	.195	(7.742)	.032	(1.267)	−.380	(−16.144)	.199
Error in Educ.							
Only: $\alpha=.81$	.224	(7.599)	.013	(0.478)	−.377	(−15.996)	.208
$\alpha=.50$	.324	(7.599)	−.062	(−1.859)	−.367	(−14.967)	.244
Error in Income							
Only: $\alpha=.81$	.192	(7.262)	.037	(1.267)	−.380	(−16.123)	.199
$\alpha=.50$	.179	(5.656)	.053	(1.267)	−.378	(−16.014)	.200
Error in Relig.							
Only: $\alpha=.81$	.190	(7.440)	.028	(1.119)	−.423	(−16.142)	.233
$\alpha=.50$	.174	(6.293)	.017	(0.605)	−.540	(−16.107)	.344
Error in Abort.							
Only: $\alpha=.81$	.216	(7.742)	.035	(1.267)	−.422	(−16.144)	.246
Error in Abort.							
& Educ. $\alpha=.81$	.249	(7.736)	.014	(0.478)	−.419	(−15.996)	.257
$\alpha=.50$	.458	(7.610)	−.087	(1.874)	−.520	(−14.970)	.488
Error in Abort.							
& Inc. $\alpha=.81$	.213	(7.327)	.041	(1.267)	−.422	(−16.123)	.246
$\alpha=.50$	.254	(5.685)	.075	(1.267)	−.535	(−16.014)	.401
Error in Abort.							
& Rel. $\alpha=.81$	.211	(7.507)	.031	(1.119)	−.470	(−16.147)	.288
$\alpha=.50$	.246	(6.334)	.023	(0.605)	−.764	(−16.107)	.689
Low Reliability in all Variables							
$\alpha=.50$	.509	(4.571)	−.204	(−1.810)	−.745	(−14.787)	.774

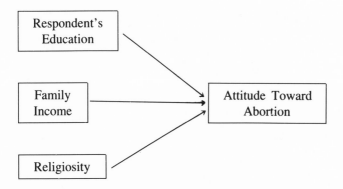

Figure 2. Regression Example for Assessing Effects of Measurement Error

Here the variables explain an estimated 77.4 percent of the variance in Attitude Toward Abortion.[3]

If we think of the variables as imperfect indicators of underlying latent variables, we can see that the assumptions of strict operationalism lead us to misleading decisions. Specifically,

1. The R^2 is .199 under strict operationalism versus .774 in a model that incorporates estimates of measurement error. *Measurement error lowers explanatory power of multivariate models.*

2. *Estimates of individual coefficients may be attenuated or exaggerated.* With the assumption of no measurement error we obtained a coefficient for income of .032, indicating an insignificant positive relationship between income and support for abortion. Assuming substantial measurement error we obtain −.204 which approaches significance in a negative direction!

Our evaluation of the effects of measurement error is complicated because not all variables have the same reliability. Assuming all the error is in the measurement of education, its coefficient is nearly as large as the coefficient for religiosity in terms of absolute value. Assuming all the error is in religiosity, its coefficient is more than twice the absolute value of the coefficient for education. Thus, the relative measurement error in these variables influences our assessment of the relative importance of different variables.

Researchers who use ordinary least squares to be "conservative" are misdirected when there are large amounts of error. They are conservative if all they want is an underestimation of R^2; they are wrong if interested in the relative contribution of different variables. Procedures that estimate measurement error (e.g., analysis of covariance structures) have advantages. Even when statistical estimates are impossible, however, a researcher should re-estimate the model varying assumptions about the magnitude of error for each variable. This determines the robustness of the findings. For instance, a sizable amount of the variance in the abortion attitude is explained by a combination of education, family income, and religiosity. Family income does not have a substantial direct effect, while both education and religiosity do regardless of assumptions about error. Moreover, religiosity has the greatest influence, but the amount of difference between it and other variables changes considerably depending on the assumptions we make about measurement error.

We lack clear standards for selecting appropriate values for the error in the absence of statistical estimates. Sorbom and Joreskog (1982) set the error variance, $\Theta_{\delta i}$, at 10 percent of $Var(X_i)$ and λ_i at 95 percent of the $Var(X_i)$. Anderson and Gerbing (in press) suggest setting $\Theta_{\delta i}$ for each single indicator at the smallest value for other estimated errors, $\Theta_{\delta i}$. A more realistic rule of thumb is trying several values between the largest and smallest estimated error for other indicators that are similar (e.g., other attitude scales, background characteristics, etc.). Both the latter approaches use information in the given research context (same sample and related variables) for making the estimates.

Systematic Error. It is often useful to distinguish between random and systematic measurement errors. However, understanding of systematic error can be obtained by conceptualizing it as specification error. If a particular scale overestimates the true score for Jews while underestimating it for Catholics, we have omitted a causally relevant variable—religion. Following Goldberger (1973) we use

$$Y = \beta^*X + u \qquad (7)$$

to estimate

$$Y = \beta_1 X_1 + \beta_2 X_2 + v, \qquad (8)$$

where X is the measured independent variable, X_1 is the true independent variable, and X_2 is the omitted variable, religion. While distinct from the effect of random error in (3), nonetheless, the problem is the same. β^* will not equal β_1 unless β_2 is 0.0. Once again, β^* represents a mixture of structural parameters.

Error with Nominal Classifications. While other fields have examined how measurement error influences nominal classifications (Bross 1954; Cochran, 1968), social scientists have paid little attention to this problem. We

Table 2. Expected Results for Dichotomous Variables When Variable Contains Measurement Error

	OBSERVED SCORE IS 0	OBSERVED SCORE IS 1	ROW TOTAL IS THE TRUE FREQUENCY
TRUE SCORE IS 0	3610	190	3800
TRUE SCORE IS 1	10	190	200
COLUMN TOTAL IS THE OBSERVED FREQUENCY	3620	380	4000

Assumptions: Reliability = .95
True rate for unemployment = .05

have assumed that nominal classifications (race, marital status, employment status, sex, nationality, etc.) were measured with so little error that we did not need to worry about them. Schwartz (1985) applied the literature on measurement error with nominal classifications to social research. His results are disconcerting to those doing categorical analysis of secondary data.

Small amounts of measurement error can create major problems (Bross 1954). The problem is greatest for the rare outcome rather than for the more frequent outcome. Schwartz (1985) provides an example where a survey is used to estimate a rare outcome, unemployment. If the true rate is .05 and the reliability is .95, the results are dreadful. Table 2 shows this. Of the 3800 people with a true score of 0 (employed), 95 percent, or 3610, will be correctly classified with an observed score of 0 and 5 percent, or 190, will be classified with an observed score of 1. Of the 200 people who are truly unemployed, 95 percent of them, or 190, will be classified this way and 5 percent, or 10, will be classified as employed. Thus, if 200 people are truly unemployed, the survey will estimate that 380 people are unemployed—half of whom will be working!

The problems with categorical data are not all the same as the problems with interval-level data (Schwartz 1985), but they are just as important. Specifically, where ψ represents the true proportion and p is the estimate in the presence of measurement error:

1. $E(p) > \psi$, $\psi < .5$;
    $E(p) < \psi$, $\psi > .5$,
2. $Var(p) > Var(\psi)$,
3. Measurement errors cannot be uncorrelated with ψ, and
4. Attenuation of bivariate correlations is greater than it is for the interval-level case.

Thus, researchers who deal with categorical data face somewhat different, but no less serious problems with measurement error. As these researchers use increasingly sophisticated forms of multivariate analysis, further research on the consequences of measurement error is urgently needed. A multivariate analysis in which half of the respondents classified as unemployed are actually employed will provide misleading results.

Full Information versus Limited Information Strategies. The impact of measurement error varies depending on whether a full information or limited information model is used. Limited information approaches to measurement base the meaning of each latent variable solely on the indicators of that particular latent variable. If there are $P_1 = 4$ indicators of political efficacy then the meaning of political efficacy is derived from a confirmatory analysis of those four items. The measurement error estimated for each of the four indicators depends solely on the information available in the covariance matrix of the four variables. This means that there are $P_1(P_1 + 1)/2 = 10$ equations used to identify the latent variable and the error variances.

Limited information approaches include summated scores in which each of the indicators receives a unit weight, factor scores in which items are weighted based on an exploratory factor analysis, and confirmatory factor analysis in which the weight of each indicator is allowed to vary, but various constraints are placed on certain coefficients. Error variance may be estimated for each indicator using the confirmatory factor analysis approach or simply set to $1 - \alpha$ if a summated score using unit weights is used. The key point when using a limited information approach is that the interpretation of the latent variable is based only on epistemic criteria and is not confounded by indicators of other latent variables or relationships in the structural model (Burt 1976).

In contrast, a full information solution defines the meaning of each latent variable in terms of all indicators in the full model and all the structural relationships. With $P = 25$ indicators in the full model, there are $P(P + 1)/2 = 325$ equations estimated simultaneously. Adding or deleting a structural coefficient, a latent variable, or even a single indicator anywhere in the model alters the meaning of each latent variable and the estimates of error variance for each indicator.

To the extent that social theory is based on the full model, then the full information approach makes sense. It is also the most efficient way to estimate parameters (Joreskog and Wold 1982). The covariance between indicators of one latent variable and indicators of a separate latent variable should have restrictions on them in a well-developed theory. However, where theoretical development is weak and new latent variables are being generated, a limited information approach should be considered. Anderson and Gerbing (in press) advocate a two-step process in which properties of the measurement model are examined thoroughly before being combined with the structural properties of the model.

MEASUREMENT ERROR: SOURCES AND TREATMENTS

Secondary data presents special problems because the researcher can do little about many sources of measurement error. Sources inherent in the sampling design, questionnaire design, interviewing methods, coding, and so on are beyond the researcher's control. Others are the result of poor decisions made by the secondary analyst. These include collapsing categories in ways that destroy meaningful variance, using inappropriate levels of measurement, failing to diagnose errors such as outliers, using procedures such as correlations of ratio variables which compound the effects of measurement error, or failing to adjust for differential levels of error when making group comparisons. Both sources of error are reviewed in this section.

Too Few Questions Are Asked. A painful limitation of secondary data is that only a few questions are asked on any topic (Kiecolt and Nathan 1985). This makes scale construction extremely difficult. At one extreme, a single item may represent a complex conceptual variable. A question asking a person's opinion about abortion in cases of rape will yield different results than one asking about abortion in cases where an unmarried woman does not want to bear a child. A single question may poorly represent the domain of a complex concept. For most conceptual variables, even two or three questions are too few to represent the domain adequately.

From Spearman's (1910) and Brown's (1910) work on reliability we can easily derive the effect the number of items in a scale has on its reliability (Carmines and Zeller 1979):

$$\alpha = N\bar{r}/[1 + \bar{r}(N - 1)] \qquad (9)$$

where N is the number of items and $\bar{r}$ is the expected value of the inter-item correlations. Thus, reliability is a monotonic function of the number of items.

With modest inter-item correlations the function approaches its asymptote when 10 items are used. The most dramatic improvement in reliability occurs as we move from one to five items. If we draw a single item from a pool of items which have an expected inter-item correlation of .5, the effective reliability estimate is .5. With five items the reliability is .83. With 20 items it is .95. While long scales used in small-scale studies have an advantage, the use of five items takes us a long way. Given this, it is regrettable that most surveys use too few indicators of complex concepts.

Increasing the number of items has no effect on systematic measurement error. A researcher who uses five items measuring attitude toward abortion that all present situations in which a pregnancy was voluntary will have different result than a second researcher who uses five items dealing with forced pregnancy. Adding more items has no effect on the systematic error.

Asking the Wrong Questions. Given the enormous cost of surveys, it is remarkable how little of the time, money, and thought is given to the wording of questions. Yet, the quality of secondary analysis of survey data depends on the quality of the information obtained in the survey. Bohrnstedt states:

> . . . too often far too little time goes into the writing of the items, and once written and employed in the field, no technique, no matter how 'fancy' or sophisticated, can salvage a set of lousy items (1983:115).

Optimism concerning how a secondary analyst can get around such limitations is boundless and new techniques are constantly being suggested. Nonetheless, there is much truth in Bohrnstedt's statement.

One example of asking the wrong question involves items that have limited discriminatory power. This results in restricted range or ceiling effects.[4] Many items have 70 percent to 90 percent of the respondents giving a single response. For example, this is common with job satisfaction measures. To the extent that there is independent evidence that the underlying variable is not this skewed, there will be considerable measurement error. Respondents may be giving accurate responses to the questions asked, but their answers do not reflect the full variance in the underlying concept being measured.

External and Internal Validity of Sample. A pervasive source of measurement error involves external validity. Many samples under-represent certain segments of the population. If the under-represented segments of the population differ on the variable, the external validity of measurement is lacking. Examples of this involve a lack of weighting or using formulas for standard errors that assume random sampling with replacement (cf. Cochran 1968). Sampling designs are often multi-stage. The GSS used a modified probability sample from 1972–1974 that included quotas at the block level.

From 1975–77 a full probability sample design was used although in 1975 and 1976 half of the sample was full probability and half used the block quota. While these designs allow researchers to disentangle true historical change from the change in design, rarely is this considered. From 1977 to 1986 a full probability sample was used. Davis and Smith (1986) suggested that a sample size of about 1,500 be treated as an effective sample size of 1,000 because of the sampling design. This sample size adjustment may or may not be used in actual research.

An example of the external validity problem is represented in Table 3 for Race, Age, and Sex. These data are from the cumulative file for the General Social Survey (through 1986) and include the WEIGHT factor. Both males and blacks are more difficult to locate and interview than females and whites. If black males have different attitudes than white females, any summary statistics (means, correlations) based on the sample will contain measurement error because of attenuated variances. Table 3 shows that only 39.9 percent of blacks between 18 and 30 are male. In contrast, 43.0 percent of blacks over 45 are males. Since black males do not have longer life expectancies than black females, it is clear that these results are not representative of the general population. Not surprisingly, young black males are under-represented in the General Social Survey as well as most other surveys. Surveys that pay less attention to sampling than the General Social Survey pose a greater problem.

Sample selection bias can introduce internal problems for validity as well. Berk (1983) shows that under-representation of people with low scores on Y results in an attenuation of the slope linking Y to X. This means that respondents who have low scores on X have a predominance of negative errors, while those with high scores on X have a predominance of positive errors. Thus, errors in Y are positively correlated with X. Other patterns of sample selection bias produce different results and in the multivariate case the problem becomes quite complex. According to Berk, "By excluding some observations in a systematic way, one has inadvertently introduced the need for an additional regressor. . ." (Berk 1983:388; see also, Heckman 1979, 1980). This is precisely the result we defined as systematic error in (7)–(8) above.

Asking the Wrong Person. Another major source of error is the use of proxies as informants. Anderson and Silver (1987) assert that many surveys have this problem (the census, crime surveys, fertility studies, and other surveys where a single individual reports for the entire household). In a comparison of spouses from the Soviet Interview Project General Survey, Anderson and Silver show that great variance exists in the accuracy of respondents as informants depending on the topic.

This problem is greatly compounded when attitudes are reported by proxies. Acock and Bengtson (1980) described this problem as "polarized misat-

Table 3.   Race by Sex Controlling for Age

First panel is for those 18–30

		MALE	FEMALE	ROW TOTAL
		1	2	
RACE				
WHITE	1	2212	2545	4757
		46.5%	53.5%	100.0%
BLACK	2	277	417	694
		39.9%	60.1%	100.0%

Second panel is for those 31–45
COUNT

		MALE	FEMALE	ROW TOTAL
		1	2	
RACE				
WHITE	1	2215	2643	4858
		45.6%	54.4%	100.0%
BLACK	2	227	369	595
		38.2%	61.8%	100.0%

Third panel is for those over 45
COUNT

		MALE	FEMALE	ROW TOTAL
		1	2	
RACE				
WHITE	1	3437	4495	7932
		43.3%	56.7%	100.0%
BLACK	2	412	546	958
		43.0%	57.0%	100.0%

tribution'' in which children underestimate differences between their parents (little differentiation reported between attitudes of mother and father) while over-estimating differences between their parents and themselves, thus exaggerating the generation gap. Informants may be expected to either over- or underestimate the opinions of others.

A second problem related to asking the wrong person is asking questions that the respondent cannot or will not answer correctly. Wyner (1981) reports an analysis of self-reported arrests which he compares to the actual number. Fewer than 15 percent of the respondents gave completely accurate responses and error was systematic. The reported rate was correlated $-.38$ with the error. Those arrested most often under-reported arrests the most. In general, socially desirable responses are over-reported and socially undesirable ones are under-reported (Bohrnstedt 1983; Pary and Crossley 1950; Lansing, et al. 1961).

Item Context. The order in which questions are asked can influence answers. Item context is a source of systematic measurement error. Scott (1987) shows this with abortion measures in the General Social Survey. Respondents give a more conservative response when asked about a married woman having an abortion because *she does not want more children* if this follows a question about abortion when a *serious defect in the child* is likely. The defect question focuses attention to a "baby's life" rather than to the woman's needs. Earlier work by Smith (1979) shows that preceding a question on general happiness by a question on marital happiness increases the reported general happiness. He attributes this to high marital happiness having a context effect.

Secondary analysts can not do much about item context. However, data sets such as the General Social Survey make it possible to compare results from different years when the context varied.[5] This is illustrated in the work of Smith (1979) where he examines long term trends in Happiness controlling for item context, seasonal context, wording of item and responses, and number of response categories.

Data Destruction. Many researchers are concerned about treating ordinal data as if it were interval. The crucial issue is whether the underlying concepts are continuous or categorical. If the theoretical or latent level in Figure 1 are continuous (age, attitude toward abortion, alienation, income), *treating the measured scores as ordinal categories increases measurement error*.

First, collapsing data into a few categories destroys variance in the data.[6] While we may not be sure of the metric, we can be sure that there is variance. For example, suppose we take an attitude score that ranges from 20 to 40 and form high and low categories (20–29 = low, 30–40 = high). We are assuming that respondents who score a 20 are indistinguishable from those who score a 29. Borgatta and Bohrnstedt describe the single item dichotomy as: ". . . a degenerate case in which the measurement has become as poor as possible. . . (1981:33)." Rather than being cautious and conservative, it systematically destroys variation in the data.

Second, collapsing data into a small number of categories produces correlated measurement error. This is evident for cases near the cut off point between categories. Observations with positive errors end up in the higher category and those with negative errors end up in the lower category. Thus, rather than eliminating measurement error, data destruction produces correlated measurement error.

Borgatta and Bohrnstedt (1981) summarize the issues surrounding forcing continuous conceptual variables into a needlessly small number of categories. They contend that while keeping as much information as possible does not insure accurate reproduction of the underlying metric, collapsing the data into a small number of ordinal categories guarantees substantial measurement error. Maximizing the amount of variance contributes to the reliability of our measurement. If it is reasonable to assign the value 0 to no and 1 to yes, then it is more reasonable to assign values of 0 to no, 1 to maybe, and 2 to yes, and so on. The contention that equal distances do not exist between the midpoints of categories is less serious a violation of the continuous conceptual variable than the assumption that every respondent either agrees or disagrees (1981:34).

Missing Data Problems. Missing data are always present in secondary analysis. The respondent may not understand the question or response alternatives, be unwilling to give an answer, skip items, or misunderstand how to record the answer. Alternatively, missing data may stem from field procedures, coding, or data entry.

There are techniques for dealing with missing data. Some solutions preserve as much information as possible (e.g., assign the mean of the variable to missing data, assign subgroup means to missing values, assign OLS predicted values on a variable for missing data, and include all cases that answer both of any particular pair of items). Other solutions preserve measurement purity (delete every case that is missing data on any item).

The literature concerning these problems is reviewed by Anderson et al. (1983). All solutions create measurement error. Assigning the mean to missing observations attenuates the variance (Marini, Olsen, and Rubin 1979). Assigning subgroup means creates serious problems if groups have different proportions of missing cases. The attenuation of variance is greatest for the subgroup which has the most missing observations. Using OLS estimates presumes that missing data have the same structural relationships as non-missing data. This is not likely given differences between those who answer problematic questions and those who do not (e.g., educational differences, class differences). Pairwise deletions produces a covariance matrix that does not correspond to any particular sample since each element is based on a slightly different sample—the covariance matrix may not be positive definite.

Listwise deletion may seem conservative, but poses a major threat to external validity since 10–20 percent or more of the cases are typically omitted. Such omitted cases may behave very differently than those who have answered every single item.

Missing data pose special problems for researchers comparing groups. When populations are compared that have different response rates, any observed differences between the samples may reflect true differences or may be an artifact of differences in response rates. For example, if mean substitution is used and 18–24 year old black males are compared to 18–24 year old white males, the attenuation of variance for the black sample may result in weaker relationships in that group than in the white group even when the population relationships are identical. In the multivariate case, biases may be either positive or negative.

Missing data pose great problems when they are systematic. Of particular importance to secondary analysts are missing observations on one predictor variable being related to scores on another predictor. Let $X = x_{ij}$ be a data matrix of predictor variables and let $M = m_{ij}$ be a corresponding matrix where $m_{ij} = 1$ if x_{ij} is present and $m_{ij} = 0$ if x_{ij} is missing. Measurement error is most problematic when any column vector in M is correlated with a different column vector in X.

For example, a 1987 survey asked nine questions measuring consistency and intensity of party identification across three election levels (presidential, congressional, and state). Fully 12.2 percent of the sample had missing data on at least one question (Acock 1987). Those with missing data averaged over 2 years less education. Thus, it is not possible to disentangle the effects of party consistency from those of education.

A number of secondary analysts include dummy variables and sometimes even interactions as a way of testing for relations between missing observations on predictor variables and scores on the effect variable. While not dealing with the dependencies between missing observations on one predictor and scores on other predictors, this approach is useful. M is included along with X in the structural equation:

$$Y = \beta X + \Gamma M + e. \tag{10}$$

If none of the estimates in Γ are significantly predictors, then missing data is less serious. Any of the γ coefficients that are significant signify that respondents who have missing values on those values have a mean shift on the dependent variable. It is also possible to allow for interactions between X and M. This tests to see if observations with missing values have different structural relationships between X and Y.

Witting and Unwitting Multi-Group Comparisons. Surveys frequently borrow scales or subsets of scales from older surveys. While this allows researchers to look at changes over time or across populations, it introduces a problem when a scale is more reliable for one sample than for another. A common statement in research is that a scale has "demonstrated reliability."

Such statements are an immediate call for caution. Unless the reliability is computed on the sample and subgroups being studied, reliability estimates for other samples, at other times, using other designs are of limited utility.

This problem sneaks into studies even when reliability is estimated (Jagodzinski and Kuhnel 1987; Converse 1964, 1970). For example, a regression analysis is conducted linking several socioeconomic background variables to school performance. The researcher introduces a dummy variables and interaction terms for race. Implicit, is the assumption that the reliability of each scale is identical for each race. However, measures of socioeconomic factors and school achievement may not have equal reliabilities for different races. As we saw in Table 1, differences in reliability produce differences in results. Unless each group has been shown to have the same reliability or unless estimates of measurement error have been incorporated to allow for differences (e.g., analysis of covariance structures), the results are suspect.

Panel studies examine stability and change in a single population across time. A single group, however, may have different measurement reliability at each time period (Kessler and Greenberg 1981; Wheaton et al. 1977). For example, sex role attitude scores may have different reliabilities at age 13 than for the same adolescents when they are 17. Differences in reliability may be due to maturation changes in the group or historical effects.

Closely related to this is the problem of invariance of measurement models across groups being compared (Porst, Schmidt, and Zeifang 1987). Some researchers are not using procedures such as LISREL to test for such invariance because of limitations in their data. They should be using such procedures *because* of the limitations in their data. If it is difficult to demonstrate that measurement models are invariant, one is not, thereby, justified in using procedures that make untested assumptions of identical measurement across groups.

These points may be illustrated using an hypothetical example from socialization research in which multiple groups are implicitly involved and in which various assumptions can be made about the measurement model. We use a deliberately simplified model linking the mother's value of education to that of her child (Figure 3).

The five panels in Figure 3 present increasingly complex and realistic measurement models. There are really two groups, namely, mothers and their children. Panel 1 shows the most typical way of treating this relationship using summed measures of the value of education. Three items are summed and the sum for the child is regressed on the sum for the mother using OLS. Implicit in this summated scale model are the assumptions that each item has a unit weighting and that the error associated with each item is zero. A re-

Panel 1:
Perfect Measures Model:

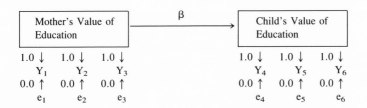

Panel 2:
Single Error Model:

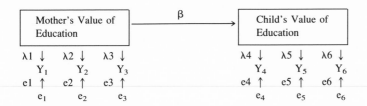

Panel 3:
Random Error Model:

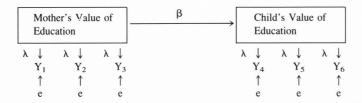

Panel 4:
Invariant Measurement Model:

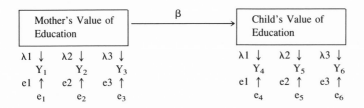

Figure 3.   (Continued)

Panel 5:

Test-specific Measurement Model:

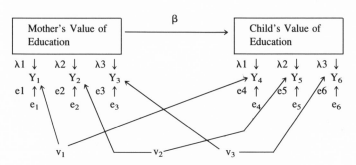

Figure 3.   Alternative Measurement Models

searcher may report that $\alpha = .80$ for the sample, but this is not utilized by OLS. Moreover, it does not mean that the mothers and children are equally reliable.

Panel 2 presents the implied model used when adjusting for attenuation (Lord and Novick 1968:69–74). This involves estimating $\alpha = .80$ for the sample, but this is not utilized by OLS. Moreover, it does not mean that the mothers and children are equally reliable.

Panel 2 presents the implied model used when adjusting for attention (Lord and Novick 1968:69–74). This involves estimating α, assuming that each item is identically reliable to every other item both within and across groups, and fixing $e = 1 - \alpha$. This is shown in Figure 3 by having e's with no subscript (because they are identical) and a single λ to represent how each coefficient is weighted identically. The problems with correction for attenuation techniques are twofold. First, they make unreasonable assumptions. Second, they become unworkable in the multivariate case.

The third panel is a random error model. Each indicator is allowed to have a different reliability (λ_i and e_i). This allows the two groups, mothers and their children, to have different reliability levels both overall and for each item. This model can be estimated using EQS or LISREL and corrects for attenuation in the estimation of β. Still, it has limitations. If $\lambda_1 \neq \lambda_4$, then the child's value of education is not the same thing as the mother's—we would be comparing apples to oranges. Differences between the corresponding λ's and e's create a serious conceptual problem of comparability—the latent variable, value of education, has different meaning for each generation.

The fourth panel, the invariant measurement model, is one solution to the problem of comparability. Here corresponding λ_i, but not corresponding e_i, are constrained to be equal. This solution constrains the meaning of value of education to be the same for both mothers and their children. Also, it allows the unique variance or error variance, e_i, to be different across variables and across populations. A more restrictive form of error variance, not illustrated in Figure 3, makes the further requirement of the corresponding e_i being identical.

Each of the first four models avoids dealing with a potentially significant aspect of unique or error variance (sometimes called test-specific measurement error). Part of each error variance is random and part of it is systematic, or test-specific error (Jagodzinski and Kuhnel 1987). Since Y_1 and Y_4 are the same question asked of a mother and her child, errors in measuring Y_1 and Y_4 may be correlated—they are specific to each question. The proper way of defining the response to each question is:

$$Y = \Lambda \eta + e + v \qquad (11)$$

In (11) we have added v to reflect the fact that the response to each item additionally depends on this test-specific variance. Part of the apparent influence of the mother on her daughter, β, may be because there is a test-specific variance that has nothing to do with a mother influencing her daughter. Failure to incorporate both the random component and the test-specific component of the error variance will bias the estimation of β (see Wheaton et al. 1977; Alwin and Jackson 1979, Joreskog 1979).

Raffalovich and Bohrnstedt (1987) partition the variance in indicators of religiosity using four items as indicators of religiosity and three time periods. They report that random error accounts for about a third, and item-specific variance for from five to twenty-percent of the variance in each item. Assuming no test-specific variance is a significant source of misspecification.

These problems are just as serious for discrete concepts. Researchers who use categorical concepts or force their measures into a categorical treatment face very serious problems when attempting multi-group comparisons. Cochran (1968) demonstrates the seriousness of this problem in other fields. Schwartz, comparing unemployment rates for men and women, shows that different classification reliability across groups makes it ". . . virtually impossible to draw any conclusions about the true differences between the groups in unemployment rates. . ." Even when the reliability is identical across groups the observed difference in unemployment rates are attenuated. Where reliability can be determined, it is possible to correct these biases. There are no standards for estimating reliability but values of between .90 and 1.0 seem reasonable for many categorical variables (e.g., unemployment, marital status, religion, sex, race). Applying these to each group would make it possible to test the robustness of the findings. Nevertheless, few such corrections are being incorporated in secondary data analysis.

Correlated Errors and Multi-dimensionality. In general, theoretical concepts should be unidimensional. ''Multi-Dimensional'' theoretical concepts are really multiple concepts. The common practice of the 1960s and 1970s of finding orthogonal aspects of concepts is really finding orthogonal concepts. If a researcher finds empirical evidence that one form of alienation is unrelated (orthogonal) to another form of alienation, the empirically orthogonal forms of alienation are not implications of a single underlying theoretical concept. Instead, they are implications of two underlying concepts. Otherwise, the loadings of the two orthogonal indicators, X_1 and X_2, on the single latent variable, ξ (alienation), would be 0.0. Such a result would make the underlying concept meaningless.[7]

Correlated error variances is an implication of more than one theoretical dimension. Whenever correlated errors appear, there is some hidden dimension that has been excluded from the analysis. There are two ways in which hidden dimensions, disguised as correlated errors, occur. The discussion of Figure 3 indicates how this happens when errors in indicators of one latent variable, mother's value of education, are correlated with errors in indicators of a second latent variable, child's value of education. This says there is another factor (hidden concept or variable) that is not included in the model (see panel 5). For this example, it may not be a test-specific factor but something else such as the attitude of the father which influences both the mother's and the child's attitude. Including such factors is the appropriate solution.[8] In secondary data analysis this is often impossible since the necessary information is not available.

A second way that correlated errors occur is when errors among the indicators of a single latent variable are correlated. This means that there are really two latent variables, each of which may be unidimensional. Acock, Clarke, and Stewart (1985) show that five standard indicators of political efficacy can be forced to fit one latent variable but result in a χ^2 of 130.56 (p < .0001) with five degrees of freedom. When errors are allowed to be correlated, the χ^2 is 5.86 (p = .618) with three degrees of freedom. Such correlated errors mask the fact that political efficacy is multi-dimensional (cf. Bagozzi 1983; Fornell 1983, Gerbing and Anderson 1984). When the items are rearranged to represent two dimensions of political efficacy, internal vs. external, the χ^2 is also 5.86 (p = .618) with three degrees of freedom. While it is easy to improve the fit of a model by correlating error variances across indicators of troublesome latent variables, the resulting improvement in fit does not make the latent variables less troublesome. Such correlations should only be used when the "other dimension" is considered a nuisance factor that is of no theoretical interest.[9] Separating variance of the nuisance factor from the variance of the primary factor improves the fit but does so only by sweeping the multi-dimensionality of the concept under the carpet.

Ratio variables present many problems to researchers.[10] This is the case with correlated measurement error. The true correlation may be exaggerated or attenuated (Long 1979). There will be a positive bias for the following relationships:

$$Y/(Z + e) = \beta[X/(Z + e)] + v; \tag{12.1}$$

$$(Z + e)/Y = \beta[(Z + e)/X] + v; \text{ and} \tag{12.2}$$

$$(Z + e)/Y = \beta(Z + e) + v. \tag{12.3}$$

There will be a negative bias for:

$$Y/(Z + e) = \beta[(Z + e)/X] + v; \tag{13.1}$$

$$Y/(Z + e) = \beta(Z + e) + v. \tag{13.2}$$

The actual impact of error on ratio variables can be enormous. For example, if the correlation between Y/Z and Z is 1.0 (equation 13.2), what happens if Z is measured with error? If the reliability of Z is .90, the observed r is .797. With a reliability of .70, the observed r is .368. With a reliability of .50, the observed r is $-.101$. When there is error in both Y and Z, the effects of small amounts of error are much greater!

Outliers, Heteroscedasticity and the Heywood Case. Two related and sometimes confused problems with measurement error involve outliers and heteroscedasticity of errors. An outlier refers to an observation that is so far from the expected response that it is reasonable to assume that their is a large error for that particular observation. Cook (1981:322–323) defines outliers as errors in measurement.

$$\mathbf{Y} = \mathbf{X\beta} + \mathbf{d\Gamma} + \mathbf{e} \tag{15}$$

where $\mathbf{d}$ is an n vector whose ith value is 1; all other coordinates being 0. A significant γ means the model for the ith case is different from the general model by a mean shift. Cook and Weisberg (1982; see also, Hoaglin and Welsch 1978) suggest a variety of ways of identifying and dealing with such outliers.

Bollen (1987) provides an example of what he describes as a problem of outliers, but actually is an example of heteroscedasticity of errors. Three people are asked to judge how much of the sky is covered by clouds. When the weather is overcast, the three judges give widely different estimates of the coverage. The rest of the time they give very similar estimates. When it was overcast one judge estimated 95 percent cloud coverage, a second 0 percent, and a third 40 percent. Thus, measurement error has enormous variance on a day in which it is overcast but little variance otherwise. Bollen shows that estimates of goodness of fit and structural coefficients are greatly influenced by the heteroscedasticity of the measurement error. By dropping three cases in which it was overcast, a Heywood case (negative error variance estimate) is eliminated. Bollen also shows ways of detecting such problems and removing those "outliers" that are causing the problem. There is little research on these procedures but Gnanadesikan (1977) and Bentler (1985) make some suggestions.

Sample size also is relevant to these problems of outliers and hetroscedasticity of errors. With sufficiently large samples many of the problems with nonconverging and improper solutions evaporate (see Dillon, Kumar and Mulani 1987, Gerbing and Anderson 1987). Where there are at least three indicators per latent variable, Anderson and Gerbing (1984) suggest that 150 cases may eliminate such problems but larger samples are needed when there are only two indicators per factor. No clear standards as to sample size exist. All the estimation procedures that deal with latent variables and measurement models that include error variance are large sample techniques. Anderson and Gerbing's figure of 150 is probably at the lower limit when assumptions are closely approximated. Depending on the estimation procedure used and characteristics of the data and model, others have estimated that at least 500 cases are necessary (see Anderson and Gerbing in press).[11]

If no outliers are present, a negative error variance estimate based on several hundred cases is due to either (a) sampling variation around a true parameter that is near zero, or (b) the model is badly misspecified. According to van Driel (1978), if a confidence interval about the negative variance is similar to other confidence intervals in width and includes zero, then the improper solution is assumed to be due to sampling error. Fixing the negative error variance at zero or at an arbitrarily small value is the suggested solution (Gerbing and Anderson 1987; Bentler 1976).

CONCLUSIONS

Two decades ago, Costner challenged social scientists to pay more attention to the rules of correspondence linking our theoretical concepts to our empirical indicators. He cautioned that we tended to focus on ill-defined abstractions alone or on strict operationalism.

> The requirement that scientific theories include both abstract concepts and concrete implications, and that the two be logically connected, has been treated rather casually by sociologists. . . . Either of these models of theory construction is costly, sacrificing either the clarity of empirical implications or the integrating potential of abstract concepts (1969:299).

In no area of research is this problem of multi-level conceptualization more important than in secondary analysis of survey data which contains substantial measurement error.

Secondary data analysts rarely acknowledge that their estimates are based on an assumption of only negligible measurement error (Schwartz 1985). We have seen that when this assumption is not met, researchers are generating unbiased estimates, but estimates of the wrong parameters.

Our review of the literature on measurement error leads to three sets of recommendations in the areas of (a) graduate training, (b) conduct of research, and (c) theory construction. Graduate training must give more attention to measurement error in questionnaire and sampling design. Borhnstedt (1983; see also, Bohrnstedt, et al. 1985) has deplored the lack of attention to measurement error in texts on survey research, questionnaire design, and statistical texts used to train those conducting secondary analysis. Training needs to stress the problems of measurement error for categorical as well as interval-level procedures. Our core statistical training is the biggest culprit because it normally assumes simple random sampling and error free measurement. Standard statistics texts used by first year graduate students neglect to show students how to deal with the problems we have outlined in this chapter. For example, much time is spent on why we divide by n-1 rather than n (e.g., 1500-1 versus 1500) when using a t distribution and no time is spent on the adjustments needed for non-random sampling designs (e.g., 1500 versus 1000). These texts do not prepare researchers to analyze secondary data.

Researchers should stop thinking they are conservative and cautious when they use procedures that ignore measurement error. Hiding our heads in the sand and relying on OLS is simply inappropriate in most secondary analysis. Similarly, collapsing a measure that represents an underlying continuum into a few categories results in inappropriate analysis and more flagrant measurement error than treating it as an imperfect interval scale. Collapsing data should not be done in the name of caution. Also, we need to stop reporting the level of reliability and start incorporating it into our analysis.

Procedures such as analysis of covariance structures allow researchers to incorporate measurement models and measurement error into their analysis.

While these methods (e.g., EQS and LISREL) are useful to experimental researchers, we have argued that they are crucial to secondary analysts. However, such procedures are not a panacea. New techniques for analyzing covariance structures are being released that will give much better estimates in the face of substantial and ill-behaved measurement error, but even these procedures require large samples.

Finally, the divergence between quantitative analysis and theory construction has been unfortunate. We need to integrate a multi-level conceptualization of measurement that bridges the gap between empirical research and theory construction.

ACKNOWLEDGMENTS

I wish to express special appreciation to K. Jill Kiecolt, Mike Grimes, Wayne Villemez, Jeanne Hurlbert, and Harold Clarke for thoughtful comments on an earlier draft of this chapter.

NOTES

1. Nunnaly (1978) indicates that for some research situations reliability as low as .50 to .60 may be acceptable.

2. LISREL is an analysis of covariance structures procedure based on maximum likelihood estimation (Joreskog and Sorbom 1984).

3. When maximum likelihood was used with LISREL to make the estimates assuming perfect measurement the results were identical to those in equation 5.

4. Berk (1983) points out that such floor and ceiling effects require a nonlinear form such as a logistic model.

5. Alwin (1987) points out that the General Social Survey uses randomized experiments (split ballots) that allow for identifying the sources of measurement errors (question wording, form, and context).

6. Andrews and Withey (1976) show, for example, that three categories reveals about 80 to 90 percent of the total variance in well-being while seven categories reveals virtually all of it.

7. It is possible to have empirically observed forms of alienation that are correlated as with an oblique factor rotation. In this instance they would be implications of two forms of alienation which in turn may be related to a higher order alienation factor. Higher order factor analysis is discussed by Bentler and Weeks (1980) as well as Bentler (1985).

8. It should be noted that correlated measurement errors are appropriate when there is compelling theoretical justification. An example is when the same variable is measured at two or more points in time. In such cases there is a priori, theoretical justification for the correlated residual and it is not included solely to improve the fit of the model.

9. Clarke, Stewart, and Zuk (1987) present an example of when a second factor is treated as a nuisance. In developing a measure of beliefs about socialist economics they find several items need correlated residuals. All of these items deal with unemployment. They can fit the model by adding another latent variable for unemployment with the troublesome items loading on both latent variables, or they can correlate the errors of the items dealing with unemployment. The two

latent variables are correlated .93 with each other and have the same pattern of correlations with other variables in their model. Since their theoretical interest is in socialist economics generally and they are not interested in unemployment, per se, the correlated errors are an appropriate solution.

    10. Debate over the use of ratio variables has continued for some time (Bollen and Ward 1979; Bradshaw and Radbill 1987; Firebaugh and Gibbs 1985; Kraft 1987). This controversy is beyond the scope of the present paper.

    11. It should be noted that the estimated χ^2 is a direct function of sample size. As larger samples insure convergence, they also produce larger χ^2 values. Joreskog and Sorbom (1984) suggest that other measures of goodness of fit are more appropriate than relying on the χ^2 when dealing with a large sample. Unfortunately, some people use the ratio of χ^2 to degrees of freedom. This is not a meaningful value since (a) its distribution is not understood and (b) it simply reduces the size of χ^2 without adjusting for the influence of sample size.

REFERENCES

Acock, A. C. 1979. "Applications of LISREL IV to Family Research." Presented at the National Council on Family Relations, Conference on theory and Methodology. Boston, MA.

Acock, A. C., and J. Huffman. 1987. "Party Consistency and Election Level." Presented at the Southern Political Science Association Meetings. Charlotte, North Carolina.

Acock, A. C., and V. Bengtson. 1980. "Socialization and the Attribution Processes: Actual vs. Perceived Similarity Among Parents and Youth." *Journal of Marriage and the Family.* 43:501–518.

Acock, A. C., H. D. Clarke, and M. C. Stewart. 1985. "A New Model for Old Measures: A Covariance Structure Analysis of Political Efficacy." *The Journal of Politics* 47:1062–1084.

Alwin, D., and D. J. Jackson. 1979, "Measurement Models for Response Errors in Surveys: Issues and Applications." Pp. 68–119 in *Sociological Methodology: 1980* edited by Karl F. Schuessler. San Francisco: Jossey-Bass.

Alwin, D. F. 1987. "The General Social Survey: Update on a National Data Resource for the Social Sciences." *ICPSR Bulletin* (December):1–3.

Anderson, B. A., and B. D. Silver. 1987. "The Validity of Survey Responses: Insights from Interviews of Married Couples in a Survey of Soviet Emigrants." *Social Forces* 66:537–554.

Anderson, J. C. and D. W. Gerbing. 1984. "The Effect of Sampling Error on Convergence, Improper Solutions, and Goodness-of Fit Indices for Maximum Likelihood Confirmatory Factor Analysis." *Psychometrika* 49:155–173.

Anderson, J. C., and D. W. Gerbing. In press. "Structural Equation Modeling in Practice: A Review and Recommended Two-Step Approach." *Psychological Bulletin.*

Andrews, F. M. and S. B. Withey. 1976. *Social Indicators of Well-Being: Americans' Perceptions of Life Quality.* New York: Plenum Press.

Bagozzi, R. P. 1980. *Causal Models in Marketing.* New York: Wiley.

Bagozzi, R. P. 1983. "Issues in the Application of Covariance Structure Analysis: A Further Comment." *Journal of Consumer Research* 9:449–50.

Bailey, K. D. 1984. "A Three-Level Measurement Model." *Quality and Quantity* 18:225–248.

Bentler, P. M. 1976. "Multistructural Statistical Models Applied to Factor Analysis." *Multivariate Behavioral Research* 11:3–25.

Bentler, P. M. 1985. *Theory and Implementation of EQS: A Structural Equations Program*. Los Angeles: BMDP Statistical Software.

Bentler, P. M. and D. G. Weeks. 1980. "Linear Structural Equations with Latent Variables." *Psychometrika* 45:289–308.

Berk, R. A. 1983. "An Introduction to Sample Selection Bias in Sociological Data." *American Sociological Review* 48:386–398.

Blalock, H. M. 1968. "The Measurement Problem: A Gap Between the Languages of Theory and Research." Pp. 5–27 in *Methodology in Social Research* edited by Hubert M. Blalock and Ann B. Blalock. New York: McGraw-Hill.

Bohrnstedt, G. W. "Measurement." 1983. Pp. 69–121 in *Handbook of Survey Research* edited by Peter H. Rossi, James D. Wright, and Andy B. Anderson. New York: Academic Press.

Bohrnstedt, G. W., P. P. Mohler, and W. Muller. 1987. "Editors Introduction." *Sociological Methods and Research* 15:171–176.

Bollen, K. A. 1987. "Outliers and Improper Solutions: A confirmatory Factor Analysis Example." *Sociological Methods and Research* 15:375–84.

Bollen, K. A., and S. Ward. 1979. "Ratio Variables in Aggregate Data Analysis: Their Uses, Problems, and Alternatives." *Sociological Methods and Research* 7:431–50.

Borgatta, E. F. and G. W. Bohrnstedt. 1981. "Level of Measurement: Once Over Again." Pp. 23–38 in *Social Measurement: Current Issues* edited by George W. Bohrnstedt and Edgar F. Borgatta. Beverly Hills, CA: Sage.

Bradshaw, Y., and L. Radbill. 1987. "Method and Substance in the Use of Ratio Variables." *American Sociological Review* 52:132–135.

Bross, I. 1954. "Misclassification in 2 × 2 Tables." *Biometrics* 10:478–486.

Brown, W. 1910. "Some Experimental Results in the Correlation of Mental Abilities." *British Journal of Psychology* 3:296–322.

Burt, R. S. 1976. "Interpretational Confounding of Unobserved Variables in Structural Equation Models." *Sociological Methods and Research* 5:3–52.

Carmines, E. G., and R. A. Zeller. 1979. *Reliability and Validity Assessment*. Beverly Hills: Sage University Papers.

Clarke, H. D., M. C. Stewart, and G. Zuk. 1987. "Political-Economic Orientations in Contemporary Britain." Paper presented at the International Society of Political Psychology. San Francisco.

Cochran, W. G. 1968. "Errors of Measurement in Statistics." *Technometrics* 10:637–666.

Converse, P. E. 1964. "The Nature of Belief Systems in Mass Publics." Pp. 206–261 in *Ideology and Discontent* edited by D. E. Apter. New York: Free Press.

Converse, P. E. 1970. "Attitudes and Non-attitudes: Continuation of a Dialogue." Pp. 168–189 in *Quantitative Analysis of Social Problems* edited by E. R. Tufte. Reading, MA: Addison-Wesley.

Cook, R. D., and S. Weisberg. 1982. "Criticism and Influence in Regression." Pp. 313–61 in *Sociological Methodology: 1982* edited by Stanley Leinhardt. San Francisco: Jossey-Bass.

Costner, H. L. 1969. "Theory, Deduction, and Rules of Correspondence." *American Journal of Sociology* 75:245–63.

Davis, J. A. and T. W. Smith, 1986. *General Social Surveys, 1972–1986: Cumulative Codebook*. Storrs, CT: "The Roper Center for Public Opinion Research.

Dillon, W. R., A. Kumar, and N. Mulani. 1987. "Offending Estimates in Covariance Structure Analysis: Comments on the Causes of and Solutions to Heywood Cases." *Psychological Bulletin*. 101:126–135.

Dilman, D. A. 1978. *Mail and Telephone Surveys*. New York: Wiley.

Feigl, H. 1970. "The 'Orthodox' View of Theories: Remarks in Defense as Well as Critique."

Pp. 3–16 in *Minnesota Studies in the Philosophy of Science 4* edited by M. Radnor and S. Winokur. Minneapolis: University of Minnesota Press.

Firebaugh, G., and J. P. Gibbs. 1985. "User's Guide to Ratio Variables." *American Sociological Review* 50:713–722.

Fornell, C. 1983. "Issues in the Application of Covariance Structure Analysis: A Comment." *Journal of Consumer Research* 9:443–448.

Gerbing, D. W., and J. C. Anderson. 1987. "Improper Solutions in the Analysis of Covariance Structures: Their Interpretability and a Comparison of Alternative Respecifications." *Psychometrika* 52:99–111.

Gnanadesikan, R. 1977. *Methods for Statistical Data Analysis of Multivariate Observations.* New York: Wiley.

Goldberger, A. S. 1973. "Structural Equation Models: An Overview." Pp. 1–18 in *Structural Equation Models in the Social Sciences* edited by Arthur S. Goldberger and Otis Dudley Duncan. New York: Seminar Press.

Heckman, J. J. 1979. "Sample Selection Bias as a Specification Error." *Econometrica* 45:153–161.

Heckman, J. J. 1980. "Sample Selection Bias as a Spefication Error." Pp. 206–248 in *Female Labor Supply: Theory and Estimation* edited by James P. Smith. Princeton: Princeton Press.

Hoaglin, D. C., and R. Welsch. 1978. "The Hat Matrix in Regression and ANOVA." *American Statistician* 32:17–22.

Jagodzinski, W. and S. M. Kuhnel. 1987. "Estimation of Reliability and Stability in Single-Indicator Multiple-Wave Models." *Sociological Methods and Research* 15:219–258.

Joreskog, K. G. 1979. "Statistical Models and Methods for Analysis of Longitudinal Data." Pp. 129–69 in *Advances in Factor Analysis and Structural Equation Models* edited by Karl G. Joreskog and Dag Sorbom. Cambridge, MA: Abt.

Joreskog, K. G. 1987. "New Developments in LISREL." Paper presented at the National Symposium on Methodological Issues in Causal Modeling, University of Alabama, Tuscaloosa, AL.

Joreskog, K. G. and D. Sorbom. 1984. *LISREL VI: Analysis of Linear Structural Relations by the Method of Maximum Likelihood.* Mooresville, Indiana: Scientific Software, Inc.

Joreskog, K. G., and H. Wold. 1982. "The ML and PLS Techniques for Modeling with Latent Variables: Historical and Comparative Aspects." Pp. 263–270 in *Systems under Indirect Observations: Causality, Structure, Prediction* edited by Karl G. Joreskog and Herman Wold. Amsterdam: North Holland Publishing.

Kaplan, A. 1964. *The Conduct of Inquiry: Methodology for Behavior Science.* San Francisco: Chandler.

Kessler, R. C. and D. F. Greenberg. 1981. *Linear Panal Analysis: Models of Quantitative Change.* New York: Academic Press.

Kiecolt, K. J. and L. E. Nathan. 1985. *Secondary Analysis of Survey Data.* Newbery Park, CA: Sage.

Kraft, M. 1987. "On 'User's Guide to Ratio Variables.'" *American Sociological Review* 52:135–136.

Lansing, J. B., G. P. Ginsburg, and K. Braaten. 1961. *An Investigation of Response Error. Studies in Consumer Savings, No. 2.* Urbana: Bureau of Economic and Business Research: University of Illinois.

Long, S. B. 1979. "The Continuing Debate Over the Use of Ratio Variables: Facts and Fiction." Pp. 37–67 in *Sociological Methodology: 1980* edited by Karl F. Schuessler. San Francisco: Jossey-Bass.

Lord, F. M., and M. R. Novick. 1968. *Statistical Theories of Mental Test Scores*. Reading, MA: Addison-Wesley.

Marini, M. M., A. R. Olsen, and D. B. Rubin. 1979. "Maximum-Likelihood Estimation in Panel Studies with Missing Data." Pp. 314–357 in *Sociological Methodology: 1980* edited by Karl F. Schuessler. San Francisco: Jossey-Bass.

Nunnaly, J. C. 1978. *Psychometric Theory*. New York: McGraw-Hill.

Parry, H. J. and H. M. Crossley. 1950. "Validity of Responses to Survey Questions." *Public Opinion Quarterly* 14:61–80.

Porst, R., P. Schmidt, and K. Zeifang. 1987. "Comparison of Subgroups by Models with Multiple Indicators." *Sociological Methods and Research* 15:303–315.

Raffalovich, L. E., and G. W. Bohrnstedt. 1987. "Common, Specific, and Error Variance Components of Factor Models: Estimation with Longitudinal Data." *Sociological Methods and Research* 15:385–405.

Schwartz, J. E. 1985. "The Neglected Problem of Measurement Error in Categorical Data." *Sociological Methods and Research* 13:435–466.

Scott, J. 1987. "Explaining the Abortion Context Effect." Presented at the American Association for Public Opinion Research. Chicago.

Sorbom, D., and K. G. Jorseksog. 1982. "The Use of Structural Equation Models in Evaluation Research." Pp. 381–418 in *A Second Generation of Multivariate Analysis*, Vol. 2. edited by C. Fornell. New York: Praeger.

Smith, T. W. 1979. "Happiness: Time Trends, Seasonal Variations, Intersurvey Differences, and Other Mysteries." *Social Psychology Quarterly* 42:18–30.

Spearman, C. 1910. "Correlation Calculated with Faulty Data." *British Journal of Psychology* 3:271–95.

Wheaton, B., B. Muthen, D. F. Alwin, and G. F. Summers. 1977. "Assessing Reliability and Stability in Panel Models." Pp. 84–136 in *Sociological Methodology: 1977* edited by David R. Heise. San Francisco: Jossey-Bass.

Wyner, G. A. 1981. "Response Errors in Self-Reported Number of Arrests." Pp. 169–86 in *Social Measurement: Current Issues* edited by George W. Bohrnstedt and Edgar F. Borgatta. Beverly Hills, CA: Sage.

EDUCATION AS A COMPONENT OF A LARGER SOCIAL SYSTEM

Krishnan Namboodiri

A number of scholars have written about the effects of "inputs" on the "outputs" of the school system. In a recent review paper Glasman and Biniaminov (1981) report that scholars have used as outputs standardized achievement tests (covering, for example, verbal, mathematics, and reading abilities), other cognitive tests (covering such dimensions as composite achievement, abstract reasoning, and general information), and student attitudes (self-concept, educational aspirations, locus of control, etc.). Among input measures used by scholars are student's family background, school-related student characteristics, student attitudes, school conditions, and characteristics of instructional personnel. By "input-output" models, Glasman and Biniaminov (1981) mean regression equations in which the output measures mentioned above are treated as dependent variables. One of the works

Research in the Sociology of Education and Socialization,
Volume 8, pages 231–258.
Copyright © 1989 by JAI Press Inc.
All rights of reproduction in any form reserved.
ISBN: 0-89232-929-7

Glasman and Biniaminov (1981) cite is a paper by Bidwell and Kasarda (1975) that presents a path model treating one set of school-district properties as exogenous, another set as intermediate, and the median reading and the median mathematics achievement test scores as the (ultimate) dependent, variables. As Glasman and Biniaminov (1981) picture it, the reduced form equations derived from the Bidwell-Kasarda (1975) recursive system are input-output models.

In this chapter I discuss three different ways in which input-output perspective can be used in education research. One approach focuses on individual pupils, classrooms, schools, school districts, and the like as the units of analysis. Another focuses on the flow of pupils through successive levels (e.g., grades) of the education system, and the third views the education system as part of a broader social system.

When focusing on individual pupils, each pupil is viewed as a producing unit. An initial trait complex, $\{X_{01}, \ldots , X_{0k}\}$, the pupil's own time during the school year, and various goods and services, including encouragement and discouragement from others (peers, teachers, family members, etc.) are viewed as the ingredients that are put together to produce an year-end trait complex $\{X_{11}, \ldots , X_{1k}\}$. In this approach, X_{0j} may be thought of as the initial level of ability of type j (e.g., quantitative skill) while X_{1j} is the corresponding level at the end of the year.

When focusing on classrooms, each classroom is viewed as transforming pupils of a certain initial makeup with respect to a trait complex into those with a corresponding year-end makeup. The initial make up may be specified as a vector of distributions: $\{f_{01}(X_{01}), \ldots , f_{0k}(X_{0k})\}$, where $f_{0j}(X_{0j})$ stands for the distribution (over pupils) of level of type j ability (quantitative skill), and $f_{1j}(X_{1j})$ is the corresponding year-end distribution.

The second approach with its focus on the flow of pupils through successive levels (e.g., grades) of the education process, permits the examination of the linkage between different processes, e.g., childbearing, schooling, and entrance to the labor force. This approach is useful also to the study of factors affecting wastage—failure to complete a cycle (e.g., high school). Of particular interest may be the linkage between the volume and educational composition of the labor-force required to get the various societal activities going, on the one hand, and the stock of pupils and teachers and flow of graduates, on the other.

The third type of input-output approach focuses on the interdependence of the various sectors (industries, strata of households, public and private schools, and so on) in society. This approach permits the examination of differences, if any, between sectors of the educational system (e.g., public and private schools) in the parameters of their interdependence with other parts of society. Variation in these differentials over population segments (e.g., regions) may also be of interest.

A FEW REMARKS ABOUT THE INPUT-OUTPUT APPROACH

Meanings of the Terms Input and Output

The terms input and output are used in different senses in different contexts. The common dictionary definition of the term input is "something that is put in" (as in "increased input of fertilizer increases crop yield.") Similarly the common dictionary definition of the term output is "something that is produced" (e.g., steel output = the amount of steel produced). With reference to computers, the term input is often used for the process of translation of incoming information into electronic patterns suitable for computer processing, and the term output is used for the reverse process. The translation is carried out by the input and output devices of the computer system. In the statistical literature on queueing theory the term input stands for "arrivals" (e.g., airplanes queueing up for take off, patients waiting their turn to see the physician) and output for departures (airplanes taking off; patients leaving after consultation). With reference to the relationship between an organism and its environment, the term input is used for everything that the organism receives from its environment and the term output stands for everything that the organism gives out to its environment. Considering the hospital as a social organization, some scholars (e.g., Herriott and Hodgkins 1973, pp. 78–79) refer to an incoming patient as a throughput; physicians, staff, etc. of the hospital as inputs; and the discharged patient as an output. Some scholars (e.g., Herriott and Hodgkins 1973, p. 79) distinguish between "organizational output" or "consumed input," (e.g., drugs, bandages etc. used in a hospital) and "production output," (e.g., the discharged patient). In economics, the inputs of an activity are the goods and services (e.g. labor and materials) used in producing its output, which may be goods or services. An output of one activity may be an input to another. Applying this point of view, one may regard pupils enrolled in school as part of the inputs to the school system, and those who graduate as part of its outputs.

A Look at the Individual Pupil as the Producing Unit

Suppose we view the individual pupil as a producing entity. With the help of goods and services a pupil with certain trait complex (e.g., verbal, reading and quantitative skills) at the beginning of a school year may be thought of as transforming himself or herself into a person with a corresponding trait complex by the end of the school year. In this case, the trait complex, $\{X_{01}, \ldots, X_{0k}\}$, at the beginning of the school year, the services received from various sources (teachers, library, laboratory), etc. may be regarded as inputs and the trait complex, $\{X_{11}, \ldots, X_{1k}\}$, at the end of the school year as the output. In the literature on the new home economics one finds this notion employed in the following fashion. The individual is thought of as producing and consuming not-for-sale "commodities," using market goods and services and own time. These "commodities" (outputs) include prestige, prejudice, pleasures of the senses, health, envy, and the like. A distinguishing feature of this notion is that the producing entity consumes all of its output; no part of it is given to any other entity.

A Model for the Output of the Individual Pupil

Now consider the following exercise (see, in this connection, Bidwell and Kasarda 1975): Suppose for each pupil in a school district we record

1. the logarithm of the average daily student attendance in the school district;
2. the per-pupil revenue received by the school district (from all sources: local, state, and federal);
3. the proportion of pupils from poor families (with family income below the nationally-defined poverty level);
4. the proportion of persons with at least 4 years of high school education, considering males 20–49 and females 15–44 together, in the school district;
5. the number of pupils in average daily attendance divided by the number of classroom teachers;
6. the ratio of administrators to classroom teachers;
7. the ratio of professional support staff to classroom teachers;
8. the percent of staff members with at least a master's degree; and
9. the score on a grade-standardized reading achievement test.

Imagine obtaining such data for all students in all school districts in, say, Colorado. [Obviously all students in the same school district have the same array of values for variables (1) through (8).] Now suppose a regression equation is estimated regressing variable (9) on variables (1) through (8). In this case, although it may seem bizarre at first blush, we may think of each student as an entity producing his or her score on the test (or the school system doing the same) using as inputs the respective values of variables (1) through

(8), plus an (unknown) residual. Conceptually, it makes no difference whether we imagine that the individual student is the entity that produces his or her test score or that the school system is the entity that concocts it. The conceptual setup is not at all different if attention is focused on (see Bidwell and Kasarda 1975) an "average" student in each school district, attributing to him (her) an average score on the reading test.

Some readers might object to interpreting the regression equation as a production function. It may not appeal to common sense to say that a student is concocting his or her test score using as inputs the logarithm of the average daily enrollment in the school district, per-pupil fiscal resources, proportion of fellow-students who are disadvantaged, and so on. The same may be said if the entity that concocts the test score from the same inputs is the school district. But if we go behind the particular "observations" and think about what they stand for, the picture may appear less bizarre. Thus, suppose (as suggested by Bidwell and Kasarda 1975, p. 61) that variables 1 through 8 are proxies for (a) student traits (e.g., ability level), (b) goods and services offered to the student (e.g., counselling), or (c) the extent of the student's use of the various learning opportunities and resources. Now imagine that the test score is a proxy for academic distinction. It becomes clear immediately that each student is viewed as producing his or her scholastic distinction using his or her own time (ability and other traits), goods and services (including encouragement and discouragement) received from others, and the facilities made available, learning opportunities presented, and so on. The academic distinction thus produced is a "commodity" in the sense the term is used in the "new home economics" model mentioned above.

A Look at the Classroom as the Producing Entity

Consider the classroom as the producing unit that takes in students of various types (analogous to different grades of raw materials) and converts them into "educated" persons. The classroom is thus viewed as a factory. There is nothing in this perspective that prevents one from recognizing that different classrooms use different inputs (including the type of students and teachers they attract). Moreover, if the pupils form a mixture of samples from, say, three "readiness" distributions (e.g., one with a "low" mean, one with a "medium" mean, and one with a "high" mean) and if data are available to separate the mixture, i.e., to classify the students according to which "readiness" distribution they belong, then we may treat the classroom as having three sectors (strata) corresponding to the three "readiness" distributions.

To pursue the point further, consider Teacher M's second grade (class) in year T in primary school Y in neighborhood Z of city C. Suppose Teacher M divides the class into three groups, say I, II, and III, according to "ability" and treats them differently in terms of goods and services given. Suppose further that Group I consists of two subgroups, say I_a and I_b, differing with respect to the facilities available to them to carry out homework assignments. For example, suppose Group I_a students have parents who help, access to an encyclopedia set at home, and so on, while Group I_b students lack all these. Under the circumstances it may make sense to consider the class as having four sectors (strata): I_a, I_b, II, and III. The guiding principle here is one of removing heterogeneity with respect to input structure.

Some Observations on Inputs (Ingredients).

Conceptually there are two types of inputs that are used in the production of an "educated" person, one having to do with personal traits, and the other the goods and services pupils receive, in the school, at home, and elsewhere. When one tries to be increasingly more specific about these ingredients, however, there is room for disagreement. Thus some scholars may attach great importance to the so-called student attitudes (locus control, self concept, academic aspirations, etc.), while others may be inclined to ignore all psychological factors.

Impacts of Inputs on Educational Outcomes.

To facilitate answering the question whether the input of goods and services (e.g., teacher-traits, peer influence, school factors) make a difference with respect to educational outcome, let us put the question in somewhat more technical terms. Suppose we agree that by educational outcome we mean change in a multi-trait complex (involving, for example, reading, writing, and reasoning ability, commitment to certain ethical codes, etc.). We imagine drawing two random samples, say, A and B, from a common universe defined in terms of the multi-trait complex just mentioned. Suppose sample A is exposed to educational process (input of goods and services) X and sample B to educational process Y. The question is whether, other things remaining the same, sample A differs from Sample B with respect to the post-exposure multi-trait complex makeup. The answer depends upon, among other things, the maximum change possible in the trait complex in question, given the corresponding initial (pre-exposure) level. Suppose there exists an education process Z that can produce this maximum possible change. Of course, when we speak of changes in a trait complex, we recognize that they are a function of duration since the completion of exposure in question. It is now easy to see that the difference that X and Y make depends upon (1) how different X and Y are from Z, (2) the magnitude of the change that Z is capable of making, and

(3) the value of the post-exposure interval t. Thus, if the change Z induces (i.e., the maximum change possible) is small, the chances are that most empirical studies will show no difference between X and Y, in the changes they produce in the trait complex in question, no matter how different X is from Y. This remark has obvious implications for studies of the so-called school effect. (See, in this connection, the Entwisle-Alexander chapter in this volume).

GRADE TRANSITION VIEWED FROM THE INPUT-OUTPUT PERSPECTIVE

Let us examine a grade transition model, focusing on primary schools. Let us assume that there are six grades in primary schools. Of course, the model is easily adapted to suit education systems in which the primary level consists of fewer or more than six grades. Treating time as discrete and focusing on the beginning of two successive school years, with a view to linking enrollments in one year with their counterparts the next year, let C_{ii} stand for repeaters in grade i, $C_{i,i+1}$ for promotions from grade i to grade i + 1, C_{iL} for leavers, and C_{Ii} for new entrants. We may depict these flows in tabular form as shown in Table 1.

The entries in the column for grade j divided by their sum give, for example

$$a_{j-1,j} = C_{j-1,j}/C_{+j}, \quad a_{jj} = C_{jj}/C_{+j}$$

As will become clear later on, these quantities can be interpreted as "direct

Table 1. A Flow Table for Primary School Pupils

Origin Grade, Year t	Destination Grade, Year (t + 1)						Leavers	Row Total
	1	*2*	*3*	*4*	*5*	*6*		
1	C_{11}	C_{12}					C_{1L}	C_{1+}
2		C_{22}	C_{23}				C_{2L}	C_{2+}
3			C_{33}	C_{34}			C_{3L}	C_{3+}
4				C_{44}	C_{45}		C_{4L}	C_{4+}
5					C_{55}	C_{56}	C_{5L}	C_{5+}
6						C_{66}	C_{6L}	C_{6+}
New entrants	C_{I1}	C_{I2}	C_{I3}	C_{I4}	C_{I5}	C_{I6}		
Column Total	C_{+1}	C_{+2}	C_{+3}	C_{+4}	C_{+5}	C_{+6}		

input coefficients'' within the economic input-output framework (if pupils constitute the sole inputs).

Another way to look at the information in Table 1 is in terms of transition probabilities. Thus from the row for grade 1 we have the following estimates of transition probabilities:

$$p_{11} = C_{11}/C_{1+}, \quad p_{12} = C_{12}/C_{1+}, \quad p_{1L} = C_{1L}/C_{1+}$$

from the row for grade 2 we have

$$p_{22} = C_{22}/C_{2+}, \quad p_{23} = C_{23}/C_{2+}, \quad p_{2L} = C_{2L}/C_{2+}$$

and so on. Of course, the proportion of leavers (e.g., p_{1L}) can be separated into its components by type of exit (graduation, drop out, death, transfer), if the relevant information is available.

Two modifications of the general idea presented above deserve notice. One is that the a's and p's can be calculated separately for each school or different levels of aggregations thereof (e.g., schools in a community or region). The other modification is that pupils when considered as inputs may be stratified on the basis of traits of one kind or another (e.g., socioeconomic background, test scores reflecting readiness, family environment).

It should also be emphasized that the a's and p's are amenable to explanatory analysis. Thus if these quantities are calculated for each individual school, it is possible to examine their time trends in each school as well as their dependence on school properties (e.g., goods and services offered to students). Note that the triplet $\{p_{ii}, p_{i,i+1}, p_{iL}\}$ is a "composition" vector, with its elements summing to unity. Methods of analysis treating such composition vectors as dependent variables are available (see, e.g., the literature on multinomial logit methods).

The grade transition model outlined above, with specific reference to primary education, can, of course, be applied to other parts of the school system, for example, to different streams of secondary education, to different streams of vocational education, and to different types of higher education. Furthermore, as already mentioned, such models can be developed for subpopulations and for different systems such as public and private schools.

Graduates as Output

When the focus is on primary schools, secondary schools, colleges, and so on, each of which may be thought of as a cycle involving entry, stay for a duration, and exit, it is natural to pay special attention to those who "graduate,'' that is, those who successfully complete the cycle. Graduates are very often regarded as the main output of the education system. It is also natural to raise the question whether those who are certified as graduates have been "adequately" trained (e.g., to pursue higher education, to perform adult roles), whether the education system has instilled in children appropriate value orientations, whether the schooling has prepared children to meet the exigencies of society (Hutchins 1953), and so on. This amounts to, in practice, focusing on traits such as reading skills, general knowledge, verbal and quantitative abilities, and attitudes and orientations. Assuming that these can be measured, for example, using standardized tests, attention turns to vectors of distributions of test scores), with emphasis on inter- and intra- cohort differences, and their determinants.

Attention may also turn to between-school variations in such measures as average pupil-years for graduation, which takes into account the time spent in school by those who die before graduation, those who drop out, and those who repeat grades. In the literature on educational statistics, the term *wastage* is often applied to pupil-years in excess of what would have been needed to produce a given number of graduates if there were no repetition, dropping out, or dying while enrolled (see, e.g., UNESCO Office of Statistics 1972). Determinants of wastage are of obvious interest.

While matters such as these have been examined, often in great detail, relatively less attention has been paid to the interdependence of the education process and its outputs, on the one hand, and other processes such as child-bearing and rearing and social change, on the other.

THE BIRTH AND EDUCATION PROCESSES

It is obvious that survivors of infants born this year are the new entrants to the school system a few (five or six) years from now. Note that this refers to an input-output relationship—output of the childbearing process serving as input to the educational process, with a time lag.

A great deal has been written on the impact on the education system, the labor market, etc., of changing birth cohort size. Thus the baby boom cohort (infants born between 1954 and 1964) had its schooling marked by over-crowded classrooms and a shortage of teachers. And the baby-bust cohort, born in the late 1960s and thereafter, seem to be having a much easier path through life. (Harter 1977; Taueber 1979). Thus as a baby- boom cohort passes through life stages (e.g., education, entry into the labor force) the institutions that deal with populations of the particular stages will undergo the strain of rapid expansion, and a decade or two later they will undertake the often difficult task of precipitous retrenchment (Plotkin 1978, p. 277).

To bring out the implications of changing birth cohort sizes, it would be helpful if we derive an accounting system showing the states occupied by a cohort as it goes through the education system and enters society as full-fledged members. Let us consider a simple case in which during the years of education a student passes to a new level (e.g., grade) each year until at some stage at which he (she) leaves the system to become a functional member of society. Let B_t be the size of the birth cohort which enters the school going age interval at time, say, $t + \alpha$. Let $p_t(0,\alpha)$ be the probability of survival from age 0 to age α, for the cohort of year t. Then in year $t + \alpha$, there will be an expected number of $B_t p_t(0,\alpha)$ pupils potentially requiring admission to the first level of schooling. Multiplying this with $e_t(1)$, the probability of entering school at level 1 for any child of this cohort reaching the school going age, we obtain $B_t p_t(0,\alpha)e_t(1)$ as the expected number of admissions of level 1 in year t $+ \alpha$. The survivors of this group consists of those who continue in school (in level 2) and those who leave the school system during or at the end of the first year of schooling. Let $e_t(2)$ be the probability of retention beyond level 1 for this cohort. Then the expected enrollment in level 2, in year $t + \alpha + 1$, is

$$B_t p_t(0,\alpha)e_t(1)p_t(\alpha,\alpha + 1)e_t(2)$$

which may written as

$$B_t p_t(0,\alpha + 1)e_t(1)e_t(2)$$

since

$$p_t(0,\alpha)p_t(\alpha,\alpha + 1) = p_t(0,\alpha + 1).$$

Similarly, the expected enrollment in level 3, in year $t + \alpha + 2$, is

$$B_t p_t(0,\alpha + 2)e_t(1)e_t(2)e_t(3),$$

and so on. In general, the enrollment in level s, in year $(t + \alpha + s - 1)$, is expected to be

$$B_t p_t(0,\alpha + s - 1)e_t(1)e_t(2) \ldots e_t(s)$$

At the end of year $(t + \alpha + s - 1)$,

$$B_t p_t(0,\alpha + s)e_t(1) \ldots e_t(s)[1 - e_t(s + 1)]$$

are expected to enter society as functional members, with s-level education, assuming of course that the survivors of the cohort who leave the school system at the completion of s-level education will all be absorbed as functional members of society immediately after leaving the school system. Notice that this number is a function of the size of the cohort born in year t, and the survival and retention probabilities applicable to this cohort.

These formulas can be made more realistic, of course, by recognizing intra-cohort variations (e.g., by race, sex, region of residence) in survival probabilities, the existence of different tracks in the education system, and possible track-differentials in retention probabilities. Further modifications are necessary in order to take into account transfers between school systems and waiting periods, if any, for leavers from the school system to be absorbed as functional members of society.

Note also that in the formulation outlined above, survival and retention probabilities have been viewed as cohort specific. Possible intra-cohort variations in these have already been mentioned. Inter-cohort variations are also of interest.

Thus there are many complexities that can be incorporated into the relationship considered above. But the simple setup considered does point to the linkage between the output of one process (births) and the input of another (entrance to society as functional members). Inter-and intra-cohort differences in this linkage shed light on the differential impact of the education system on segments of society with respect to educational attainment.

EDUCATED PERSON-POWER NEEDS OF SOCIETY

Let us turn now to the stock of pupils and teachers and flow of graduates necessary in order to satisfy *given educated person-power needs*. Following Thonstad (1968) let us focus on stationary conditions (i.e., when there is no change in the stock or flow characteristics of interest). Let

P_s = the number of pupils enrolled in level s ($= 1, \ldots, S$);
G_e = the number of persons in the labor force, with e-level education;
T_e = the number of teachers with e-level education;
N_e = the number of non-teachers in the labor force with e-level education;
T_{es} = the number of e-level educated teachers teaching in level s;
g_e = the number of leavers from the school system with e-level education;
μ_{es} = the number of e-level educated teachers needed per student at s-level (these being usually referred to as teacher-pupil ratios);
ω_e = the average length of working life of those with e-level education.

Also let π_{es}, $e = 1, 2, \ldots, E$, be the distribution by education of teachers teaching at s-level ($\Sigma_{e=1}^{E} \pi_{es} = 1$). These may be called *qualification coefficients*. Let λ_{se}, $e = 1, 2, \ldots, E$, be the average duration of occupancy of level s per leaver with e-level education. These may be called *duration coefficients*. To understand what these latter stand for consider the information given in Table 2. In preparing this table, it has been assumed that every child is expected to complete 6 years of Elementary and 3 years of Junior High school. Children with "less than High School" education include those who complete the 9 years of compulsory education and those who take additional years of High School, but not enough to graduate from High School. It has been assumed that on average this group completes one year beyond the compulsory level. Completion of High School requires 12 years of formal schooling. Only one average type of vocational training is shown in Table 2, this one requiring on average 0.65 years in High School and 1.75 years in Vocational school. Similarly only one average type of teacher training is recognized in Table 2. This involves High School graduation plus two years of Teacher's college. University education is treated in Table 2 with just three cycles—the usual four-year degree cycle, a master's degree cycle or equivalent, and others (e.g., Ph.D.) requiring longer durations.

It is easily seen that

$$G_e = N_e + T_e \quad (e = 1, \ldots, E) \tag{1}$$

that is, that the "gross" labor force consists of teachers and nonteachers. Also

$$T_e = T_{e1} + \ldots + T_{eS} \quad (e = 1, \ldots, E) \tag{2}$$

$$\pi_{es} = T_{es}/T_e \tag{3}$$

that is, that e-level educated teachers can be classified into S mutually exclusive and collectively exhaustive categories on the basis of the level which they have primary responsibilities for. And the *qualification-specific teacher-pupil ratios* are

$$\mu_{es} = T_{es}/P_s \tag{4}$$

From (2) and (4) it follows that the total number of e-level educated teachers required by the system, given enrollments $\{P_s\}$ and the teacher-pupil ratios $\{\mu_{es}\}$ is

$$T_e = \Sigma_{s=1}^{S} \mu_{es}P_s \quad (e = 1, \ldots, E) \tag{5}$$

Table 2. Average Duration of Occupancy of Each School Category, by Level of Education

			Level of education completed				
	<H.S.	H.S.	Vocational training	Teacher training	College degree	Graduate degree	Other
School level	e = 1	e = 2	e = 3	e = 4	e = 5	e = 6	e = 7
s = 1 Elementary	6.00	6.00	6.00	6.00	6.00	6.00	6.00
s = 2 Junior High	3.00	3.00	3.00	3.00	3.00	3.00	3.00
s = 3 Senior High	1.00	3.00	0.65	3.00	3.00	3.00	3.00
s = 4 Vocational school	0	0	1.75	0	0	0	0
s = 5 Teacher's college	0	0	0	2.00	0	0	0
s = 6 University	0	0	0		4.00	6.00	9.00

And, given the level-specific duration coefficients $\{\lambda_{se}\}$, we have the average number of years to complete e-level education given by

$$\lambda_e = \Sigma^S_{s=1} \lambda_{se} \quad (e = 1, \ldots, E) \tag{6}$$

If we ignore mortality and rule out transfers, it is possible to express enrollment in each school category as a function of final graduations of each type and duration coefficients:

$$P_s = \Sigma^E_{e=1} \lambda_{se} g_e \quad (s = 1, \ldots, S) \tag{7}$$

The reasoning behind this relationship is the following: Those enrolled at level s can be categorized in accordance with the level at which they eventually leave the school system. Thus those enrolled in High School (see Table 2) can be categorized into those who eventually leave the school system while enrolled in High School, at High School graduation, after x years of college, and so on. Now recall that λ_{se} is defined as the average duration of occupancy of level s per leaver at level e. Let us write

$$P_s = \Sigma^E_{e=1} P_{se} \tag{8}$$

where P_{se} stands for those among P_s who leave at level e. If we assume that exits from school occur only at the end of school year, the total duration of occupancy of level s is the same as enrollment at level s. It immediately follows that

$$P_s = \Sigma^E_{e=1} (P_{se}/g_e)g_e = \Sigma^E_{e=1} \lambda_{se} g_e \tag{9}$$

Extension of the argument to cover exits at all durations is straightforward.

By inserting the expression (7) for P_s in (5) we obtain

$$T_e = \Sigma^E_{j=1} [\Sigma^S_{s=1} \mu_{es}\lambda_{sj}]g_j \quad (e = 1, \ldots, E) \tag{10}$$

giving the teacher requirements as a function of graduations from each level and the qualification and duration coefficients.

We can express the teacher requirements in terms of educational composition of the labor force, by noting that $G_e = g_e\omega_e$ or

$$g_e = G_e/\omega_e \tag{11}$$

using which we obtain from (10)

$$T_e = \Sigma_{j=1}^{E}[\Sigma_{s=1}^{S}(\mu_{es}\lambda_{sj}/\omega_j)]G_j \tag{12}$$

The quantity within brackets on the right-hand side of (12), that is,

$$(1/\omega_j)\Sigma_{s=1}^{S}\mu_{es}\lambda_{sj} \tag{13}$$

can be interpreted as the number of person-years of e-level educated teachers, i.e.,

$$\Sigma_{s=1}^{S}\mu_{es}\lambda_{sj} \tag{14}$$

per person-year of work of a j-level educated labor-force participant. From (7), on substitution for g_e, we obtain

$$P_s = \Sigma_{j=1}^{E}(\lambda_{sj}/\omega_j)G_j \tag{15}$$

as the required enrollments at level s (= 1, . . . , S).

It is of course possible to derive formulas for non-teaching labor force corresponding to those derived above for ''gross'' labor force (teachers plus non-teachers). Thus substituting for T_e its equivalent $G_e - N_e$, we obtain an equation system

$$G_e - \Sigma_{j=1}^{E}[\Sigma_{s=1}^{S}\mu_{es}\lambda_{sj}/\omega_j]G_j = N_e \tag{16}$$

wich can be solved for the G's in terms of N's. Substitution of the solutions in (15) gives P_s in terms of N's. And similarly using (11) we can obtain g_e in terms of N's.

Thus we have seen how to express $[P_s]$, enrollment by level, $\{T_e\}$, the teacher labor force by educational qualification, and $\{g_e\}$, graduation by levels, in terms of the educational distribution of the non-teacher labor force. These relationships tell us explicitly, for example, the enrollments, teacher labor force, and graduation flows needed to maintain a given steady supply of non-teacher labor force. What remains now is to link the labor force to the production, distribution, and consumption of various goods and services, a task attended to a little later.

It should be emphasized that the relationships mentioned have been derived keeping a stationary setup in mind, that is, when there are no shifts in the stocks or flows of interest. They are nonetheless useful in comparative static analyses of given stock levels and flow patterns.

The Non-Stationary Case

The formulation given above can be extended to the non-stationary setup. To simplify matters, let us ignore for a moment mortality and migration. Further let us assume that students leave the school system at year end only. Let

$P_s(t)$ = the enrollment in level s at the beginning of year t;

$g_e(t)$ = the number of leavers (graduations) at the end of year t after completing level e;

μ_{es} = the number of e-level educated teachers needed per student enrolled in s-level;

$T_e(t)$ = the number of e-level educated teachers in the labor force at the beginning of year t;

$G_e(t)$ = the number of e-level educated participants in the labor force (teachers and non-teachers combined) at the beginning of year t;

$N_e(t)$ = the number of e-level educated non-teachers in the labor force at the beginning of year t;

Then the enrollment in level s at the beginning of year t is given by

$$P_s(t) = \Sigma_{j=1}^{\lambda} g_{s+j}(t+j) \tag{17}$$

where λ is the maximum educational duration. This equation simply says that those who are enrolled now consist of those who leave (graduate) at the end of this year, at the end the next year, and so on. The teacher requirement is then given by

$$\begin{aligned} T_e &= \Sigma_{s=1}^{S} \mu_{es} P_s(t) \\ &= \Sigma_{s=1}^{S} \mu_{es} \Sigma_{j=0}^{\lambda} g_{s+j}(t+j) \end{aligned} \tag{18}$$

And the number of e-level educated persons at the beginning of year t in the labor force (teachers and non-teachers combined) is given by

$$G_e(t) = \Sigma_{j=0}^{t-1} \sigma_j g_e(t - j + 1) \tag{19}$$

where σ_j is the fraction of those graduating at the end of year $(t - j - 1)$ who are still in the labor force at the beginning of year t (which is the end of year t − 1).

Formula (17) is modified as follows when mortality is taken into account. Let $q_s(t)$ be the probability of dying during the year for those enrolled in level s at the beginning of the year. Then $[1 - q_s(t)]P_s(t)$ is the expected number of survivors to the end of the year. Out of these survivors a fraction $[1 - e_s(t)]$ leave the school system, and the rest continue at the next higher level, assuming that there are no repeaters. Thus the enrollment in level $s + 1$ at the beginning of year $t + 1$ is given by

$$P_{s+1}(t+1) = [1 - q_s(t)]e_s(t)P_s(t) \tag{20}$$

and the full accounting of $P_s(t)$ becomes

$$P_s(t) = q_s(t)P_s(t) + g_s(t) + P_{s+1}(t+1) \tag{21}$$

where

$$g_s(t) = [1 - q_s(t)]P_s(t)[1 - e_s(t)] \tag{22}$$

is the expected number of leavers (graduations) from the school system at the end of year t (after completing s-level education). It is now easy to see that

$$P_s(t) = [p_s(t)]^{-1}g_s(t) + [p_s(t)]^{-1}P_{s+1}(t+1) \tag{23}$$

where $p_s(t) = 1 - q_s(t)$ is the annual survival probability of those enrolled in level s at the beginning of year t. This last formula immediately leads to the following expression for the enrollment in level s at the beginning of year t in terms of graduations at the end of years $t, t + 1, t + 2, \ldots$, and the annual survival probabilities:

$$P_s(t) = \Sigma_0^{t+\lambda} \frac{g_{s+j}(t+j)}{p_s(t) \cdots p_{s+j}(t+j)} \tag{24}$$

where the last term in the summation on the right-hand side corresponds to the highest level of education. One of the uses of such a formula is to compute current enrollment, given desired future flow of graduates.

INTERDEPENDENCE OF VARIOUS PARTS OF THE COLLECTIVE LIFE PROCESS

Let us now take a look at the broader socioeconomic context of the education process. As is widely recognized, the education system competes with other social and economic sectors for the same set of resources (funds). The resources allocated to the education system, and, in turn, the quality and efficiency with which the system operates and the degree to which everyone is offered equal opportunity to take advantage of the services the system offers are a function of the interdependence of various parts of the collective life process. In this section this interdependence is viewed from the perspective of the input-output approach first developed by Leontief (1936).

Leontief's Input-output Approach

The basic features of the Leontief approach can be grasped by imagining an economy segmented into a number of sectors. For example, a seven-sector model for the United States economy may be based on the following sectors: (1) agriculture, forestry, and fishing; (2) mining; (3) construction; (4) manufacturing; (5) transportation and trade; (6) services; and (7) other. Ritz, et al. (1979) present a model using close to 500 sectors. Note that a sector, in this context, may be a specialized industry or an aggregation of industries.

The data needed to construct the input-output model of an economy consist of inter-sectoral flows of products, usually for yearly intervals and expressed in monetary terms. Other time intervals can be used, and one could express the flows in terms energy units or the physical units themselves.

Let $z_{ij}(t)$ be the monetary value of the ith sector's product flowing to the jth sector during time interval t. The distribution (by destination) of the ith sector's product then gives the balancing equation:

$$x_i(t) = z_{i1}(t) + z_{i2}(t) + \ldots + z_{in}(t) + y_i(t) \qquad (25)$$

where $x_i(t)$ is the monetary value of the total output (production) of sector i, n is the number of sectors, and $y_i(t)$ is the part of $x_i(t)$ going to exogenous purchasers, usually consisting of households, government, and foreign enterprises. These flows can be conveniently presented in tabular form with origins on the rows and the destinations as columns. For numerical tables see, for example, Chapter F of *Historical Statistics of the United States* (U.S. Department of Commerce 1975).

In the Leontief input-output approach, one is often interested in examining the implications of the assumption that inputs are combined in fixed proportions, that is, that $z_{1j}(t), \ldots, z_{nj}(t)$, the jth industry's inputs, are respectively equal to $a_{1j}x_j(t), \ldots, a_{nj}x_j(t)$, where the a's, called *technical coefficients,* are time-invariant.

The coefficient a_{ij} is interpreted as the dollar value of inputs from sector i needed to produce a dollar's worth of output of sector j. In terms of the technical coefficients, the balancing equation (25) can be written as

$$x_i(t) = a_{i1}x_1(t) + \ldots + a_{in}x_n(t) + y_i(t), \quad i = 1, \ldots, n \quad (26)$$

Any component of the exogenous purchasers can of course be endogenized. For example, suppose a model with seven endogenous sectors treats the household sector as exogenous. To endogenize the household sector we create an eighth row and an eighth column for the household sector, the entries in the eighth column representing flows of money to households as payments for labor services rendered, and the entries in the eighth row representing flows of money from households to the various sectors as values of purchases made for household consumption. Instead of treating the households as a single sector, one could stratify them into, say, upper-class, middle-class, and lower-class households, on the basis of socioeconomic status or other criteria, reflecting goods and services consumed, and treat each stratum as a sector in its own right. In a similar fashion any other component (e.g., government) which is traditionally treated as exogenous can be endogenized. When there is no exogenous component to a model, it is called a closed model.

The educational system has not been explicitly mentioned so far. This will be done shortly. But before doing that it might be worthwhile to examine a simple society to fix the basic ideas of the approach outlined above.

An Example of a Closed Model

Hunter-gatherers approximate the type of society relevant here. For the present purpose let us assume that the collective life process of such societies consists of three activities: food production, reproduction and training, and maintenance, the last having to do with taking care of human individuals. The outputs of these activities are food, new members to carry out various activities, and person time (measured in person-years of life) respectively.

It is reasonable to assume that none of the activities require inputs other than person time. It is also reasonable to assume that the food produced goes in its entirety to the maintenance sector, no part of it being needed for the production of food. The following flow table captures the interdependence of the three activities in such a society:

The input-output structure of the activities can be represented by the following Leontief system of equations:

$$x_1(t) = a_{13}x_3(t)$$
$$x_2(t) = a_{23}x_3(t)$$
$$x_3(t) = a_{31}x_1(t) + a_{32}x_2(t) + a_{33}x_3(t)$$

where

Table 3. A Flow-Table for Hunter-Gatherers

Origin Sector	Destination Sector			Total output
	Food production	Reproduction and training	Maintenance	
Food production			$z_{13}(t)$	$x_1(t)$
Reproduction and Training			$z_{23}(t)$	$x_2(t)$
Maintenance	$z_{31}(t)$	$z_{32}(t)$	$z_{33}(t)$	$x_3(t)$

a_{13} = food produced per person year of life
a_{23} = number of new entrants to functional membership in society per person-year of life,
a_{31} = person time absorbed in the production of one unit of food, on average
a_{32} = person time absorbed in the production of one new functional member, on average
a_{33} = person time absorbed in the production of one person-year of life, on average (= fraction of human power absorbed in the maintenance sector).

Interdependence of Functions

It should be obvious from what has been said above that basically the Leontief input-output framework formalizes the interdependence of various activities (functions) comprising the collective life process. Each activity produces an output, which serves as one of the ingredients necessary for the production of the output of the same activity or of some other one.

It is important to recognize the distinction between an activity and a unit that performs that activity. A given activity may be performed by a number of units. Thus there may be two or more gatherers in a hunter-gatherer band. Also what may be thought of as one activity may indeed be a complex of a number of subactivities. Thus maintenance (taking care of human individuals) may involve rendering a number of services. Ideally one would like to subdivide an activity into its components as minutely as possible. But observational difficulties set severe limits on how far one can go in this respect. A major problem with lumping together a number of activities into one activity is that the specification of the corresponding production function in accordance with the input-output approach may be invalidated. Similarly, when many units carrying out a given activity are lumped together in one sector, the possible between-units variation in production functions is glossed over.

A Closed Model That Takes into Account Growth

When we shift attention from hunter-gatherers to simple horticultural societies, we begin to see the need for explicitly recognizing the creation of production capacities. The simple gardening tools of early horticulturalists, namely, wooden hoes and digging sticks, may be treated for our present purpose as free goods available in unlimited quantities. But clearing the land for cultivation and building structures for habitation invite special attention.

Let us assume that nothing more than person time is needed to clear land and to construct dwellings. Change is then needed only in the row for the maintenance sector in the flow matrix. Part of the person time in the setup under consideration goes to current maintenance, food production, and reproduction and training. The remaining part goes to the creation of production capacities (e.g., clearing land; construction of dwellings).

In general, creation of a production capacity involves a gestation period. Also, a capacity once created and installed, its productive life is finite and its productivity age-dependent. These apply to land cleared for cultivation, to dwellings constructed for habitation, and to male-female pairs coupled for procreation.

a_{ij}'s be defined as before, referring to current production, and let

$c_j(t+\theta)$ stand for the increment to the production capacity of sector j (measured in some appropriate unit), becoming effective at time $t + \theta$;

$b_{3j}(\theta)$ for person-time required to be invested at time t in order to increase by one unit the production capacity of sector j by time $t + \theta$;

α_j for the maximum gestation period required for the creation of a unit increase in the production capacity of sector j;

L_j for the maximum life span of any unit of production capacity newly installed in sector j; and

$w_j(u)$ for the age-dependent productivity of production capacities created in sector j.

In place of the simple flow matrix created earlier for hunter-gatherer societies we have the following flow matrix for simple horticulturalists: where

$$b_{3j}^* = \int_0^{a_j} b_{3j}(\theta) c_j(t+\theta) d\theta \tag{27}$$

Now if the production capacities created and installed are fully utilized, the output of sector j at time t is given by

$$x_j(t) = \int_0^{L_j} w_j(u) c_j(t-u) du \tag{28}$$

This equation simply says that the total output at time t is obtained by summing the outputs of cohorts of units of production capacities, the oldest cohort installed at time $t - L_j$ and the youngest at time t.

Stationary Setup

When overall production capacity remains time invariant, production of new production capacities is also time invariant; that is

$$c_j(t - u) = c_j(t) \tag{29}$$

for all u. Consequently Equation (20) becomes

$$x_j(t) = c_j(t) \Sigma_0^{L_j} w_j(u) du \tag{30}$$

which implies time invariance for outputs, i.e., $x_j(t + \theta) = x_j(t)$.

An Input-Output Flow Table Applicable to a Complex Society

Let us consider a closed economy. Let there be M sectors producing the usual types of goods and services. Let the household sector consist of H strata, corresponding to what is ordinarily understood as different life styles. Such a stratification is necessary in order to take into account the possibility that each lifestyle has its own peculiar input-structure. Each stratum thus conceptualized qualifies to be viewed as a sector in its own right, in the input-output flow table. For convenience of reference let these strata of households be collectively called the maintenance sector. Its output is person-years of life, a substantial portion of which is used up within the sector itself to produce the sector's output (person-years of life).

Let us assume that childbearing and rearing take place in C different sec-

Table 4. A Flow Matrix Showing Capital Investment, i.e., Allocation of Resources
for the Creation of Production Capacities

	Current			Future		
	Food production	Reproduction and training	Maintenance	Food production	Reproduction and training	Maintenance
Food production	0	0	a_{13}	0	0	0
Reproduction and training	0	0	a_{23}	0	0	0
Maintenance	a_{31}	a_{32}	a_{33}	b_{31}^*	b_{32}^*	b_{33}^*

tors, each producing, in its own style, new functional members of society. The corresponding inputs include services rendered by the education system. For analytical convenience the childbearing and rearing sectors are distinguished from the maintenance sectors. Data problems may prevent applying this strategy in practice.

Turning to education system, let us assume that there are many different tracks (channels) in the education system. Each track can be further stratified by levels (e.g., first, second, etc., grades in schools; freshman, sophomore, junior, and senior years in college), school characteristics (e.g., private or public), and so on. Each level in each track forms for the present purpose a sector of the education system.

If there are M industrial sectors, H strata for the maintenance sector, C childbearing and rearing sectors, and S sectors constituting the education system, the input-output flow table has $N + M + C + S$ rows. These may be augmented, of course, with rows for environmental inputs (e.g., land, water, minerals, etc.), government, and so on.

Remark 1:   The idea of stratifying a sector (mentioned above in connection with the maintenance sector, for example) can be carried over to the industrial sectors also. Thus, for example, the apparel industry may be stratified by "style" (fashion line).

Remark 2:   In a straightforward manner, the input-output flow table just described can be extended to cover multi-regional interdependence.

Remark 3:   Population is viewed as human resource. The duration of pregnancy plus the period of socialization and training constitutes the gestation period in its creation. There is, however, a major difference between material capital and human resource. The former is scrapped after its productive life is over. The human individual on the other hand, is taken care of even after his (her) productive life ends. This is understandable because human individuals are consumers as well as producers. In most societies, it is permissible to be exclusively a consumer, when there is no productive life left.

Remark 4:   Reproduction and training can be viewed as outputs of units created to perform those functions. From this standpoint reproduction-cum-training units are similar to any other production capacity, in that they have a gestation period, an age-dependent production capacity, and a finite length of productive life, the first and last of which are not easy to determine, although certainly menarche and menopause set definite bounds for the reproductive life of women.

Open Systems

If two societies, say, A and B, are engaged in exchange relationships, one could construct an input-output model for either of them treating the exchanges with the other as imports and exports. An alternative is of course to treat A and B as parts of one interdependent whole. This latter option requires the model builder to pay attention to the internal flows in both, whereas in the other option, the internal structure of the foreign society is not of interest.

RELATIONSHIP BETWEEN INDUSTRIAL OUTPUTS AND SCHOOL ENROLLMENTS IN A STATIONARY ECONOMY

Suppose the education system is endogenized in a Leontief input-output model, but the maintenance and the reproduction (childbearing and rearing) sectors are treated as exogenous, as are the government, foreign enterprises, and the biophysical environment. Let us assume stationarity. The output of a given (endogenous) sector goes to various endogenous sectors, including the education system, and to exogenous destinations. The inputs used up in maintenance of production capacities and in the creation of new production capacities in order to keep production level stationary, are all treated as current consumption for notational convenience. Let the number of industrial sectors be M, and the number of sectors in the education system be S. Let ξ_{js} be the dollar value of the delivery required from industry j per pupil in sector s of the education system, and a_{ij} be the dollar value of the ith industry's product required to produce a dollar's worth of industry j's output. Then the flow equation for the output of industry i can be written as follows (assuming fixed prices)

$$x_i(t) = \sum_{j=1}^{M} a_{ij}x_{ij}(t) + \sum_{s=1}^{S} \xi_{is}P_s(t) + y_i(t) \qquad (31)$$

Let us assume that the required education-specific person-power in each industry is proportional to the output of the industry. Let υ_{ej} stand for the requirement for e-level educated person-power per dollar value of output of industry j. Then the requirement for e-level educated persons is given by the sum of the requirement for e-level educated non-teachers and teachers, that is,

$$G_e = \sum_{j=1}^{M} \upsilon_{ej}x_j + \sum_{s=1}^{S} \mu_{es}P_s \qquad (32)$$

where, μ_{es} is, as already defined, the number of e-level educated teachers needed per pupil in sector s of the education system. And as derived earlier [see Equation (15)]

$$P_s = \sum_{j=1}^{E} (\lambda_{sj}/\omega_j)G_j \qquad (33)$$

The equations (31) - (33) can be solved for the x's, the G's, and the P's, in terms of the y's. Once we know the G's we can determine g's using the definition $g_j = G_j/\omega_j$. We can thus express the level-specific annual final graduations in terms of flow of goods and services to exogenous destinations. It is easy to see that this relationship depends on

- length of working life for persons with given level of education (ω's)
- educational duration coefficients (λ's)
- teacher-pupil ratios (μ's)
- person-power coefficients (υ's)
- traditional input-output coefficients (a_{ij}'s)
- input coefficients of the education system (ξ's)

SUMMARY AND CONCLUSIONS

Scholars agree that the education system is hierarchically organized: pupils within classroom; classrooms within school; schools within school district; and so on. Outputs of the education system can be similarly conceptualized. It is common, for example, to focus on test scores (reflecting various skills, attitudes, etc.) when thinking of individual pupils as the units of analysis. For each individual pupil one thinks of a vector of scores: $\{X_1, \ldots, X_k\}$. At the classroom level, the corresponding output becomes a vector of distributions: $\{f_1(X_1), \ldots, f_k(X_k)\}$, where $f_i(X_i)$ stands for the distribution (over pupils) of the scores on the ith test or some other measure of, say, "Type i ability." At the school level, there are as many vectors of distributions as there are classrooms. And so on. One form of input-output analysis of educational outcomes is to treat as *explanandum* $\{X_1, \ldots, X_k\}$, $\{f_1(X_1), \ldots, f_k(X_k)\}$, or some such output complex. Commonly, when, for example, classrooms are the units of analysis, one of the distributions from among $\{f_1(X_1), \ldots, f_k(X_k)\}$ is chosen and a summary statistic (e.g., median score) is calculated, which is then used as the score on the explanandum. The explanatory variables chosen usually are interpreted as inputs. Many of the studies that focus on school effect can be thought of within this framework.

Another type of input-output analysis focuses on the flow of pupils through different levels (grades) of the school system. Recognizing that the output of the childbearing process serves as input (with a lag) to the school system and the output of the school system serves as input to the labor force, the input-output analysis that focuses on the flow of pupils through successive levels of the education system permits linking different processes (birth, education, and entrance to the labor force) with each other. Also the focus on the flow of pupils through successive levels permits an examination of school effects insofar as the flow pattern differs between schools or over time within a school. Particular interest often centers on the wastage, having to do with dropping out or dying before completing a given cycle such as senior high school. The flow pattern, of course, may show intra- and inter-cohort variations, where by cohort is meant pupils who enter the school system at the same time, e.g., year 1980. Differences in socioeconomic background, readiness, family environment, and the like are known to account for intra- and inter-cohort variations in the flow pattern.

Yet another type of input-output analysis focuses on sectoral inter-dependence in society. Households, classrooms, schools, etc. can be treated as sectors analogous to industrial sectors for this purpose. Also, instead of treating households as a single sector, it makes sense to stratify them on the basis of socioeconomic status or similar criteria and treat each stratum as a sector in its own right. The same applies to classrooms, tracks, schools, etc. This type of input-output analysis permits linking the output of the education system with the flow of various goods and services in society. In this way the education system is viewed as part of a broader social system. The parameters of the education system that receive particular attention in this approach include teacher-pupil ratio, the number of leavers from the education system at different levels (e.g., high school graduates), level-specific duration coefficients (the average number of school years of life at each level per leaver at the end of the cycle involved), qualification coefficients of teachers (composition by qualification of teachers instructing each level of students), and input coefficients of the education system (the flow of goods or services from each industry to each sector of the education system per pupil enrolled in the sector). This approach can be extended to cover intra- and inter-regional interdependence. By considering different regions and different sectors of the education system within each region, it is possible to examine variation of parameters of the education system between regions and between sectors (e.g., public and private) within regions.

REFERENCES

Bidwell, C. E. and J. D. Kasarda. 1975. "School District Organization and Student Achievement." *American Sociological Review* 40:55–70.

Glasman, N. S. and I. Biniaminov. 1981. "Input-output Analyses of Schools." *Review of Educational Research* 51:509–539.

Harter, C. L. 1977. "The "Good Time" Cohort of the 1930s." *Population Reference Bureau. Report 3.*

Herriott, R. E. and B. J. Hodgkins. 1973. *The Environment of Schooling: Formal Education as an Open Social System.* Englewood Cliffs, NJ: Prentice-Hall.

Hutchins, R. 1953. *The Conflicts in Education.* New York: Harper and Row.

Leontief, W. 1936. "Quantitative Input-output Relations in the Economic System of the United States." *Review of Economics and Statistics* 18:105–125.

Plotkin, M. 1978. "Future Size and Growth Rate of the U. S. Population." In *Consequences of Changing U. S. Population: Baby Boom and Bust, Vol. II, Hearing Before the Select Committee on Population, Ninety-Fifth Congress.* Pp. 741–766. Washington, D. C.: Government Printing Office.

Ritz, P., E. Roberts, and P. Young. 1979. "Dollar Value Tables for the 1972 Input-output Study." *Survey of Current Business* 59:51–72.

Taueber, C. 1979. "A Changing America." *American Demographics* 1:9–16.

Thonstad, T. 1968. *Education and Manpower: Theoretical Models and Empirical Applications.* Toronto: University of Toronto Press

UNESCO Office of Statistics. 1972. *A Statistical Study of Wastage at School. Studies and Surveys in Comparative Education.* UNESCO, Paris/Geneva.

U. S. Department of Commerce. 1975. *Historical Statistics of the United States.* Washington, D.C.: U.S. Government Printing Office.

Research in Sociology of Education and Socialization

Edited by
Ronald G. Corwin
The Ohio State University

Volume 1, Longitudinal Perspectives on Educational Attainment
1980, 271 pp. $58.50
ISBN 0-89232-122-9

REVIEWS: "The volume is a valuable addition to the literature since it does do what it promises to do. It does provide clear summaries of most of the major research going on currently!"

— *The Review of Education*

"... a valuable resource for students of educational stratification in the form of introductions to six longitudinal data sets that have been used for analysis of educational attainment processes."

— *Contemporary Sociology*

CONTENTS: Foreword, *Alan C. Kerckhoff.* **Elementary and Secondary School Progression, High School Graduation, and College Entrance of the American Population: 1950 to 1978,** *Larry E. Suter, Population Division, Bureau of the Census, Washington, D.C.* **The "Explorations in Equality of Opportunity" Survey of 1955 High School Sophomores,** *Karl L. Alexander, The Johns Hopkins University and Bruce K. Eckland, University of North Carolina, Chapel Hill.* **The Wisconsin Longitudinal Study of Social and Psychological Factors in Aspirations and Achievements,** *William H. Sewell and Robert M. Hauser, University of Wisconsin, Madison.* **Educational Attainment of the High School Classes of 1980 Through 1983: Findings from Project Talent,** *Lauress L. Wise and Lauri Steel, Project Talent, American Institute for Research.* **The Youth in Transition Series: A Study of Change and Stability in Young Men,**

Jerald G. Bachman and Patrick M. O'Malley, University of Michigan. **Perspectives on Educational Attainment from the National Longitudinal Surveys of Labor Market Behavior,** *Herbert S. Parnes and Malcolm C. Rich, Ohio State University.* **The National Longitudinal Study of the High School Senior Class of 1972,** *Bruce K. Eckland, University of North Carolina, Chapel Hill and Karl L. Alexander, The Johns Hopkins University.* **Looking Back and Looking Ahead,** *Alan C. Kerckhoff, Duke University.*

Volume 2, Research on Educational Organizations
1981, 316 pp. $58.50
ISBN 0-89232-158-X

Guest Editor: **Ronald G. Corwin,** *Department of Sociology, Ohio State University.*

REVIEW: "The volume makes the case for bringing sociology back into the study of school effects, and more generally, into research on educational organizations."
— *Contemporary Sociology*

CONTENTS: Foreword, *Ronald G. Corwin, Ohio State University.* **Using Standardized Test Performance in School Effects Research,** *Karl L. Alexander and James M. McPartland, The Johns Hopkins University and Martha A. Cook, Indiana University.* **Review of Recent Case Studies on Equity and Schooling,** *Kathryn Borman, University of Cincinnati.* **Time in School,** *Nancy L. Karweit, The Johns Hopkins University.* **Organizational and Institutional Socialization in Education,** *David H. Kamens, Northern Illinois University.* **Careers of Academic Administrators in the U.S.A.: An Approach to Elite Study,** *Edward Gross and James C. McCann, University of Washington.* **Sociology Looks at Team Teaching,** *Elizabeth G. Cohen, Stanford University.* **Research on the Implementation of Educational Change,** *Michael Fullan, Ontario Institute for Studies in Education.* **Images of Organization and the Promotion of Educational Change,** *William Firestone, Research for Better Schools, Philadelphia and Robert Herriott, Private Consultant, Cambridge, Mass.* **Patterns of Organizational Control and Teacher Militancy: Theoretical Continuities in the Idea of "Loose Couling,"** *Ronald G. Corwin, Ohio State University.*

Volume 3, Policy Research
1981, 323 pp. $58.50
ISBN 0-89232-187-3

Guest Editor: **Ronald G. Corwin**, *Department of Sociology, Ohio State University.*

Volume 4, Personal Change Over the Life Course
1983, 286 pp. $58.50
ISBN 0-89232-303-5

Volume 5, 1985, 350 pp. $58.50
ISBN 0-89232-424-4

University, and Maureen T. Hallinan, University of Notre Dame. **The Educational Attainment of Religio-Ethnic Groups in the United States,** *Charles Hirschman and Louis M. Falcon, Cornell University.* **Part II: Education, Work and Personal Development, Education as a Valid but Fallible Signal of Worker Quality: Reorienting and Old Debate About the Functional Basis of the Occupational Hierarchy,** *Linda S. Gottfredson, The Johns Hopkins University.* **Adolescent Work Hours and the Process of Achievement,** *Michael D. Finch and Jeylan T. Mortimer, University of Minnesota.* **Work and Self-Concept: Selection and Socialization in the Early Career,** *Kenneth I. Spenner, Duke University and Luther B. Otto, Boys Town, Nebraska.* **Part III: Perspectives on Gender and Social Development. Gender Difference in Interpersonal Relationships and Well-Being,** *Dorie Giles Williams, The University of Michigan.* **Impact of Changing Gender Role Expectations Upon Socialization in Adolescence: Understanding the Interaction of Gender, Age, and Cohort Effects,** *Diana Mitsch Bush, Colorado State University, Fort Collins.* **Education and Gender Equality: A Critical Review,** *Jean Stockard, University of Oregon.* **The Relationships of Marital Status and Career Preparation to Changing Work Orientations of Young Women: A Longitudinal Study,** *Therese L. Baker and Judith A. Bootcheck, DePaul University.*

Volume 6, International Perspectives on Education
1986, 302 pp. $58.50
ISBN 0-89232-712-X

CONTENTS: List of Contributors. Foreword, *Alan C. Kerckhoff.* **Higher Education in an Era of Equality: A Cross-National Study of Institutional Differentiation on the Tertiary Level,** *Larry Sirowy, Stanford University and Aaron Benavot, University of Georgia.* **Educational Mobility in Hungary and the Netherlands: A Log-Linear Comparison,** *Jules Peschar and Roel Popping, State University of Groningen.* **High School Attendance in a Sponsored Multi-Ethnic System: The Case of Israel,** *Abraham Yogev and Hanna Ayalon, Tel Aviv University.* **Social Inequality in Education Attainment in Norway, Marianne Nordli Hanson, University of Oslo. Sponsored and Contest Education Pathways to Jobs in Great Britian and the United States,** *Alan C. Kerckhoff and Diane E. Everett, Duke University.* **Contrasting Achievement**

JAI PRESS

Rules: Socialization of Japanese Children at Home and in School, *Bruce Fuller, The World Bank, Susan D. Holloway, University of Maryland, College Park, Hiroshi Azuma, Tokyo University, Robert D. Hess, Stanford University, and Keiko Kashiwagi, Tokyo Women's Christian University.* Neighbourhoods, Schools, and Individual Attainment: A Better Model For Analyzing Unequal Educational Opportunities?, *J. Dronkers, Tilborg University and H. Schijf, University of Amsterdam.* Certification, Class Conflict, Religion, and Community: A Socio-Historical Explanation of the Effectiveness of Contemporary Schools, *Andrew McPherson, University of Edinburgh and J. Douglas Willms, University of British Columbia and University of Edinburgh.*

Volumes 1-6 were published under the editorship of Alan C. Kerckhoff, Department of Sociology, Duke University

Volume 7, Out of School
1987, 312 pp. $58.50
ISBN 0-89232-755-3

CONTENTS: List of Contributors. Foreword, *Ronald G. Corwin.* PART I. CONTEXTS. The Education of the Baby Boom Generation, *Robert A. Dentler, University of Massachusetts, Boston.* Theories of the Labor Market and the Employment of Youth, *Toby L. Parcel, The Ohio State University.* PART II. INSTITUTIONAL LINKAGES. The Floundering Phrase of the Life Course, *Krishnan Namboodiri, The Ohio State University.* Consequences of the Process of Transition to Adulthood for Adult Economic Well-Being, *Margaret Mooney Marini, William Chan and Jennie Raymond, Vanderbilt University.* PART III. THE SCHOOL-TO-WORK TRANSITION. Leaving School for Work, *Kathryn M. Borman, University of Cincinnati, and MaryCarol Hopkins, Northern Kentucky University.* What Do We Know About Dropping Out of High School?, *Theodore C. Wagenaar, Miami University.* Curriculum Effects on Early Post-High School Outcomes, *Lawrence Hotchkiss and Linda Eberst Dorsten, Vocational Education National Center for Research.* Interrelations and Parallels of School and Work as Sources of Psychological Development, *Jeylan T. Mortimer and Catherine*

Yamoor, University of Minnesota. **PART IV. NON-SCHOOL EXPERIENCES. Involvement in Task Activities Outside of School: A Preliminary Investigation,** *Dale Dannefer, Christina Frederick and Harold L. Munson, University of Rochester.* **Work and Maturity: Occupational Socialization of Non-College Youth in the United States and West Germany,** *Stephen F. Hamilton, Cornell University.*

Volume 8, Selected Methodological Issues
1989,258 pp. $58.50
ISBN 0-89232-929-7

Edited by **Krishnan Namboodiri** and **Ronald G. Corwin,** *Department of Sociology, The Ohio State University*

CONTENTS: Preface, *Krishnan Namboodiri and Ronald G. Corwin, The Ohio State University.* **Schools and the Distribution of Educational Opportunities,** *Aage Sorensen, Harvard University.* **Early Schooling As a "Critical Period" Phenomenon,** *Doris R. Entwisle and Karl L. Alexander, The Johns Hopkins University.* **Comparing Individual and Structural Levels of Analysis,** *Hubert M. Blalock, Jr., University of Washington.* **Conceptual and Measurement Issues in the Study of School Dropouts,** *Aaron M. Pallas, Teachers College, Columbia University.* **The Meaning of Educational Attainment,** *Charles Bidwell, University of Chicago.* **Have Individuals Been Overemphasized in School-Effects Research?,** *Ronald G. Corwin and Krishnan Namboodiri, The Ohio State University.* **The Advantages and Disadvantages of Longitudinal Surveys,** *Robert W. Pearson, Social Science Research Council and Columbia University.* **Measurement Error in Secondary Data Analysis,** *Alan C. Acock, Louisiana State University and the Agricultural Experiment Station.* **Education as a Component of a Larger Social System,** *Krishnan Namboodiri, The Ohio State University.*

JAI PRESS INC.

55 Old Post Road - No. 2
P.O. Box 1678
Greenwich, Connecticut 06836-1678
Tel: 203-661-7602

Research Annuals and Monographs in Series in SOCIOLOGY

Research Annuals

Advances in Group Processes
Edited by Edward J. Lawler, *University of Iowa.*

Advances in Health Economics and Health Services Research
Edited by Richard M. Scheffler, *University of California, Berkeley* and Louis F. Rossiter, *Virginia Commonwealth University.*

Advances in Information Processing in Organizations
Edited by Lee S. Sproull and Patrick D. Larkey, *Carnegie-Mellon University.*

Advances in Social Science Methodology
Edited by Bruce Thompson, *The University of New Orleans.*

Comparative Social Research
Edited by Richard F. Tomasson, *The University of New Mexico.*

Current Perspectives in Social Theory
Edited by John Wilson and Scott G. McNall, *University of Kansas.*

Current Perspectives on Aging and the Life Cycles
Edited by Zena Smith Blau, *University of Houston.*

Current Research on Occupations and Professions
Edited by Helena Z. Lopata, *Loyola University of Chicago.*

Knowledge and Society: Studies in the Sociology of Science, Past and Present
Edited by Robert Alun Jones, Lowell Hargens and Andrew Pickering, *University of Illinois.*

Political Power and Social Theory
Edited by Maurice Zeitlin, *University of California, Los Angeles.*

Research in Community and Mental Health
Edited by James R. Greenley, *University of Wisconsin Medical School.*

Research in Corporate Social Performance and Policy
Edited by Lee E. Preston, *University of Maryland.*

Research in Economic Anthropology
Edited by Barry Isaac, *University of Cincinnati.*

Research in Human Capital and Development
Edited by Ismail Sirageldin, *The Johns Hopkins University.*

Research in Inequality and Social Conflict
Edited by Michael Dobkowski, *Hobart and William Smith, Colleges* and Isidor Walliman, *School of Social Work, Basel.*

Research in Labor Economics
Edited by Ronald G. Ehrenberg, *New York State School of Industrial and Labor Relations, Cornell University.*

Research in Law and Policy Studies
Edited by Stuart S. Nagel, *University of Illinois.*

Research in Law, Deviance and Social Control
Edited by Steven Spitzer, *Suffolk University* and Andrew T. Scull, *University of California, San Diego.*

Research in Micropolitics
Edited by Samuel Long, *Pace University, Pleasantville.*

Research in Organizational Behavior
Edited by Barry M. Staw, *University of California, Berkeley* and L.L. Cummings, *Northwestern University.*

Research in Organizational Change and Development
Edited by Richard W. Woodman, *Texas A&M University* and William A. Pasmore, *Case Western Reserve University.*

Research in Personnel and Human Resources Management
Edited by Kendrith M. Rowland, *University of Illinois* and Gerald R. Ferris, *Texas A&M University.*

Research in Philosophy and Technology
Edited by Frederick Ferre, *University of Georgia.*

Research in Political Economy
Edited by Paul Zarembka, *State University of New York at Buffalo.*

Research in Political Sociology
Edited by Richard G. Braungart, *Syracuse University.*

Research in Politics and Society
Edited by Gwen Moore, *Russell Sage College.*

Research in Population Economics
Edited by T. Paul Schultz, *Yale University.*

Research in Public Policy Analysis and Management
Edited by Stuart S. Nagel, *University of Illinois.*

Research in Race and Ethnic Relations
Edited by Cora Bagley Marrett, *University of Wisconsin, Madison* and Cheryl Leggon, *University of Chicago.*

Research in Rural Sociology and Development
Edited by Harry K. Schwarzweller, *Michigan State University.*

Research in Social Movements, Conflicts and Change
Edited by Louis Kriesberg, *Syracuse University.*

Research in Social Policy, Critical Historical and Contemporary Perspectives
Edited by John H. Stanfield, *Yale University.*

Research in Social Problems and Public Policy
Edited by Michael Lewis, *University of Massachusetts* and JoAnn L. Miller, *Purdue University.*

Research In Social Stratification and Mobility
Edited by Arne L. Kalleberg, *University of North Carolina, Chapel Hill*

Research in Sociology of Education and Socialization
Edited by Ronald G. Corwin, *The Ohio State University.*

Research in the Sociology of Health Care
Edited by Julius Roth and Sheryl Burt Ruzek, *University of California, Davis.*

Research in the Sociology of Organizations
Edited by Samuel B. Bacharach, *New York State School of Industrial and Labor Relations, Cornell University.*

Research in the Sociology of Work
Edited by Ida Harper Simpson, *Duke University* and Richard L. Simpson, University of North Carolina, Chapel Hill.

Research in Urban Economics
Edited by Robert D. Ebel, *Northwestern Bell, Minneapolis.*

Research in Urban Policy
Edited by Terry Nichols Clark, *University of Chicago.*

Research in Urban Sociology
Edited by Ray Hutchison and Ronald K. Baba, *University of Wisconsin, Green Bay.*

Research on Negotiations in Organizations
Edited by roy J. Lewicki, *Ohio State University*, Blair H. Sheppard, *Duke University* and Max H. Bazerman, *Northwestern University.*

Social Perspectives on Emotion
Edited by David D. Franks, *Virginia Commonwealth University.*

Sociological Studies of Child Development
Edited by Patricia A. and Peter Adler, *Washington University, St. Louis.*

Studies in Communication
Edited by Thelma McCormick, *York University.*

Studies in Qualitative Methodology
Edited by Robert Burgess, *University of Warwick.*

Studies in Symbolic Interaction
Edited by Norman K. Denzin, *University of Illinois.*

Monographs in Series and Treatises

Contemporary Ethnographic Studies
Edited by Jaber F. Gubrium, *Marquette University.*

Contemporary Studies in Sociology: Theoretical and Empirical Monographs
Edited by John Clark, *University of Minnesota.*

Contemporary Studies in Applied Behavioral Science
Edited by Louis A. Zurcher, *University of Texas at Austin.*

Contemporary Studies in Economic and Financial Analysis
An International Series of Monographs
Edited by Edward I. Altman and Ingo Walter, *New York University.*

Handbook of Behavioral Economics
Edited by Stanley Kaish and Benjamin Gilad, *Rutgers University.*

Monographs in Organizational Behavior and Industrial Relations
Edited by Samuel B. Bacharach, *New York State School of Industrial and Labor Relations, Cornell University.*

Political Economy and Public Policy
Edited by William Breit, *Trinity University* and Kenneth G. Elzinga, *University of Virginia.*

Public Policy Studies: A Multi-Volume Treastise
Edited by Stuart S. Nagel, *University of Illinois.*

Please inquire for detailed subject catalog

JAI PRESS INC., 55 Old Post Road No. 2, P.O. Box 1678
Greenwich, Connecticut 06836
Telephone: 203-661-7602   Cable Address: JAIPUBL